WHEN CHINA WAKES

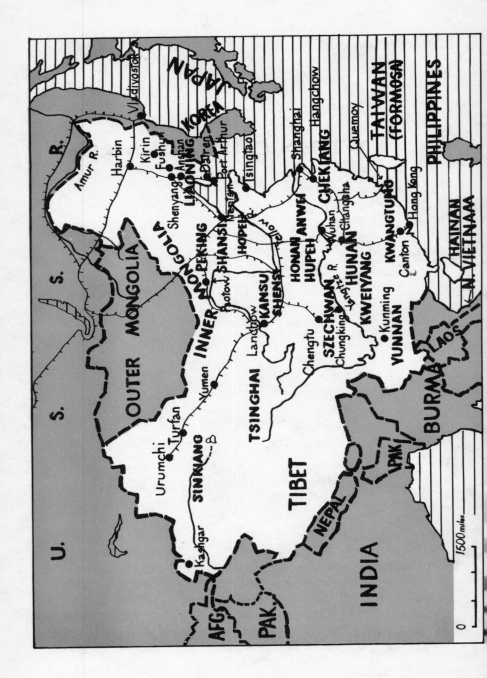

WHEN CHINA WAKES

ROBERT GUILLAIN

"Let China sleep. When she wakes the
world will be sorry." Napoleon

WALKER AND COMPANY
NEW YORK

CONTENTS

FOREWORD

The balance of power and the very march of history have undergone, at the end of this the twentieth century, broad alterations thanks to the "emergence" (to make use of a neologism that means just what it says) of a new China. In another thirty years China will have definitely taken her place among us as one of the new giants of modern times. After that, the world will never be the same as it is now in these days of China's long "absence."

Unfortunately, this formidable opponent in the international game is for the most part unknown to the other players. Today the task of understanding China—her actions, thoughts, and plans—is a must for everyone who wants to understand the shape of times to come. However, to understand a country one must first recognize her existence, and it is certainly because at the beginning of 1964 France reestablished diplomatic relations with Peking that I was allowed to visit China again. Having returned, I am more than ever convinced of the necessity of keeping such channels open and developing them as much as it is possible.

Given such an attitude, all travelers, especially journalists, must exercise a certain restraint over both their tongues and their pens. Thus in writing what follows I have frankly attempted to enforce a certain amount of self-censorship—to avoid unimportant incidents, personal reactions, and passing judgment; instead I have tried to understand more and to simply describe, thus leaving to the reader the task of drawing conclusions. In any case, ideologically based criticisms and objections to means or results are of absolutely no importance to the Chinese. They go their way without giving any thought to what the world thinks.

In addition, they have the advantage of being able to point out that their system has succeeded. Yes, after my long trip through Communist China, I want to admit right away that when the rulers in Peking claim that on the whole they have succeeded, I must agree. "On the whole"—the phrase is a prudent one, and they are careful to use it frequently. For the time being, the phrase does describe reality—for the majority of their problems, the time of failure is past. It allows the reasonable claim that the regime is on its feet and once again making headway, even though it is true (as we are free to gather) that obstacles and errors almost brought it to the verge of disaster. And if it allows the Communists an optimism that boasts of tremendous progress on all fronts, it implicitly concedes that there are still areas, sometimes enormous, of difficulty and suffering such as the Chinese have long known, and such that any objective traveler can spot.

Enemies of China or of Communism, if they could get to Peking, would often be dismayed, I believe, by the tremendous visible progress that the regime has made in this country. But at the same time friends of China or of Chinese Communism must often feel overwhelmed, when they travel across the country or consider the situation carefully, by the unbelievable problems that still await resolution.

In addition I should add, when I claim success for Communism in China, that such a claim by a Western observer includes two very different aspects. To begin with, Communism won a victory worthy of the highest praise when it conquered all sorts of former plagues: corruption, disorder, sickness, opium, prostitution, etc. The greater part of the changes, already extraordinary during my last trip in the autumn of 1955, have not only withstood backsliding, but have indeed been consolidated: reunification, education within the means of all, honesty, morality, sanitation, etc. A single example will suffice: the flies have made no comeback. And if it is true that the Chinese have known semi-famine, they now eat their fill.

As for the second aspect of their "success," the state has succeeded in its attempt to rebuild the Chinese character in its own image, to produce seven hundred million yesmen. Here too there is no retreat—if anything "progress" in comparison with my last visit. The desire to steamroller the individual under the wheels of Maoist Marxism seems to grow stronger as "on the whole" it succeeds. But "successes" in this quarter—whatever their merits and advantages—I leave to the Chinese themselves to praise.

CHAPTER ONE

NINE YEARS AFTER: FIRST IMPRESSIONS

ON THE TRAIN BETWEEN HONG KONG AND CANTON. THE TYPHOON that I saw passing over Hong Kong has continued its path through South China and left the countryside in Kwangtung Province drenched but radiant. Yes, there are beneficent typhoons too, typhoons that cause almost no damage and distribute water abundantly over a wide area in need. I caught sight here and there of peasants obviously overjoyed to direct the course of so much water, and children splashed joyfully in ponds or buckets while women watered gardens or did the laundry.

In the paddies the rice is green, close-planted, healthy. Almost no one in the fields in the South at this season, and I see no trace so far of the "people's communes." How picturesque these villages are with their pointed eaves: the houses built of black brick stand as close together as possible to save arable land. Yet this landscape is poor and joyless. Aside from irrigated paddies there are fields of sweet potatoes, corn, peanuts and beans; then come eroded hills covered with sparse brush. Here and there, however, these slopes show the recent planting of pines—which promises to modify this scene considerably. ¬Reforestation is apparent

almost everywhere, and I believe it might change this countryside into something as charming as Japan. . . .

I have just entered China and from my window I watch the
first frames of that technicolor film, endless, fascinating, that
film which is the Chinese countryside. Besides the stretch between Hong Kong and Canton, I will spend the better part of
the day for three days running in untiring observation of this
changing spectacle that takes place on the empty screen of my
window.

When you go to Peking . . . Yes, you'll go to Peking. Today
everyone goes to Peking—except Americans. When you go to
Peking, take my advice: go by train. I mean, enter by way of
Hong Kong and take the train from there.

It isn't an expedition any longer—if it ever was. Entering China
today I can no longer enjoy the sensation of my entry of twelve
years ago: the feeling that I was seeing things never seen before,
like Marco Polo, or, like the astronaut of the future touching
down on an unknown planet. Many travelers have visited Peking:
Communist China is more open and is less far away.

Yet it is this shrinkage of our world that makes me wonder if
the trip by train may not in the end become the expedition it
once seemed, but from another point of view. No one will be
doing it in the future, everyone will go by plane. Even now I
could have gotten to my destination quicker by air; leaving
London this afternoon I could have lunched on Peking duck
the day after tomorrow. That route would have taken me to
Shanghai by way of Pakistan. I could have arrived even sooner
by way of Moscow. And in the near future, when we can fly
directly from Paris to Peking in a single day, who will detour
to Hong Kong and then spend two nights in a train?

As for me, though, I shall remain faithful to this means of
transportation, if I return! I pity anyone whom a tight schedule
parachutes into Peking straight off. The bewilderment following
on such a sudden arrival is too hard on the system. And that
way one begins with the atypical—the capital; the necessary
background, this Chinese countryside, will be lacking when he
makes his first observations. The train provides the traveler with
something the plane cannot, an initiation into China.

Such an initiation is important even for such a visitor as myself, who has been to this country several times. I knew the China of Chiang Kai-shek as a young correspondent in 1937–38 during the Sino-Japanese War. I saw the country again toward the end of 1945 as the Americans entered Shanghai in triumph after winning the Pacific War. In 1949, as a special correspondent for *Le Monde,* I underwent the Communist siege of Shanghai and after its capture saw the installation of a new regime. In 1955, still a special correspondent for *Le Monde,* I covered more than 6000 miles of the "New China."

But the upsets of the last thirty years have been so staggering that each new voyage must begin with the discovery of an even newer China! Thus this train ride is a welcome initiation for an old China hand. My eyes immediately provide me with material concerning the most important sector of China's economy—life in the fields and provincial centers. Rarely seen by outsiders, it demands deciphering. These sights interest me all the more since it was only two years ago, after the three black years (1959, 1960, and 1961) that followed "The Great Leap Forward," that heavy industry lost its priority to agriculture in the national effort. Chinese agriculture, this hardly known background and at the same time basis for all their economic progress, has become even more important. What is it like in this the fifteenth year of their new regime?

Suddenly it strikes me: there's not a square foot of arable land that is not under cultivation! The most unexpected places yield evidence of varied crops—cereals, beans, peanuts, and vegetables. They creep up railroad embankments, almost reaching the tracks, invade the roadside ditches, cover sandbars seasonally exposed by the rivers, spread over canal banks, and attempt to grow on pieces of earth reclaimed from the brush or terraced out of ravines. This compulsion to make use of every last bit of earth provides a striking demonstration of the Chinese peasant's industry. But it also unavoidably betrays the terrible pressure that drives him to such lengths. The passion with which new bits and pieces of land are added to agriculture gives the impression of urgency, of crisis, of a state of emergency. These fields translate into pictures the pressures of the population explosion. These

fields evoke the great food crisis of those three black years. Often
this marginal cultivation also betrays a heartbreaking waste of
labor. No amount of effort can produce a harvest on the little
hills that strengthen the pylons of power lines, or on the embank-
ment of an earlier railroad. Anything planted there turns yellow
and dies. They have gone too far onto the rocks and into impossible soils, but next year, who knows, it may work.

And besides, this is only a minor aspect of the agricultural
effort, a sort of snipers' battle on the periphery of arable lands.
. . . And on the main front of China's war for food, the crops
are magnificent and spread out on a larger scale than ever before:
socialization has torn down former boundaries to do away with
the limitations of small farming. The paddies of the lowlands as
well as the grain fields of drier ground have expanded to extraordinary dimensions on which a promising harvest ripens.
Never on any previous trip through China have I seen the land
so well worked. Never before did it so closely resemble one immense garden worked by millions of gardeners.

But I have allowed myself to be carried away by observations
made later, during my trip through Central China, and now I
must retrace my steps to speak of another aspect of my initiation—Canton, and a new experience, my first city. And I must
immediately add that all the cities that I visited afterwards were
better off than this one. Right off I felt that life had suffered
some slowdown, that poverty here was deep. It had just stopped
raining and perhaps the humidity accounted at least in part for
the slightly sinister atmosphere this town gave off. Or perhaps I
was still under the influence of Hong Kong's fabled charm and
too much aware of the differences between these cities. Leaving
one and entering the other reminded me of a film in black and
white following immediately on one in technicolor. After the
riches, the sounds, and the elegance of Hong Kong came the
uniform gray of this world.

Of course certain improvements are obvious and the presence
of the new regime makes itself felt in many positive ways. The
streets are clean, although the buildings that line them are as
run-down as ever. Magnificent parks have appeared and the pub-

lic places are well kept. Some sort of city planning is evident. The "floating slums" of the old days are gone: the dirty water of the canals no longer supports thousands of poor people in a city of sampans. And at least part of the population wears clean clothes.

There are differences in the crowd that overflows the sidewalks into the autoless streets. Among the people in good clothes or in clean ones there are a considerable number in old clothes, and bare feet, too (which I hardly noticed anywhere else). In addition, there are old-fashioned costumes—often black ones, mixed with the blue favored by the new regime, as though the revolution had touched South China somewhat less. There are even a few people in rags.

One of the characteristics of Hong Kong is the profusion of signs—advertisements, posters, and announcements fill the sky and cover the walls from one end of town to the other with a fabulous confusion of Chinese ideograms. In Canton, a poor man's Hong Kong, socialism has wiped all this out. Socialism has also done away with thousands of little shops that lined the arcaded sidewalks, replacing them with state stores and cooperatives. Former shops now serve for housing. With these shops have disappeared much of the life and local color of a Chinese street scene. However there are sufficient foodstuffs and a number of restaurants: people look poor, but they appear to get enough to eat. . . .

And I did eat well—Chinese cooking—at the hotel where I spent my first night in China before spending my second and third on the train. But in this large and luxurious hostelry constructed for the annual visits of those foreign businessmen who converge on Canton for the great Export Commodities Fair, I became again aware, for the first time this trip, of the climate of boredom and undefined mistrust that marks the hotels of this country.

All in all Canton wrings my heart, makes me wonder what sort of country I've come to this time. (The rest of the trip was to reassure me, I repeat. And I believe this stop in Canton is profitable. It serves as a warning, a warning that one must be ready for everything in this country. Conditions cannot be uni-

form over such an enormous territory, and the differences between the best and the worst will often be glaring.)

What a joy it is to find my seat in the train and sit for the next
installment of that interrupted film, the Chinese countryside. And
besides, it's very comfortable: I have a compartment for four all
to myself. Later I learned that this was one of the measures
taken to make sure that the traveler in China does not come into
contact with anyone other than than the officials to whom he is
entrusted. I might add that these officials exercise great cour-
tesy.

When the white-shirted cook in the dining car sees how ap-
preciative I am of his Chinese cooking, he tries to stuff me. The
porter in my sleeping car wears a suit of dark blue cotton and a
stiff cap, and he is also careful to see to it that I'm happy. Just
as I did on my trip nine years ago, I find someone zealously
tracking down the few remaining flies, chasing them passionately
and killing them with an infallible fly-swatter. One of the porter's
assistants (each car has its own personnel) also looks after me,
and lets me know, by signs that cannot be misinterpreted, that
he has been detailed to keep an eye on me. He manages this
task conscientiously but with a pleasant discretion. But all the
same, and so much the worse for possible consequences, I keep
right on making those notes that mark me as a journalist under
way.

After Leaving the Kwangtung Province

The country still looks drenched by the recent typhoon. The
beautiful green of young rice adds the only color to the rather
dull countryside where there are few signs of change: the eternal
villages of China and the ancient plows pulled by gray water
buffaloes; not a new building, and hardly a trace of the new
communes. But there are many irrigation reservoirs, and reforestation continues. As we turn to the north at the province's
boundary, the train for a long time follows a river, the Pei, which
is approaching flood level. It is heavy with mud and cuts through
wild hills covered with sparse brush. How much sterile land
this over-populated country contains! Night falls on this scene. . . .

Through Mao Tse-tung's Home Province

Now it's Hunan, always known for its rice, that presents me with another river, not a wild, deserted one like yesterday's; instead there are white-sailed junks that carry merchandise, and there are also smaller junks for fishing. The train passed not far from the village where Mao Tse-tung was born, but now here we are in the capital of his province, Changsha, where at the turn of the century he almost became an unimportant teacher. But could he have remained unimportant long? In Changsha people seem better off than they do in Canton, better dressed— but they are no better housed. A large percentage of their merchandise is still transported on human backs: this is quite striking in the rail, coal and lumber yards seen from the train. And nobody seems in much of a hurry. . . .

As my train returns to the Hunan countryside, communes and other transformations appear. For a long time we wind around the foot of a mountain where cultivation has risen higher and higher, almost to the top, and the pale fields trace a harlequin costume on the dark mountain side. The fields are at an almost 40-degree angle and the fatigue of working under such conditions must be considerable.

Then something absolutely new catches my eye among the green of young rice—chemical fertilizer! The communes distribute it to the villages. In the flooded paddies peasants manually spread a powder that turns the three-week-old rice shoots white. I've never seen anything like this in China before, and I must admit it's very moving. Much will change when the earth of this country, like that of Japan, will be able to produce all it promises, thanks to chemical fertilizer. (I should mention here that nowhere else in my travels did I see chemical fertilizer spread over the fields.) In every village and in the fields the peasants, men and women in teams of fifteen to twenty, head for work. Wheelbarrows make their appearance. Until now, and especially in the Kwangtung, I haven't seen any wheeled vehicles in the fields, and very few beasts of burden—except human beings.

And another interesting observation: I begin to notice here and there the famous "individual plots" that the regime allowed the peasants, alongside their collectivized fields, when the shortages during those three black years forced a slowdown in the systematization of the people's communes. They really are infinitesimal parcels of land, often "no bigger than a pocket handkerchief," and they are never irrigated. Most often they have been snatched from the bits and pieces of land of which I have spoken, remnants that were previously left fallow. The peasant and his family work them after hours, whenever collectivized labor leaves them the time, and keep the produce for themselves. Typical scene: On one of these plots I see three children, stripped to the waist and energetically plying the earth with hoes and picks. They are obviously three brothers, and after school it is their job to cultivate the family plot while father's working on the collective.

Hunan composes its landscapes from these three elements: paddy, red clay, eroded hill. The colors are two: the red ochre of the soil and a very new green. Villages with scaly roofs, mud walls. Trees are rare and thin. Irrigation works are everywhere. Peasants dressed in blue cotton work small paddle wheels by either foot or hand, and raise water into the channels of the rice paddies. Men carry their loads in two small baskets balanced at either end of a pole slung across one shoulder. The plows are the ancient model.

Hupeh Province

Lots of water, many flood-control reservoirs in this rather poor country. Hupeh means "north" (*Peh*) of the "lake" (*Hu*), while Hunan means "south" (*Nan*) of the "lake" (*Hu*). We are passing through the country near those great lakes which are situated in the very heart of China, halfway between Canton and Peking, and which regulate the flow of the Yangtse. As summer begins, the harvest is under way and in the courtyards of farms grain is threshed with wooden flails. In the villages new houses with red tile roofs or simple straw thatch indicate—among the blackened roof tiles of older cottages—that there is growth due to increasing population.

More red clay and denuded hills, touched very gently with the green growth of low brush. In the afternoon, as we approach Wuhan, the land spreads out, but still there is brush and sad hills. How really poor this Chinese earth must be! Then there are some white herons in a rice paddy. One thing strikes me: how few songbirds I've seen. One bird all alone on a power line. He seems to be waiting for a friend—but the last bird I saw was almost fifteen miles back, and he too was alone and waiting. Several years ago the Chinese people were ordered to kill birds because they ate too much grain. Approaching the problem with their usual energy, the Chinese seem to have surpassed themselves. I'm told they're sorry. A cobblestone road! I believe that this is the first time since Canton that I've seen anything but a path or a dirt road. Not a car or truck to be seen. Only further down the line, almost to a town, are there any signs of industrial activity: one truck on the road, a factory; a few chimneys in the distance, just a few and besides most of them aren't smoking.

But at last, after a stop in Wuchang at a huge station, huge but incomplete and obviously so for the last several years, I am allowed to experience something tremendous: I'm crossing the Yangtse on a train, on the celebrated bridge! In 1955 I saw the first eight gigantic piers growing out of the river, but we were still obliged to cross by ferry, which caused costly and time-consuming transfers. This gigantic river literally cuts China in two. An easy grade for the two-level bridge raises the tracks to a height of 60 yards above the river, and the road with its trolley-buses and a walkway to 80 yards. High above the great panorama of the Yangtse, the train proceeds slowly for almost a mile. Below are fleets of junks with oblong gray sails upon the reddish water, and the banks are lined with industries. Here the chimneys are more numerous, but few of them are smoking. Could it be because today is Sunday?

Now the train slowly passes through Hankow. No city is beautiful seen from a train. In this case the train cuts through a mess of ancient hovels, shacks and really sinister dormitories for working men. There has obviously been a great effort to rebuild, but the new tenements of red brick already look weather-worn and present every sign of incredible overcrowding, of the sardine-like piling up of the poorest population. After the stop in Hankow's new terminal (well cared for: beds of flowers, women selling ice cream or Chinese rolls, employees impeccable in their dark blue cotton, etc.) we pass again through the suburbs, different but the same, where an unbelievable multitude moves along streets bordered with weathered buildings. I have the impression that many of the factories we pass have laid off or even closed down. But I note that everything which even in the West we would consider public (here of course everything is!)—roads, bridges and accessory installations and even the personnel of the railroad—is in excellent condition: scrupulous maintenance and absolutely irreproachable costume!

After the river it's still Hupeh, land of rice, but wheat fields make their appearance. Everywhere commune peasants are to be seen busy collecting straw or reeds. Fields full of people in this really rich countryside where, around the farms and villages, something new has been added, trees in little bunches and greater expanses. Buffaloes, pigs, fowl and, a real event, a few agricultural machines, even a few metal plows! In these extensive paddies to which the endless plain lends itself, an ox still pulls the plow. Rice here is planted closer together than it is in Japan. At about six-thirty in the evening, the peasants return in groups from the fields, single file along the paths, tools on their shoulders: it's beautiful to behold. They are well-dressed, and if you get close enough you can see they are also well-fed.

Across Hopeh

My second night on the train and the afternoon of the third and last day before arriving in Peking. This morning I find the northern plain outside my window—wheat fields. We crossed the Yellow River and the whole of Honan in the dark. (*Ho* means "river"; Honan is south of the river; Hopeh, north of the river.)

Now I see the peasants going to work with long-handled hoes over their shoulders—I hear that all over China these handles have been lengthened in order to spare the peasants fatigue. The women wear colored smocks, the men light-colored shirts and blue trousers, everyone wears wide-brimmed straw hats. No bare feet in the country, and this observation proved true of China as a whole, except (as I have already noted) for Canton and the Kwangtung Province. Peasants always appear in teams—that's how far the collectivist organization of the communes has gotten. But no one seems in a hurry to get to work. Many stand chatting —this is something I'll note very often. Sleep in the shade of poplars or acacias is also frequent. No one seems in a rush and their activity is nowhere very lively.

I have an opportunity to see the country people up close in a depot, where several hundred of them are boarding a train on the next track. Young people, old people, children, every possible age, they all had to stand in line in front of the station, and the long procession climbing and descending the walkway over the tracks moves without the least shoving. All are well-dressed, in trousers or brightly colored smocks, and their baggage appears easily carried, bundles fore and aft generally, or string-bags. Their faces radiate health, and by comparison with the peasants of the old days the difference is not only in a change of costume, but in something undefinable: I have the impression they're somehow "modern," at ease, and in control of the situation.

Across the Hopeh countryside many trees have been planted and villages now are shaded by willows, poplars and acacias. Low houses built like great railroad cars show the world nothing but their backs, like windowless walls, but open on narrow courts or passages that remain invisible. More and more as we advance into the North I notice that houses have been fixed up, walls rebuilt out of clay or unbaked brick. The earth is dry and water is brought up from innumerable wells by means of bucket-chains worked by donkey or mule. Innumerable too, in this region, are the power-pumps that supply the necessary irrigation. For a long time now a dusty but well-tended road has paralleled the railroad. The absence of vehicles still startles me. We hardly ever pass a truck; a few carts, almost always in convoys and often pulled by a mixed pair of animals, a large mule and a little donkey, or a donkey and a horse, even a donkey and an ox—as though there were some shortage of animals that precluded matched pairs.

Changes, Progress, Slowdowns

As in the South, the northern peasant has dug and planted every last morsel of arable soil. But there is another phenomenon

that I have not yet considered. There is no longer "the" peasant
in the singular; he appears to have vanished.

China now contains only peasants in the plural: not one man
by himself, always groups of fifteen to twenty, single file on the
paths, a long line thrown out across the fields and making almost
the same movements with almost the same tools. Nowhere else
have I ever seen these collections of human beings in regular
little clots on the landscape, nor such obvious systematization
of field work, divided up among sections and sub-sections that
share the terrain, like combat groups on maneuvers. From
Kwangtung to Shenyang (Mukden in Manchuria) and from
Shanghai in the East to Hankow in the West, I saw this over and
over again throughout my trip. At a glance anyone would know
that he was in the land of people's communes, and that these
communes continue their regimentation of the Chinese peasant.

Since I have arrived at these general remarks, I shall attempt
to add some comments on the more obvious improvements all
over China as I saw it in the course of my last trip: innumerable
water works (dikes, canals, ponds, wells); ubiquitous reforestation, which, especially in North China, has worked a real change
in their broad plains; chemical fertilizer; power pumps, either
Diesel or electric; and last of all, rural electrification. On this
trip for the first time I have begun to feel that at last electricity
is making its way to the villages, and I find this change extraordinary. Many wires parallel the tracks, but just as many run
off into the landscape at right angles to the right-of-way. The
high-tension lines are supported by great wooden pylons—obviously metal must be used sparingly.

In addition to these signs of progress, however, there are also
surprises of another sort: poverty and slowness are everywhere
apparent. I find them scrawled across a generally monotonous
background, wide but sad horizons. For long stretches, as I have
remarked, the soil of China looks awfully poor, and too often
the rice paddies or other fields give way to low mountains or
hills, where nothing grows or lives. I have already given a few
examples of this poverty: empty roads, absence of trucks (which
are rare even in towns), and the lack of beasts of burden. The
farther north one gets, the more hand-carts one sees, some of

metal. And of course the more men, and women, thousands of them, whose job it is to pull or push them.

The most surprising thing though is the almost total absence, now as nine years ago, of any visible mechanization—except for the pumps I've mentioned. Not a tractor on the fields, only a very few small agricultural machines, and with a few rare exceptions no modern plows. On the other hand I could see everywhere the general use of ancient implements and ancient methods: wooden plows, old-fashioned flails of wood or bamboo, stone rollers for threshing, or even more frequently threshing done completely by hand. What can those factories be up to? We have been told that agriculture has the priority.

I am unable on the basis of what is visible from the train to answer that question. Besides, I saw very few factories during the first half of my trip, south of the Yangtse. It is only north of that river, and especially as one approaches Peking, that the number of factories, and of modern constructions of all sorts, begins to increase noticeably. One thing I could be sure of: there were a great many. In 1955 I had to admit my surprise that the communists had built a great deal more than I had been led to expect. This year, as well prepared as I believed myself to be by my previous trip, my expectations are again exceeded. One can't help seeing, for instance, that "The Great Leap Forward," although so often described abroad as a complete failure, was nothing of the sort, even though it ended badly. At least it left behind a considerable number of buildings, factories and constructions of all sorts. Factories for the most part, and an almost unbelievable number of workers' developments; and besides these, an immense number of public buildings and public works.

But there is something in this landscape that is equally striking and that is surely one of the liabilities left by the Great Leap. I was aware of course that the 1959–1961 crisis that followed the hurried advance on all fronts, and the "Readjustment" policies that were its consequence, had reduced or stopped a portion of China's industrial output. But I had never expected to witness along the right-of-way (as I was to see everywhere else on this trip) such an impressive number of "victims" of the Leap. It was not only the heartbreaking spectacle of all those deserted "village blast furnaces" we'd heard so much about—and which no one has bothered to remove. There were other more important ghosts: lifeless factories, obviously abandoned for a long time, their dormitories empty; factories slowed down or cut back to nothing, as the empty shops, unpeopled yards, and the high proportion of smokeless chimneys announced; unfinished structures, facades without windows or roofs, depots without a sign of life, piers meant to carry bridges but left standing in the middle of nowhere waiting for roadbed and rails or a highway that should have gotten there but is nowhere to be seen.

Then again I noticed, especially as we approached the capital, another curious phenomenon (and again one that I would see over and over again during my trip): vast quantities of goods heaped up out in the open behind walls or barbed wire fences, but protected from the weather by nothing more than thick straw matting in place of tarpaulins. What sort of goods? A mystery. These yellow mats form peaked roofs and resemble nothing so much as rows of thatched peasant cottages. But they hardly allow a guess as to what they hide. Metal or machine parts? Building supplies? Inventories? Foodstuff in reserve? It all appears to have been there a long time and is often near enough to warehouses or sheds to prove that these were unable to open their doors to this surplus because they were already filled.

All that one can be sure of is that these accumulations are somehow a result of the economic imbalances produced in China by The Great Leap Forward. Even if this program did not end in total failure, it was largely a tremendous waste, particularly paradoxical and tragic in this country that ought to be the last in the world to mismanage its resources or the efforts of its people.

Nevertheless, the men and women of China appear to have completely recovered from that crisis. This first contact with them shows them well-clothed and well-fed. But I must not allow myself to forget the stop in Canton, where I soon learned that the differences from one place to another can be startling. Nor can I base my impression simply on my fellow travelers on the Peking

Express, men who for the most part are quite obviously officials, functionaries, and Party cadres. What impressed me most is the liveliness of the provincials and peasants seen in their everyday surroundings.

Upon arrival, I can see that Peking also shows evidence of improvements. That oppressive sameness of clothing that struck me in 1955 has disappeared. Their costume still lacks variety, I admit, and charm still seems forbidden to women, or at least still in hiding because of the trousers and straight bangs or braids. All the same, this summer men wear white shirts, while women and girls wear flowered smocks, and these additional tints, together with a sprinkling of real dresses, have put an end to the reign of blue.

And morale? I don't want to attempt too rapid a judgment, but I believe I recognize, and did from the first, a certain relaxation of the stiffness I felt in 1955. I felt it in the friendly treatment I received on the long journey from Hong Kong to Peking, in the less controlled, less closed faces of people, and in their somewhat more relaxed manner with each other. China's famed good humor has not vanished. No one seems in a hurry, no one seems to be nourishing an ulcer.

And yet . . . Nothing indicates that *discipline* has been relaxed. On the contrary. All over China people are lined up in single file —in stations, leaving school, pulling carts; Communist slogans are everywhere—platforms, walls of stations, factory fronts, city intersections; portraits of the leaders show Mao Tse-tung next to Stalin; loudspeakers in the train blare the latest instructions from the *People's Daily* instead of the latest news. All this proves the existence of a Communism as thoroughgoing as it was nine years ago.

I made the trip from Hong Kong to Peking alone, but was met on the platform by Mr. Ni, the smiling agent detailed to keep an eye on me, an interpreter and employee of China International Travel Service—I almost wrote Chinese *Intourist*, but that word is no longer current. . . .

The station is new, immense and in the conventional style favored by the regime: two big square towers are turbanned with yellow tiles. In front of it, at the end of avenues of approach, is a tremendous crowd lined up under red banners; I hear fanfare and choruses. What is it? Judging from the size of the crowd, the entire population of Peking must be taking part. But my interpreter says he isn't sure what it is. Well, let's go see, I exclaim. That would be too difficult, he answers, and we would easily lose ourselves in such a crowd; the delay would be annoying. So he takes me to my hotel in a taxi that makes long detours. Can I return to the demonstration on foot? My guardian angel dissuades me with polite firmness. . . . No, I must rest after my long trip, I must wait until my program has been outlined to me —and that, he will have the pleasure of doing tomorrow.

Later I discovered that the day I arrived in Peking was a holiday, an organized holiday of course, in honor of the visit of the president of Yemen. One hundred thousand persons converged on Red Square to greet him. But this whole colorful noisy festival was concealed from me. Anywhere else they would have told a journalist, "Drop everything and come see this!" Here, nothing of the kind. Although I am a journalist and this demonstration of one hundred thousand people took place in the vicinity of my hotel, I am expected to pretend it never happened because it isn't on my program—which has not yet been settled by the authorities.

CHAPTER TWO

PEKING IN THE FIFTEENTH YEAR OF THE NEW REGIME

SUMMER EVENING IN PEKING. MY TAXI HEADED WEST ON THE "Champs Elysées" of Peking, the new boulevard that runs in front of the red gate of Celestial Peace. It turned a corner and went north, then west again and then north again. Peking is laid out regularly on a north-south axis, and so streets cross at right angles: to go northwest you have to zigzag.

I don't know the exact moment at which we left the old city because unfortunately the ancient wall has been almost completely removed. I do know that I have entered a new world, a startling world, the world of the new Peking outside the walls in the direction of the University. In 1955, this area was sad and the signs of disordered construction about the dusty, treeless plain appeared to promise little. Today, in the Year XV of the new regime, the whole quarter looks more like a park than a suburb, but it is obviously destined to become a balanced mixture of greenery and buildings.

The blueprint is visible even though the abundant landscaping along the splendid avenues does much to mask it. The trees have

not been planted in single files to the left and right of the road
as they usually are abroad; instead they march in battalions, in
rank of two, four, eight, and often as many as ten. Behind these
dense yet light curtains of willow or poplar rise new apartment
houses. They do not yet form anything but isolated islands of
red brick of from eight to ten stories high—buildings that high
are only to be seen in Peking—and the waiting empty lots behind
them retain the traces of farms or barracks, or even fields of corn.
But planned groupings of administrative buildings have already
appeared: ministries, commercial offices, governmental bureaus
or those of public corporations, provincial delegations, scientific
institutes, academies, hotels for official visitors, and a few factories
to round out the picture.

Seven o'clock in the evening. Whole tribes of Chinese pour
along beneath the close-planted poplars and willows and into
the beautifully laid asphalt road; workmen and white-collar
workers making their long way home on foot—or rolling along
on new bicycles—school children, strollers, families, and students.
All are in bunches and clusters, as if the Chinese in town as in
the country are never alone: bunches of school girls, groups of
women in trousers, an Indian file of tiny Pioneers in red neckerchiefs—the boy scouts of Communism—and groups of workmen
whose shifts have ended for the day. Many aren't moving though;
they just stand around enjoying the evening cool near their dwellings. Others stand waiting for the blue trolleybuses or the red
buses that always tow another (to carry more people for less gas)
and are the only motor vehicles to be seen. Now those are pictures of an absolutely new world, of a resurrected China, one
unbelievable to the eyes of someone like myself, who knew the
former country. This world has lost almost everything distinctly
"Chinese"—as we think of that word in the West. There has been
a tendency in the direction of a sort of elementary Occident or
America, everything sketched in a shade we might call decent
poverty, or satisfied artlessness, a world ugly and uniform in its
externals, yet somehow beautiful because of the youth and liveliness of its inhabitants. I can't help thinking that for all these
people life must really be all new and clean. Men in unironed
white shirts and blue trousers or shorts, women in white or

flowered smocks and some in trousers or skirts; such clothing may not be elegant, but it is always decent and suitable.

And I believe that beneath the shade trees of this proletarian Champs Elysées everyone, or almost everyone, must be thinking something very close to, "My life has stability and that's the important thing. I earn little, but no less than the people next door; my job is protected—as long as I'm not suspect politically. My family can expect a future without too many jolts. My father and mother never knew anything like this. And compared to everyone who lives in the old parts of Peking I am really a member of a privileged class!"

And there's the contradiction. Although a new Peking has been created and its new quarters spread, all of the former capital remains within the rectangle once formed by those vanished walls, and there another city lives in conditions that are only average, when not bad or revolting. Against the ancient backdrop of gray alleys, in *hutungs* formed of low secretive dwellings that only open toward the central court, people may live almost decently by Chinese standards, I suppose, but they live in a state of terrible overcrowding. But alongside these quarters, hundreds of thousands live in other large old city areas that have not been cleaned of shacks that shelter the most absolute poverty.

I will never forget the first time I ran across these quarters on a summer evening, although I have often returned to them on my exploratory walks—without the company of my guide-interpreter, of course. For more than two hours, until nightfall, I zigzagged back and forth among these shacks. Through open doors I could see the overcrowded miniature interiors, black with squalor and antiquity. As in the old days, I found the windows glazed with old newspaper or yellowed paper. How cold it must get inside when winter grips Peking! But now it is the heat of summer that makes them uninhabitable and drives their occupants out for air.

Along the alleys, many too narrow for anything but pedestrians, everyone was out of doors squatting on his threshold. All were half undressed, the women hardly less so than the men, and the few clothes they wore were worn and very poor. Housewives had pulled their primiitve stoves in front of their doors and were

cooking suspicious porridges and faded pancakes. Whole families, seated on benches or stones or even squatting on their heels,
dined with chopsticks off brown rice and a few vegetables, while
naked infants, blackened by the dust of these by-ways, played
at their feet. Water was evidently something rare—which might
explain the filth of the inhabitants: I saw a few bearers of paired
wooden buckets headed for a distant fountain.

From time to time my walk caused me to leave these back
alleys and cross or follow some thoroughfare for a moment. There
again I found a more prosperous population in blue trousers and
light-colored smocks in front of less dilapidated scenery. Along
these sidewalks a certain amount of refurbishing and restoration
has added infrequent socialized shops that stand out almost like
new and certainly look serviceable. But there were always a great
number of former stores that have been closed down, killed by
the socialization. Their facades—formerly the opportunity for so
much complicated decoration, in sculptured wood, for instance,
lacquered and even gilded, or those inevitable Chinese subjects
for laughable bad taste, dragons, phoenixes, peonies and chi-
maeras—flake away and vanish under the thick gray dust. Shutters nailed in place transform these old shops into dwellings. On
the sidewalks and even in the streets (where except for those red
buses there were only carts with their human draught animals)
the crowd was thick and the sweat that covered so many of the
passersby indicated how far they must return on foot from their
jobs.

Then, on the other side of the avenue, behind the front row of
houses built in a style that has hardly changed in the last 400
years, I entered again the world of back alleys. Here and there
were unbelievable structures whose unlikely shape and fragility
seemed hardly able to stand the poke of an elbow. The half-
effaced Chinese inscriptions, the bright red of children's clothes
hung out to dry, the ancient baskets, and a great many other
objects all formed a tempting ensemble for a film director on the
lookout for footage for a movie about the lower depths. This
whole world seemed to consist of dwellings that only stood up
and held fast because of a continuous patching with nails and
boards, or paper and paste. And yet the inhabitants seemed in

no way affected by their surroundings, and least of all the bands of children who filled these labyrinths with their joyous games.

In on alley two little girls squatted over their task, carefully separating a mound of garbage that had not yet been collected, although it was already evening. In one pile they put bits of coals that had been lost in the ashes, in another any vegetable refuse, and in a third pile was left unclassified garbage. But more impressive than the scene was the fact that it was repeated two more times in the same street. Once the uncollected garbage was worked over by an old man, another time by a mother and daughter.

Where was I? Not really very far from my hotel, the Hsin Chiao, between the Temple of Heaven and the Wall of the Legations, in the southern quarter that used to be called The Chinese City, and was distinguished from The Tartar City. This part of Peking deserves to be leveled, and I hear that this is planned. But work was to begin during The Great Leap Forward and as yet nothing has been done. Will they wait much longer? Yes, I'm afraid so, and indeed I wonder how, when so many little Chinese are growing up to swell the multitude, the regime will be able to shoulder the added burden of lodging the excess population and housing *these* millions whose present dwellings should be destroyed.

I must admit that even in these superseded areas life has decidedly improved. Sanitation rules are for the most part adhered to. The poor can make use of the hospital now and personnel from various clinics visit their homes. Children are vaccinated. At one corner a board set up for posters allowed me to assimilate in passing the advice of a local committee: precautions to take against diarrhea in summer—simple rules of hygiene like washing ones hands before eating, killing flies, etc. As a matter of fact there are no more flies, I'm a witness to that, and no more vermin, I hear. Vanished too are the swarms of beggars, prostitutes, and thieves. And the red-light districts that used to cover a great area no longer exist. And all those gangs that used to exploit the coolies by dealing in labor have vanished.

The tremendous clean-up by the regime has extended to the very dregs of Peking. In order to pass judgment fairly on sections

such as I have described one must keep in mind what they used
to be like—much worse. We must remember that for centuries
now these great cities have contained sections in which part of
the population lived under frightful conditions and that the shacks
of today are a heritage from yesterday.

In reality China looks very different from the photographs
in Peking's illustrated magazines in which well-fed, well-dressed,
smiling workers enjoy a happy life in a flowered landscape.
Reality for China is made up of lights and shadows that contrast
strongly, just how strongly I had not previously been aware.
China presents a series of pictures that shade from the very dark
to the very light. That there was so much black is something that
I am much more aware of on this trip than I was nine years ago.
Perhaps the reason for this is that the progress made in those
nine years lends more contrast to the remaining black. In order
to give an accurate idea of China today it would be necessary to
take certain black, very black, pictures and never show the
numerous brilliant ones without them. And I add for the sake
of clarity that any pictures taken today, no matter how black,
could never equal in quantity or quality those that could have
been taken everywhere under the previous regime.

I have not yet seen a film or a selection of photographs that
gives a picture of the new China whose total accuracy I can con-
sent to. So far none has combined the correct proportions of
shadows and lights. If such a film or book exists I have not yet
found it. The fault may lie with editors who have their political
axes to grind or who wish to cater to the prejudices of their
audience and therefore cut those pictures that seem to them to
give too flattering an image of the regime, or who on the other
hand reject anything that seems too disobliging.

But an even more probable source of cinematic insufficiency
vis-à-vis New China comes from the difficulty of taking any
"black" pictures at all. This has been my own experience. I had
arrived in China with the necessary stock of cameras and film
to make a photographic report for my own pleasure as well as
for the reportage I was to write for my paper. After reconnoiter-
ing the terrain, I gave up immediately any idea of taking pictures.

I discovered that it would be easy to take pictures that would flatter the regime by their "brilliance" and that even the documentation of the neutral aspects of everyday life could be had, but that it would be difficult to take any pictures of the darker side, and that therefore I would be unable to attain my goal, a balanced presentation of the highlights and shadows.

The authorities allow an almost complete liberty to foreign photographers. Doubtless they realize that they aren't risking much in so doing. Three factors at least make the visitor hesitate to turn his lens on the darker side. First of all there's a possibility that his film will be confiscated either during the trip or as he leaves China. If he behaves prudently and shows a "positive" attitude in his choice of subjects, his films aren't even looked at as he leaves, and this is usually the case. But if he should take any pictures the regime doesn't approve of, he is likely to be denounced to the authorities and lose his films. The second factor is the ever-present guide-interpreter. His duty is to direct his charge to favorable impressions and divert him from anything else. The third factor is the Chinese people: passersby create difficulties for the photographer as soon as they notice that his camera has angled around to unflattering subjects. The subject himself will protest, a shopkeeper will refuse to allow his shop to be snapped, the schoolboy in a red neckerchief shouts "Spy!" or a man steps out of the crowd and turns to agitate other passersby who demand that the foreign photographer take the new but ugly building on the left, instead of the fascinating shack on the right. Of course unflattering photographs have been taken, but only "on the run," from a moving car for example; it is impossible to peacefully and quietly take as many as are necessary to present every aspect, every darker side of what reality means today in China.

I therefore made up my mind that it was better not to complicate the already ticklish situation of a journalist. After all, I decided, my pen or my typewriter will allow me to export from China as many "written pictures," as much "written footage" as I like, and those pictures, no matter how "black," no one can prevent my taking, or taking out, or publishing. So I left my equipment unused in my hotel room.

"Formidable problems, remarkable progress"; there, in a nut-shell, and on the material plane, are the contrasting phenomena of which life in China consists today. And it is a contrast that asserts itself, to begin with, in the capital, Peking. But at the same time this city loudly demonstrates that when a balance is drawn it is progress that wins. Extensive changes have been made in the very heart of Peking since my last visit in 1955. Al-though my hotel is close to the slums of the past, it is also close to the monumental surroundings in which the regime stages its festivals. And the stage is tailored to the size of the crowds. An enormous east-west boulevard opens out into a gigantic square, the Red Square of Chinese Communism, rivaling the one in Moscow. Since I was here in 1955 its area has been tripled or quadrupled, and it now seems every bit as large as the Place de la Concorde. One of its sides makes use of an ancient decor, the Forbidden City and its red gate of Celestial Peace. On two other sides the decor is new and modern: on the west the tremendous Great Hall of The People, on the east the no less tremendous Museum of Chinese History and of the Communist Revolution. Both of these were constructed during The Great Leap Forward: in 1958 an army of 100,000 workmen completed them in a few months, and those few months the coldest part of the winter. I had feared that their high facades and vertical lines would ruin the flat landscape and horizontal lines of the Forbidden City. Nothing of the kind! I had not reckoned with the vast distances separating these structures.

Other buildings that date from The Great Leap Forward can be found in the heart of the ancient city: Peking Station, the traditionally styled green-roofed palace that houses representa-tives of China's various nationalities, the luxury hotels, Radio Peking—which imitates Stalinist architecture—and the new Mu-seum of Art with its roof of yellow tile in the style of the Empire. And beyond the old wall of which only the gates remain there stretches the checkerboard of a growing city, Greater Peking, which already boasts a population of seven million inhabi-tants.

It is there that the new sections appear, sections such as those I have described in the northwest of the old city, sections in which administrative buildings and cultural or scientific institutions are grouped. It is the same to the east and northeast, where embassies are now being built. Still further out and predominantly to the east a network of highways divides up industrial parks now under construction. Peking is already an important industrial center and boasts important modern textile mills, steel mills, machine tool works, chemical plants, etc. The countryside with its gray villages has been completely invaded by working-class suburbs, apartment houses, and large factories—some still under construction.

In China the roads never go very far. Thirty miles out of town the asphalt stops and all that is left is a track of hard earth or the worst sort of dusty road. But the highways that do exist are excellent: the roadway has breadth and is kept in perfect condition; a curtain of trees accompanies it everywhere and grows rapidly.

Reforestation has been considerable in Peking and the surrounding province. The capital has become a city of parks. All the older ones have been spruced up and replanted, so that they flower in profusion. In fact this reforestation extends to the whole country, and it is possible that there has been heavier rainfall during the last few years because this vegetation has changed the climate. I recall the days when trees never grew because they weren't given a chance to. All that has changed radically and now they are carefully tended. In the cities I even saw teams supplied with hand pumps out watering the groves of trees: they squirted water—probably improved with insecticide—generously over the foliage. Even more startling: one night I saw street-washing trucks roll through the streets and boulevards of Peking and douse the trees with streams of water under enough pressure to fight fires—dust here gets very thick in summer.

Greenery has also invaded the city in the form of vegetables. It is more in the nature of a flood! The regular markets no longer have room for it all, so it spreads over the pavements, where each day peasants unload their produce from the communes. Cabbages, in particular, form real little mountains. There is a certain amount of waste. One sees a veritable exhibition of Chinese vegetables—their versions of our spinach, lettuces, sorrel, beets, fennel, broccoli, etc., besides less easily classified varieties of herbs or greens along with roots and gourds of every shape, whole fresh ginger, and dried spices. All this surrounded by a sea of tomatoes.

As a result of the food shortages of 1960–1961, a tremendous effort has been made to improve the provisioning of cities in vegetables. Each city has taken under its wing the surrounding farmlands and each section has taken a neighboring sister commune whose job it is to provide foodstuffs. The plan has worked so well that it overshoots the mark. And the peasants don't suffer because the state has held to the fixed price in spite of overproduction. The consumer buys very cheaply, and to keep their displays in order, the venders often beg housewives to take two pounds of tomatoes for the price of one, or even as much as they can carry away. If anyone loses, it is the state.

In general, nutrition no longer seems an urgent problem in Peking, and I can say the same thing for the other cities visited. The abundance of visible foodstuff suggests it even more than the healthy faces. The Chinese seem to eat anywhere and even though the meals I see do not look appealing, they are never scant. The grain ration has once again returned to normal—I don't want to enter into detail on this rather complex subject. Eggs, fowl and pork make up much of what is sold in the markets. Inexpensive restaurants abound and there are even a few very good ones. Today once again one can have in Peking a Chinese banquet that rivals "the good old days," as delicious, as inexhaustible, washed down with yellow wine or *mao-tai* (alcohol). This is relatively inexpensive for the Western pocketbook, but obviously a great luxury for the Chinese on their austere salaries.

The clothing seen in Peking is decidedly presentable, much above the level in Canton. Rags and tatters, formerly so much in evidence, have completely vanished. The ancient Chinese costumes are less and less to be seen, and the slit dress of the old days hardly exists. The long gown formerly worn by the men, the ones with long sleeves in which the Chinese hid their crossed hands, is no more than a memory. That is not to say that everyone has turned to suits with vests and ties. The Sun Yat-sen collar above a rather military tunic remains fashionable. But now that there are a few smocks and bright skirts to liven it up, in the cut of their clothes and the colors a crowd in Peking more and more resembles any Western crowd. Just as in Japan (or even more than in Japan—the kimono dies hard), in China people will soon be dressed like us and have lost every trace of a specifically Chinese or even oriental costume. For example, this crowd waiting on the curb for a bus has already lost everything distinctly Chinese—except facial features.

Buses that burn fuel oil and the increasing number of trolleybuses assure Peking of the bare minimum of public transportation. To save fuel almost all of them are double, a motorized vehicle towing another. In Peking there is hardly any other motorized traffic—trucks are rare and taxis both rare and expensive. In Peking as elsewhere in China, the insufficiency of motorized vehicles, especially for the transportation of goods, remains a mark against the regime. All that these beautifully planted boulevards lack is the traffic of a great city. Lacking that, a mass of heteroclite vehicles invades the roadway, and the only common feature is their power; it is supplied by one or more pairs of naked legs. There are all kinds: rickshaws of the classic sort but often provided with tires, little metal pushcarts on bicycle wheels, or bulkier wheels—today these pushcarts double for trucking in China—and bicycle-carts, which are also used to transport goods.

Pushcarts and porters, just these two subjects would supply me with the "blackest" photographs! How many times I've felt my throat tighten at the sight of an unending caravan of human carriers, of tricycle delivery wagons worked by men doubled over the pedals, half-dressed and dripping with sweat; and the other pushers or pullers of assorted carts, all of them straining forward and often miserably clothed—because here at work the tatters reappear on the very poorest.

Take this group. By means of wheeled platforms supplied with shafts, they slowly transport an unidentifiable load of heavy machinery, perhaps large castings. Between the shafts they've hitched an old man in his fifties, shaved head, naked to the waist, thin. Why a man where the work calls for a horse or mule? Three helpers pull at long ropes that cut their naked shoulders;

one is only a boy of thirteen or fourteen who looks very proud to be allowed to toil with his elders. At the rear two women push; their arms and torsos are so nearly horizontal that their whole bodies parallel the earth, faces hidden; indeed nothing shows but their sweat-darkened blue clothes and their sandaled feet seeking better footing. Men pass in an Indian file of heavy bicycle-carts that look rusty and patched together; they carry clumsy crates of unpainted pine. They too are dripping with sweat. Some are already old and their fatigue, rags, thin naked legs and tragic faces suddenly bring back the image of the coolies of the past.

It is important to remember, however, that such an image is as old as China. Formerly the situation was even worse, the loads even heavier, and the coolies more miserable than these workers of today, who for the most part are organized and enjoy a fixed salary. If any criticism of the new regime is possible on this account, it is simply that this primitive system of transportation is not being replaced rapidly enough.

Provisional conclusion after my first explorations of Peking: whatever remains of filth and squalor belonged to the old China and is in the process of disappearing, even though it is true that many isolated bits remain. On the whole, material conditions have improved, the most important needs are satisfied and everyday life looks less monotonously gray than it did on my last trip. Let me give a few more examples.

While still in Paris I would dream of revisiting Peking. I used to wonder what Wang Fu Chin, the principle business street of Peking, looked like now. Well, here, with all the dryness of a documentary, are a few frames from the movie my notebooks contain.

Wang Fu Chin, 4 P.M. on an afternoon in June. First I will pan in slowly along one side of the street to show the kind of shops beneath the Chinese acacias. Leathergoods: handbags, wallets, and portfolios. Photographer's shop: equipment, portraits, hand-colored photos of young-marrieds (dressed in blue cotton), of infants, and brave soldiers. Clothing: shirts, smocks, summer dresses, etc. Dyer's shop. Furniture: chests of drawers and tables.

Works of art, old-style paintings, Communist statuettes (the brave soldier, the model peasant wife, the worker) and classical calligraphy. Chinese pharmacy. Liquor store: rice wines, spirits, Chinese vermouth, white and red wines, beers, etc. Hardware. Another photographer. Cafe—and all sorts of beverages appear to be sold and drunk there. Children's shop: clothing and toys. Hats. Another dyer's. Books about music and sports. Linen and bedding. Optician. Third photographer. Furs. Radios. At the corner, an open-air exhibition by the Political Propaganda Services: pictures from the life of Lenin . . .

Accompanied by my guide-interpreter I entered the blue interior of the cafe and sat there over an orangeade watching the passersby. The orangeade was served in its bottle; the brand was "Polar Bear." The straw was waxed paper. Other customers at nearby tables enjoyed vanilla ice cream, purchased candied fruit, or went off with something like ice-cream pops. But let's watch the street . . .

A lady in a gray dress with a flowered blouse, white plastic shoes . . . An unarmed soldier in khaki, cloth helmet, musette bag at his side, felt shoes . . . A young man with a green cloth sack . . . A lady in a blue white-dotted split skirt (rare as they are) whose little girl wears a doll-like raspberry dress . . . Two girls with long hair buy ice-cream cones at this cafe . . . A little old lady with bound feet, wearing black trousers and a white blouse, both of silk, style that dates from the Empire . . . An old man comes in and takes a seat; he wears a straw hat, white vest and blue trousers, has Confucian beard in three strands, and his fan unfolds black ivory . . . Two little girls from a poor neighborhood, four and six years old—badly washed dolls . . . A student, hair cut short, white shirt and blue trousers, leather shoes (rare), leans his bike against a tree and chains it before he goes off . . . Two young women go by in modern printed dresses, bourgeoise or even "decadent," with curled hair and waggling hips—very rare—filmstars? Ready for a period of "re-education," I'm afraid.

Wang Fu Chin has always been a street with a great deal of chic. And this chic has not disappeared completely even though it has taken on proletarian coloration. So let's visit, for our last strip of "footage," an ordinary neighborhood, where we can document the little man's Peking. It's a short walk from my hotel. Past the rose and gray of the Chung Wen Gate in the Wall of the Legations. This wall has already been almost cleared of its crenellations (indicating that it is marked for destruction). Areas are being cleared on the other side of the gate: a canal is being cleaned, an open-air sewer which is being led into black pipes and buried. This walk cuts a square into the depths of Chinese life. We are not far from the hovels previously described.

First, a broad avenue toward the south. The housing is of the old style, never more than one story, except for places of business, many of which have their shutters nailed to; others are closed because it's Sunday. These secretive lodgings present nothing more to the street than a covered porch and a wall of brick. . . .

Gray walls, bloodshot walls, ancient patina everywhere visible, a wearing down that verges on decay, honest poverty that lacks self-awareness . . . This China stands still or only moves forward inch by inch. And even it is no longer the same. Look! There's a woman sweeping the street, a civic employee. There's a butcher's display without flies, and there are blocks of ice on their way to some shop that sells ice. An old shopkeeper dusts his display of loose caramels and dry litche nuts. A few portals allow one to catch sight of poor housewives busy in the courts onto which open lines of dwellings that pour forth a confusion of junk.

Sunday and it's five in the evening. A large crowd flows from the "other Peking," the new one that surrounds Red Square, toward the old Peking, the poor neighborhoods to the south. They return in families. A father in a white jacket and black trousers, a mother in the same costume only brighter, neat, well laundered. Their little girl wears red ribbons in her hair, a flowered blouse, black dress, white socks, and red shoes. Her little brother also wears red, the neckerchief of the Pioneers; shaved head, white shirt, shorts with suspenders, no socks, and new plastic sandals. The mother pushes a third child, an infant, in a wickerwork carriage. Bicycles, new bicycles and not so new, each provided with a license plate and a red reflector on the rear mudguard. A pretty girl in a western skirt, an eighteen-year-old, rolls along next to her boyfriend who looks as though he's already passed thirty. He has a crease in his trousers (very rare) and a really white white shirt. They've returned from a picnic: utensils empty in a string-bag, brightly colored thermos.

An ancient tree supplies this quarter's only greenery, except for here and there, before some gray entry, pots of flowers or a tub of laurel. Elsewhere along the same street a heap of scrap iron, great tree trunks in heaps. Beneath a shed covered with a tarpaulin of plaited straw are quantities of vegetables: mounds of round cabbages, bunches of herbs, of leeks, unidentifiable varieties of gourd. Although today is Sunday, some shops are open, one of which looks splendid, the only one freshly painted; it has a sign in beautiful calligraphy, gilded, posters in the old style, lacquer and blue porcelain: a pharmacy. Delicious smelling medicinal herbs are being put into paper packets by white-smocked girls whose faces are hidden by sanitary masks of gauze.

Farther on I see a machine shop with circular saws and primitive blowtorches. A shabby grocery looks appetizing enough on entering: canned goods, cakes, meat, sausages and glazed duck. There are spirits and other beverages with bright labels, and the usual accumulation of vegetables. Vegetables all over the place. A peasant on the sidewalk sells what is probably the produce of his own little plot, but he cannot possibly dispose of the whole pile by nightfall. Squatting against a wall, a man repairs shoes. He adds rubber heels or patches up soles with pieces of an old bicycle tire.

On the avenues, red buses, an occasional truck, and bicyclists harnessed to heavy trailers; they are everywhere, everywhere, in caps, in straw hats, in gray shirts or nude to the waist, glistening with sweat, young and old, in sandals or gripping the pedals with bare feet, hundreds of them! An occasional wagon pulled by a donkey, often paired with a much larger mule. Another rare item passes, a three-wheel motorized bike, its great cube of brown wickerwork piled high with vegetables. Those blue trailer-trolleybuses are full to bursting.

And all the while a flood of pedestrians rushes along toward the south. A young girl leads a band of brats home, little brothers and neighbors, but pushes the four smallest ones in front of her in a crate on wheels. The very caricature of an old Chinaman, bamboo walking stick, chin whiskers, silk toque, embroidered silk jacket with cloth buttons, and narrow stuffed trousers above old felt slippers. An old-fashioned costume like this is so unusual that it looks like a disguise. An old blind woman with her hand in the small hand of a Pioneer. But old people are in the minority, children are everywhere. Noisy laughing girls in bright bodices; two young fellows showing off their track suits, big red numbers; two little three-year-old girls whose hair has been tied up with red ribbons, so that it resembles a Christmas candle, go by licking ice-cream cones. Workmen in blue. A policeman and his buddy, one behind the other, white summer jackets, blue trousers, revolvers, hurry to an intersection where the traffic must be regulated.

And at that intersection I cross the avenue and make a turn toward the west into a slightly smaller street of the truly Chinese city, shabby but clean. The houses are squat and square, their low fronts of blackened brick beneath the heavy roofs of tile. Dust and age make this spot as oriental as can be imagined. Except for the smooth roadway and the honking buses, Marco Polo might have seen a corner little different from this one in the Chinese cities of his day. Then I make another turn, this time to the north, for the third side of my rectangular walk. (In Peking no one says "turn to the left" or "take the next right" or "in front of" or "behind," but "to the west," "to the east" "to the north" or "to the south"—the noble idiom of times in which people felt related to the basic geometry of the universe.

I'm back in the *hutungs,* in narrow alleys between walls grayed by faded paint, dust and age. Another world of children. There must be thousands. Every one of them must date from 1960 or thereabouts. Clean and amusing, they are all of them, both boys and girls, dressed in shorts and shirts, and they are all wearing shoes. They run races, or play ball, or a Chinese version of jacks, or tag. They also "skip rope." Here, however, the point isn't to jump over the stretched rope, it's to jump right on it; the elasticized rope springs back, and the jumper hooks it with one foot or the other, from the front, from behind, with pirouettes, with sudden bounds, and all the while her little friends give the rhythm with a Chinese song.

Nothing in this alley but children; the sculptured stone markers beside doors with ironwork fittings represent young lions playing drums. All the fine old houses, solid, square—square as all buildings are in China—must have been middle-class homes. Are they still? The walls say nothing. As is the rule, the entire alley forms two long walls, a corridor. Under eaves of scaly tile an infrequent window appears, and once passed the worn threshold into the central court, the inquisitive passerby finds that a wall prevents both investigation and entry.

And now we come to the fourth side of this tour. I turn again, toward the east, and approach my point of departure through a larger street. This one is lined with the shops of craftsmen. Some of these fellows cut and assemble pieces of iron wire, others work over laundry in a peculiar shed: in front of a vast cauldron they pile oddly twisted gray linen. In an empty cafe the radio blares at oilcloth-covered round tables. On a doorstep a father reads a tiny illustrated magazine while his child squats on the threshold, dining on a bowl of hot soup. An old man, dressed like a Party member, walks into a building with a big red star over the door. That's the only trace of the Party I've seen all day. The new regime hardly made itself felt during this walk. Perhaps the true representatives of the Party are all those children, saturated as they are with politics (as I shall see later) from the moment they enter school.

On my return the Chung Wen Gate is still waiting, thrusting its old, unpainted surface into the evening sky. How different it is from the restored gates of the Forbidden City. High above the old, dilapidated pavilions with their faded rose columns, weeds have invaded the green tiles. Have things really changed much in Peking? Will China ever finish being renovated? I seem to hear these silent questions as I approach the ancient gate. Swallows congregate here at dusk, idiotically happy and full of movement: they graze in flight the green enamel glistening upon motionless dragons lined up with the joints of the roof, those dragons who wonder about the passage of time and men's attempts at change. Under the sonorous arch of this gate little children in blue jackets shout—to hear the echo's reverberation.

CHAPTER THREE

THE CHINESE RALLY TO THE REGIME

VISITS, CONFERENCES, INTERVIEWS; MY PROGRAM WAS ARRANGED BY the authorities and occupies every minute of my day. Hardly a moment for walks through Peking, even fewer for going off on my own. Such excursions aren't forbidden, and indeed they would be difficult to prevent. But they are not well loved in high places. The authorities would rather that the foreign journalist's time be completely taken up with the official program, even if, as in my case, he is not here as a guest of the Chinese government but is on his own and paying his own way. Just as on my previous trip, the Information Bureau of the Ministry of Foreign Affairs has arranged the program after ascertaining what questions particularly interest me.

The China International Travel Service supplied an interpreter detailed to accompany me every day I stayed in the capital. For an agent of the Police, Mr. Ni is very discrete; as a source of information, he is extraordinarily cautious. Evidently it is not his business to advance any information or opinions of a personal nature, and there is every indication that as a good Chinese Communist he simply has none. But as a translator he is excellent, and as a Chinese, indefatigable, because the Chinese cannot be fatigued. Nor can a journalist, so I force Mr. Ni to undergo a veritable "Great Leap Forward" in the travel field, not to mention the Great Leap the thermometer took into the upper nineties. It's June.

Here is a partial list of our expeditions. Under the heading *visits*: a textile mill, a cokery and chemical works, a printing house, a factory producing hand tools, two rural people's communes, three museums, a hospital, several schools, kindergartens, a university, a technical school, a gymnasium, department stores, the buildings of the National Assembly, the local TV station, etc. Under the heading *conferences and interviews*: spokesmen of the Foreign Office, of the Office of Economic Planning, from industry, agriculture, commerce, education, public health, and municipal government. In addition, numerous engineers, workmen, housewives, students, professors, peasants, and white-collar workers. Under the heading *tours* (because after all I am a tourist): the ancient quarters, the parks, the Temple of Heaven, and the Forbidden City.

But even sightseeing in this country is colored by politics. At least I found this to be so in the former imperial city, where the visits of the common people are now received at all hours. Obviously all the members of the proletariat looking up at those roofs of yellow tile feel that all the formerly imperial splendor which they have come to behold now belongs to them. Even more, it isn't at all hard to believe China's new masters when they say that today all of the glories of the past have come to life again in the government that they have given China.

The people and the regime: both confidently confirm my first impressions of a relaxation of their demands on each other, as compared to 1955. The atmosphere of terror and mute resistance in those days has for the most part evaporated. In 1955 there was fear in the air. Arrests were a matter of course. There was a steady stream of denouncements. Propaganda was violent. Nine years later I have the feeling that the regime no longer pushes people around, or not in the same way. It seems as though it has become part of their life, as though the immense majority has been won over, or made its separate peace, or simply given in.

If I call up my memories of arrival in 1955, it seems to me that there were two sorts of people: on the one hand the fanatics, and on the other the mass of the population—which the fanatics were busy working into shape. The fanatics threw themselves at every visitor and began their work of persuasion on him too, but their excesses of zeal always had an effect contrary to the one intended. They all said something like this: "Repeat after me: Everything is new! Everything is perfect! Everything is admirable!" That sort of importunate excess has ceased. Now the visitor is subject to fewer demands for his applause, and apparently so is the average Chinese. The pressure doesn't seem to be as high.

This is suggested by the way people stroll in Peking, by the laughter in the hotel elevator, by the relaxed attitude of friends who run into each other downtown—formerly I had the impression that people avoided each other. In the streets passersby look busy but neither hurried nor tense. They give the impression that "everything's under control." At work, at home, or in the street one no longer hears, as one did nine years ago, "We are perfectly happy!" spoken too loudly and accompanied by a prefabricated smile. Today it's a relaxed and modest "Things aren't so bad." Of course, to a certain extent Peking is a model city, and it would be dangerous to pass judgment on the whole of China from one's impressions of the situation here; but allowing myself to draw on later experiences, let me say that what I felt here was hardly corrected "on the whole" by what I saw while traveling through the provinces.

China seems, again "on the whole," to have accepted its Communist government. There are hundreds of millions who require no more than a nod from their superiors to render homage to the regime. The regime on the other hand has worked out certain ways of doing things, created new institutions. Not only has it found its everyday self, but it has invented its parade dress, as it were, as Peking at almost any hour bears witness.

It is ten in the morning in front of the red *Tien An Men* (Gate of Celestial Peace). For exactly an hour now every street and alley in the capital has spewed forth demonstrators, in long serpentine chains, in veritable Chinese dragons, directed without hesitation, according to prearranged schedule, to this gigantic square with its monumental avenue. Is it the celebration of some great victory? A welcome home for some high-up in the Party? Not at all! This is simply the regular welcome in honor of a visitor from the Afro-Asian block. The other day it was the president of Yemen. Soon it will be the general who is prime minister of Burma. Today is the turn of the vice-president of Zanzibar, Mr. Kaouaoua. He is entitled to a crowd of medium size: 800 yards of human wall made of 50,000 participants. The festivities are always tailored to the importance of the guest and whatever "quotation" the regime puts on his friendship. Prince Sihanouk received the greatest yardage so far recorded, while Prince Souvanna Phouma, prime minister of Laos, only saw a modest volume of demonstrators.

Demonstrations: the word calls up a host of men and women in a rage. But these welcomers come from an immense hive of students, boys and girls, beefed up by something like 25 percent of workmen and white-collar workers of both sexes—and hardly any older. This whole mass, let off for the morning, converges on the square by delegations, by schools, by unions, by factories, by neighborhoods. Those wild red flags, made once for the barricades of Revolution, lead the van of today's carnival of flowers—artificial flowers. A battalion of girls, in bright skirts for once instead of trousers, ready their red flowers, and the ones behind, the green flowers, while a group still coming along places caps of crimson paper on their heads. Elsewhere colored ribbons are distributed, or fans, or balloons made of gut. In addition, immense balloons, each held in place by four cables, rise into the sky, decorated with thousands of red streamers. In the background rises the Gate of Celestial Peace, framed to the right and left by four groups of four immense flags of red silk, which float easily in the hot summer breeze.

Will it all end with the disorder of a country fair? No, the stones of the whole gigantic square were at some time in the past all numbered with white paint so each file can take its position without hesitation. The tall electrical lights rise on posts that disguise loudspeakers shouting orders. Each battalion lines up with precision in its preordained location.

At the center of this engine appear several delegations of costumed dancers. Girls with enormous fans and embroidered aprons, boys in velvet jackets and shirts trimmed in an ancient style, surround ancient gongs and monumental drums. Soldiers from some dance group and drum majorettes from the People's Army in turquoise tunics, heads in turbans wound from blue silk scarves. Young women from the Army prettily clad in pants of blue cotton. Workers' bands with musicians in white shirts and blue trousers. And as a climax to all else, dancers and musicians from the "minorities," meaning non-Chinese peoples, all in their national costumes. A miracle! The women here, and especially those from the minorities, are entitled to their beauty. Contrary to that unwritten law of Communist China which forbids girls to appear attractive, these have been chosen for their ravishing features, so for a morning, here they are assembled, beauties such as one no longer sees in China; and they don't attempt to hide their charm—they'd made up their faces and combed their hair, and they appear even more exquisite in the ancient costumes that lengthen and slim their delicate grace "like a bamboo in the breeze."

Everyone is ready at the appointed hour when the illustrious visitor from Africa is to appear. And indeed at a quarter to eleven, under a sudden outburst from the drums, gongs and cymbals that make an infernal racket on top of high platforms; in a mad activity of flags, crowns, garlands, streamers, ribbons, parasols; in the midst of people letting go balloons that clash with the blue of the sky, Vice-President Kaouaoua and the members of his suite, the delegation of Tanzanian friendship, get out of an automobile procession and walk to the center of the square. Waiting for them there with all those costumed characters just described are the folk ballets of every province and minority in China. Cat-eyed girls of the Miao and Hui costumed as ancient princesses of the East; Uighirs in furred silk bonnets; Tibetans toga'd in brown wool; Mohammedans in white tarbooshes and blue surplices, with metal castanets, booted Mongols; Korean girls in raspberry dresses and others in pistachio dresses twirling immense fans decorated with peonies: a whole book of Chinese pictures dances for black Africa.

And suddenly another miracle. Without a sound, certainly

without an order, all at once the crowd begins to disperse. In ten minutes the whole congregation has become an orderly retreat irreproachably executed. Each participant finds his group and his position, each line knows precisely the time and route for its withdrawal. I am beholding the perfectly ordered dismantling of a performance already repeated hundreds of times, the final moments of a "production number" at the pitch of perfection.

The regime, like a new machine, had to be broken in, and this, along with the training of the personnel who serve this machine, has been accomplished. What few malcontents or enemies still exist are lost in the multitude of believers and followers. For someone who has followed Chinese affairs closely over the years, this was a surprise. As everyone knows, China has just managed to get out of a difficult situation. These same Chinese who today cheer the regime were all too recently on the verge of starvation and at the same time suffering further privations from a very serious industrial crisis.

Let me go over these events briefly; we shall have more than one opportunity to return to them in detail. In 1958 China's rulers decided on a frenzied acceleration of the national effort. In cities and factories it was called The Great Leap Forward. In the country it took the form of the creation of the "people's communes" that then undertook a great leap forward on the agricultural front. The people were promised that three years of strenuous work would significantly raise their standard of living. But by autumn, 1959, everything had gone sour. After having quite literally worked themselves to death, the Chinese found themselves in the black years—1960, 1961 and 1962. Communes, Great Leap, and their extensions such as industrialization on the village level, the creation of urban communes, etc., proved to be mostly failures. The Chinese were hungry and lacked consumer goods; China reached the very limit of shortages and poverty. The worse time of scarcity lasted from autumn, 1960, to spring, 1961.

How did they manage to survive? What did they do to come through? These are questions that it is no use asking now. They maintain a total silence about their recent misery. Is it because the regime demands their silence? Or is it only discretion? Everyone behaves as though this recent past had never been. Now even a curious silence shrouds that great moment of the history of the regime, The Great Leap Forward. And the "readjustment" that followed was presented to me only as a manner of short pause after the successful completion of a period of rapid growth. Functionaries affirmed whenever they had a chance that the policies of the Party have always been "correct," nor did I ever hear a single Chinese question this official truth.

The only mention occasionally made of these past misfortunes concerns the explanations given by the regime for its difficulties: the various natural calamities that struck China for three successive years beginning in autumn, 1959. No doubt about it, China's food shortage can be largely traced to changes of climate. During the three bad years there was a succession of droughts and floods, parasites and locusts. In 1960 half the cultivated land was affected. During these three years there was not a province in China, except for Tibet and distant Sinkiang, that was not visited by disaster. The large-scale public works, the pride of the regime, doubtless diminished the area of the catastrophe, but they did not live up to the imprudent assurances of their planners, who had announced in the days of The Great Leap Forward that the country was henceforth "fundamentally protected" from floods and droughts.

Although these natural disasters were an important cause of the misfortunes of the Chinese, they were by no means the only causes. In the explanations manufactured by Peking for internal consumption, a carefully worded and more exact formula comes up repeatedly: "Grave natural calamities" and "*some* shortcomings and mistakes in our practical work." Liu Shao-chi, president of the People's Republic, in a speech delivered in July, 1961, on Party Day, went so far as to throw aside the official formula and say, "*Many shortcomings and two disastrous years.*" His words were carefully weighed and human errors were found to be primary. In October, 1962, Chou En-lai, announcing in his turn that the worst was passed, attributed these difficulties both to nature and "to errors in our work." He might also have mentioned another cause for the crisis in industry, but at the time it was always passed over in silence: "The perfidy of Khrushchev revisionists."

However the problem of responsibilities is to be decided, there remains a fact that silence cannot completely hide: during those three black years hundreds of millions of Chinese suffered from hunger and malnutrition. On this point the wealth of information available at that time leaves no doubt. We do not owe this information simply to refugees (the exodus of May, 1962, to Hong Kong was part of this drama); it filtered out of all China in many ways. Travelers confirmed it, as did letters received abroad from mainland Chinese. The reports of the diplomatic corps in Peking confirmed it too, as did the gossip of resident foreigners. And there were appeals for help which asked for packets of food; and it is a fact that for a time the expediting of such packets, to the number of several hundred thousand, was an industry of the well-fed British colony of Hong Kong at the gate of famished China. And last of all, these stories were confirmed by the Communists themselves in newspapers published in China, in official bulletins, in instructions to their members, etc.

Just once, in February, 1961, a word that was never printed or uttered in Peking, not by any government official, made an appearance in an article for *Red Flag*, organ of the Central Committee, by the minister of agriculture; that word was "famine." The minister was speaking of the situation in those regions most severely hit by floods and droughts. The word never appeared again, and the spokesmen of the government denied all the while that a condition of famine had been reached. But "scarcity," the word they did use, was surely serious enough. This "scarcity" affected the whole of China; in fact that was its unique quality: never before in China's recent history have we seen a food crisis so widespread, distributed so equally over the entire breadth of the country. The regime came out of this trial with at least one thing to its credit: the handling of the equal distribution of insufficient supplies.

Those provinces traditionally rich in rice or wheat were no better nourished than the others, nor were villages better off than cities. All surpluses were collected and shipped to the poorer areas. In the cities all over China the grain ration became smaller and smaller until the maximum for a worker of the first category sank to thirty pounds a month; others often had to make do with the half of that. Thirty pounds a month can nourish a man if the rest of his diet keeps to the same level, but there was also a tragic shortage of other essential foodstuffs such as meat, fish, sugar and fats.

In 1961 the population of Shanghai received small quantities of meat only four or five times; they got a quarter of a pound of fish per month and a quarter of a pound of sugar. In May, 1961, the grain ration in Shanghai fell from thirteen pounds a month to eleven. In the old days during a famine the peasants ate bark and weeds. In 1961 things hadn't gotten that bad, but the authorities were encouraging the search in the countryside for various *ersatz* products to fill out the meager rations. The Party systematically organized a hunt for wild fruits, for mountain greens, and for marsh plants which, to quote a Peking paper, "can ease hunger." From Manchuria in the north to Kwangsi in the south commune peasants, by the hundreds of thousands, were out looking for natural additions to their diets: game, fish, edible plants.

"Eat the mountain" was one of the slogans in Szechuan, formerly one of China's granaries. "Plan your meals" became a national password, and local cadres turned out propaganda aimed at making everyone eat less by "eating according to plan." These shortages were accompanied by all the expected side effects: beri-beri, sicknesses due to undernourishment or bad food, increase in the death rate, and physical weakness that decreased worker production or even forced lay-offs.

In the absence of conversation with the Chinese themselves about the hard times, I have read with interest the firsthand accounts by a foreign journalist who can hardly be suspected of overemphasizing the bad side, indeed one who is often rather inclined to gloss over anything unfavorable to Peking: Anna Louise Strong, a Communist journalist from the United States, is an active propagandist for Mao's China.

I do not know her personally but I have looked up articles that were first published in 1962 and then re-issued as a pamphlet in Peking in 1963 under the title *China Fights for Grain*. "There were great hardships in many areas," she writes. She explains that much of the privation resulted from the lack of secondary commodities that should have eked out the rice ration—vegetables, eggs, and poultry vanished or were only to be had at astronomical prices on "the free market," *i.e.*, the black market.

"The worst time was in the winter of 1960–61, and this was especially bad in cities located in disaster areas. Among these were Tientsin and Kaifeng, whose surrounding areas suffered from long drought. Several people I know in those cities lost as much as thirty pounds in weight, and some even went to hospitals. . . ."

Elsewhere, Anna Louise Strong cites a case, the worst she had personal knowledge of: a section in Liaoning Province, in Manchuria, where 80 percent of the harvest was lost. There the people manufactured what they called "a carbohydrate cake," which the Communist reporter describes as "a ground mixture of cornstalks, sorghum stalks, leaves, and tender bark, with the addition of edible roots and some grain. . . . Its main function was to keep the stomach full and still the pangs of hunger. The people slept as much as possible, rising once a day for a full meal and to do house or farmyard chores. In this way, they kept in fair condition on little food."

Anna Louise Strong ends with a most significant remark. Every Chinese peasant, she explains, knows how to manage in a situation like that after centuries and centuries in which catastrophic harvests have not been rare. "They do not even call it *famine*," she remarks. This remark is enlightening. When we hear that "There was no famine in China" we now know approximately what is intended. . . .

We must recognize, however, that even the worst period did not bring about that one classic phenomenon of Chinese famines —the exodus of peasants onto the roads. In earlier famines something very like the decomposition of social units took place; village and family divided into young and old and went off in every direction to beg for food—and die far from home, wherever chance took them. Let us keep in mind other observations of Mrs.

Strong on this point, and set them down to the regime's credit. "All communities," she writes, "even when hungry, stood, fought and were given aid." A system of mutual help on three levels was built up under the guidance of the Party: "self-help" thanks to the discovery of local *ersatz;* communal aid from neighboring communes; and state aid of two sorts, either from the province, or, when the province could do no more, from the central government.

Naturally, in the country as in the towns, these black years did not pass without certain disorders breaking out, nor without the suffering and discontent of the people causing disturbances here and there. But again, nothing "gave way." Whatever explosions of anger or disorder there were, remained sporadic. Judging from the echoes that reached the outside world, in scattered localities there were demonstrations against agents of the Party, attacks on silos or public warehouses, local revolts of peasants or workers, and acts of sabotage. The situation was particularly strained in the South and at Canton, where the local garrison had to be replaced by troops from the North. If in certain places the feelings of the people gave the regime serious concern, nowhere did they appear truly to endanger its continuity. Thousands of isolated malcontents found themselves unable to form a hostile front for organized action.

That version of the story dear to Americans and to the Formosan Nationalists, that the Chinese people were on the verge of overthrowing their Communist masters, seems completely unfounded. The most rational explanation of why nothing of the kind happened is perhaps that state of physical weakness of the better part of the population, which was tired out by The Great Leap Forward and then sapped further by hunger. People obliged to stretch out and sleep during the day are hardly in a state suitable for rebellion. Especially when they see before them the formidable apparatus of the Party, of the police, and of the army—those three pillars of government.

Every sector of the defensive-repressive apparatus was kept in a state of alert. The army and the police, as objects of the special attentions of the government, were entitled to preferential treatment and thus escaped from the general weakness. Well-fed and

well-paid, their fidelity was total, though it is also true that a
stiffening of discipline was necessary to prevent morale being
unfavorably affected by the misery to be seen everywhere. That
the army was not just the guardian of China's borders but had
become the regime's principal support of internal security, is
obvious from the fact that in 1962 Peking concentrated large
numbers of troops in the South—as much to tighten its control
on the populace as to discourage any attempts on the Mainland
by Formosa. For its part, the Party reenforced its provincial
organization by creating the six regional offices of the Central
Committee. Its total strength showed a marked rapid rise during
the height of the crisis—from fourteen million in 1959 to seventeen million on the first of July, 1961.

Indeed the very essence of the Chinese Communist Party
resides in its concern for immunizing itself against popular protest. The formation in China of any sort of group that would remain outside the surveillance of the regime would be impossible:
either an organization is their creation—or they infiltrate it. Even
the very beginning of opposition would be impossible, further
organization and continuity are downright unthinkable. Agents
of the Party are everywhere. Moreover the Party can rely on the
aid of millions of unpaid agents.

Anyone who criticizes the Party out loud or translates such
criticism into action is denounced immediately by those around
him. Every Chinese, not simply out of his sense of civic duty but
from prudence as well, accepts as a rule of life that he is to report
to the Party anything contrary to its wishes or decisions. There
is another reason for his playing stool pigeon: if he fails to report
anything he becomes liable himself. Just as in the old days in
China no trees ever turned into forests because as soon as one
began to grow it was cut down, today in the new China discontent and opposition are dealt with by the regime on the individual level, and suppressed before they can grow into resistance on
a comunity level.

In December, 1964, Premier Chou En-lai appeared before the
National Assembly to justify the regime's anti-resistance measures
during the bad years. His analysis of the situation is worth
repeating. What he describes is hardly a tendency to revolt

rumbling among the masses; rather it was a political pressure on the part of certain reactionary elements in favor of a move by the regime toward liberalization in a capitalist sense. He admitted that these elements amounted to "quite a few people," and that they found their strength among class enemies and revisionists.

"Quite a few people have actively become the advocates," he writes, "of an extension of individual plots and of the free market, of an increase in the number of privately-owned enterprises whose profit or loss is in their own control, of the setting of quotas according to family size, of a return to an individualist economy, of the liberalization and reversal of previous correct decisions, and of capitulationism in our labor for a united front."

The prime minister added that the opposition demanded a new foreign policy as well, consisting of "the cessation of our struggle with imperialist powers, reactionaries and the new revisionism, and the reduction of our assistance and support for the revolutionary efforts of other peoples." He also added that since September, 1962 (it was then, let me add, that the great crisis came to an end with the first evidences of an upturn) "a powerful counteroffensive" had been launched by the people against the forces of capitalism and feudalism—the Central Committee of the Party having decided at that date that the time had come for a tightening of discipline on a nationwide scale.*

Moreover I was repeatedly able to confirm that since my 1955 visit there had been a complete transformation, involving the destruction of classes or social categories that might give birth to an opposition. In 1955 this destruction went on under my very eyes: the regime was in the process of launching the kolkhozes (which they called cooperatives of production). Private property was abolished; commerce was put into the hands of the state and small shops were socialized; the "remolding" of the bourgeoisie and intellectuals was under way and hobbled the various religious sects, especially Catholicism. This tremendous machine that was going to socialize China still made some hideous noises, and they lasted into 1957 and the well-known crisis of the "Hundred Flowers." But by the end of that year the organized conversion of a whole people to the disciplines and obligatory

*Chou En-lai, "Report on the Work of the Government," *Peking Review*, January 1, 1965.

tenets of Socialism was almost complete, allowing the regime to launch The Great Leap Forward and the communes. And in its turn the upheavals caused by The Great Leap and the communes finally achieved the total pulverization of the Chinese people. The human dough that remained was uniform and malleable.

I find this transformation, so striking by comparison with 1955, confirmed by the analyses of the leaders of the Party, Mao Tse-tung and Liu Shao-chi. Mao in his report on "The Contradictions in the Hearts of the People," published in June, 1957, declares all organized resistance to the regime to have been wiped out in 1956, leaving nothing behind but sporadic acts of counter-revolution. "*After 1956*," he writes, "*the situation changed radically. In the country as a whole the principal forces of counterrevolution have already been destroyed.*" He goes on to protest against those in the Party who have prolonged a too-rigorous manner beyond that date, and orders that in the future the accent be placed on methods of "persuasion" among the people.

In 1958 Liu Shao-chi (who was not yet President) was pleased to relate that the sure remedies of the Party for obtaining permanent obedience of all good people, and what might be called "the mowing-down" of the opposition, had brought about a satisfactory conclusion. His claims seem to be demonstrated by the facts. It would be a good idea if today one reread the grand proclamation of May 5th of that year in which Liu Shao-chi inaugurates The Great Leap Forward. There he speaks of "criticism and self-criticism"—which is the name for that process of political steamrolling to which the Chinese are submitted. Rather than "criticism and self-criticism," they ought to say "accusation and self-accusation."

In principle it means that every fault, every error, every omission and, in a manner of speaking, every sin against socialist order and thought must be reported to the Party or its representatives. Just as elsewhere in the world the faithful go to confession, here the Chinese citizen is bound to regularly accuse others, as well as himself, of any "shortcomings," and this in the presence of the authorities as well as of his equals. In this speech, Liu Shao-chi points out the most important merit of this system. It not only brings the straying citizen to order, he explains, but it provides the masses with an arm against those officials who become guilty of "bureaucratism." This method, he goes on to say, insures "an equality among people" which would be inconceivable in a capitalistic country. "Until the present day there has been no political party [meaning: not even the Russian Communist Party] brave enough to practice democracy on such a tremendous scale." "In the future," he says, "this system of criticism and self-criticism will become the regular means by which the Party reforms ideology and improves labor," and it will be periodically used in enormous political campaigns. Liu Shao-chi congratulates himself for being able to base the action of the regime upon "facts disclosed by the masses" and the mutual criticism of Chinese "who name names." All this adds up to the fact that the reporting of every incorrect action or thought as well as the denunciation of all recalcitrants has become the duty of every Chinese citizen—beginning with his own thoughts and actions.

If, two years after the end of the great crisis through which China passed, there is on the whole only obedience and approval of the regime, the explanation, it seems to me, must be at least in part that a system of political measures has grown up which isolates and evacuates—to borrow an image from hygiene—discontent and resistance as swiftly as they develop. This explains why the Chinese are as silent about their former misfortunes now as they were at the time of the troubles. It explains why the past receives the same approval as the present, and why not a voice is raised to criticize their leaders for the fashion in which the country has been run in the last few years.

Now that the crisis has ended I believe the gamut of public opinion must be something like this. For millions of Chinese, finally, increased confidence in the regime: "They are really powerful! They got us out of that mess!" For still other millions, discreet obedience: "Let's repeat the slogans when called on. We learned what they're worth, but at least they'll let us be." For the rest, fatalism and resignation: "No, we'll never beat them. Let's face facts; they're here to stay."

The Chinese now docily take part in the exercises of conformity that are demanded of them. That conviction was formed during the course of my trip, and I shall give examples. The Chinese, formerly a people of individualists, even anarchists, seem to have lost their capacity for being shocked by such customs as the Party's enforced unanimity, universal denunciation and the humiliating experiences of self-criticism.

Today a generation has ripened which has never known any spirit or method other than those that have formed it. And this gives another explanation of their rallying to the regime. Anyone under thirty-five in China bears within him, in body and soul, the red seal of these new times. And those young people whom the Communists found in kindergarten when they came to power, how old are they now? Twenty, twenty-one. And what proportion of the population is "less than 20"? About a half.

Half of the people one sees on the streets have never known anything other than the present regime. Those who are now thirty fell into the hands of the Party at fifteen, and they too bear the marks. As for those who are forty and more, who were twenty-five and over when the new regime began, it seems to be enough that they obey and that in the ranks of the servants of the new order, they take their places behind those younger than themselves. Doubtless the regime has problems with the young, but the regime will belong to them one day, and even now one can say that youth is the regime.

It is they who furnish the largest battalions of demonstrators. It is they who produce the noisiest ovations for welcomes and the most vociferous shouts if a protest is scheduled. Indeed the regime has perfected a whole series of production numbers as its public rites. There are meetings to voice approval. There are protests during which weapons appear in their hands; they shout, carry bannered slogans, and roar their anger—to order. There are victory celebrations too. And the commemorative meeting. That is the most elaborate model, and both National Day (October 1st) and May Day play an important part in the cult that the regime devotes to its glory and its leader. Then there are the receptions that the people of Peking stage in honor of visiting dignitaries—one of these, for Kaouaoua, we saw ourselves.

No matter what the occasion, it owes all the color it has to

these young people who are able to save even the most luster-
less meeting from boredom, simply by being there; for example,
those meetings that take place indoors. We are at a reception in
honor of the president of Yemen, a Moslem country that is
"progressive and friendly to China." The Great Hall of the People,
in which this reception takes place, seats 10,000 and that means
that there are 10,000 people sitting there, all, or almost all, young.
According to the invitation, they represent "every section of Peking," and the Hall contains a carefully selected sampling of the
capital's inhabitants, male and female: officials, workmen, housewives, white-collar workers, soldiers, peasants from nearby
communes, etc. Since President al-Salal is a Mohammedan, a detachment of the local Islamic community has been given a con-
spicuous place. You recognize them by their little white caps.

Instead of resembling a legislative chamber, the room resembles
a movie theater. And that should not be astonishing. When the
deputies are in session, they do not debate; they merely listen to
and record the decisions made by the government. They are
nothing more nor less than seated spectators. Today's session has
been carefully staged. At every point in these speeches, which
have become classic (anti-American anathemas, diatribes against
Russian revisionism, exaltation of China's generous treatment of
progressive peoples, etc.), powerful spotlights built into the decor
of the chamber come into play to point up the climax, while the
cameras of Peking Television and the newsreel cameras grind
away at speaker and audience.

One striking peculiarity of this room is the perfect alignment
of the seated spectators. In the West, a room full of people has a
mobile and irregular surface. Here 10,000 boys and girls are
arranged like caramels in a box, and the vertical lines are as
regular as the horizontals. Like 10,000 model students, they all
sit at attention, their backs stiff and their eyes fixed on the
speaker. These boring speeches contain propaganda that they
have heard a hundred times, but this model audience acts as
though the speaker were making extraordinary revelations. Then
suddenly, the audience lets go! As soon as a suitable passage has
been enunciated, the speaker is immediately overwhelmed with
applause. The applause has been perfectly drilled: it comes all

at once and everybody participates. Not one palm is off beat, not one hand is missing. It is nothing if not perfectly unanimous. It begins and it ends cleanly. This audience forms a single being, and that being has excellent reflexes.

I try to pick out the individuals who form this mass. At a word from the speaker I see them pass instantly from a state of good conduct worthy of boy scouts to a positively revolutionary frenzy; then as the speech takes another turn they each become attentive students. When the next ovation explodes, 20,000 hands beat violently and yet it is only the hands that move. The bodies they belong to remain motionless, deep in their chairs. And finally, when silence returns and the speaker returns to his theme, I catch a significant gesture: thousands of hands at chest level in an attitude of interrupted applause, ready for the next sudden renewal of thunderous unanimity. I believe that those hands are translating into a visible image the real passion for approval and applause that all these young people feel for those who lead them.

CHAPTER FOUR

MANCHURIA: CHINESE FACTORIES AFTER THE RUSSIANS' DEPARTURE

IN THE MANCHURIAN PLAIN THREE GREAT CITIES BRISTLING WITH chimneys lie close together: Anshan, Fushun and Shenyang. I arrived by train for a tour of the factories in the highly industrialized Northeast. "The Northeast," that is the new name for Manchuria, land of progress, industrialized before the rest of China but since long before this began, in the Twenties, a pawn in the struggle between Russia and Japan for spheres of influence.

My itinerary through China's provinces will bring me to only two other major cities, Wuhan—in central China—and Shanghai. Compared to my previous visit this itinerary is singularly restricted. In 1955 I journeyed into the far-away Northwest, as far as Lanchow where I was fascinated by the spectacle of the industrial revolution reaching the confines of Central Asia; then

I flew to Chungking in the West where I took a boat down the Yangtse, through the celebrated Gorges. This year when I presented my projected voyage to the authorities in Peking they courteously rejected my request to revisit Lanchow and Szechuan, the richest agricultural region in the country, or to see Kunming, "city of eternal Springtime," in the mountains of Yunnan near the Vietnamese border.

China is more secretive in 1964 than she was in 1955. The list of cities that are open to foreign journalists and diplomats (if they have permits) is very short. On the list are the principal cities of Manchuria, a few in North China (Tientsin, Taiyuan, Tsinan, Sian), and the great centers on the Yangtse: Wuhan, Nanking, Shanghai. In the spring of 1964 a group of diplomats saw Chungking but had the feeling that their visit was carefully watched and carefully staged. Three months later journalists were barred from the city.

Note that except for Canton, which cannot be avoided if one enters China by way of Hong Kong, all these authorized cities lie north of the Yangtse. Is South China "less edifying"? Are they afraid to allow visits to the provinces farther removed from Peking, where the economic recovery may not yet be satisfactory? Is the Northwest disturbed, as we hear, by difficulties with the Mohammedans in the population? Or do they simply wish to keep closed the window it opens on far away Sinkiang, in the heart of Asia, where there have been border incidents involving the Russians? As for Lanchow, that a visit there should be forbidden is perhaps motivated by the rumored presence, in a city which Marco Polo described, of the newest and most sensational addition to China's industries: atomic reactors. If there is one subject that is never mentioned to the visitor it is the atom—I mean atomic technology.

—This new China, like the eternal China of the past, remains a land filled with mysteries. By the end of his stay the traveler should have some means of measuring the extent of his ignorance and the modesty of his information. All the same, this trip, even though it will be much shorter than the one I made in 1955, can tell me a great deal, beginning with what I learned in Manchuria.

In 1955 I was aware of a tremendous surge in development and modernization under the impetus of the first Five Year Plan. In Anshan, China's industrial capital, where the Japanese had already built a complex of modern factories and trained a first generation of qualified Chinese workers and engineers, a new wave of model factories and a new generation of engineers of the Communist era and the first Plan has changed everything. Russian aid played an important part in all this, it is true. But it is also true that the Chinese learn quickly and were quick to demonstrate their abilities, so that now there are automobiles marked "Made in China," and there are also trucks, tractors, planes and machinery—all made in China by the Chinese. In the nine years since my last visit, Manchuria and the rest of China have known terrible setbacks. After the Great Leap came the black years of crisis, 1960, 1961, 1962. In what condition is the industrial effort at the present day? What will Anshan be like?

Larger, older: those were my first impressions. Larger, because Anshan has been building. Older, because all that construction seems for the moment to have slowed almost to a standstill, and instead of the birth of factories and the influx of machinery, so noticeable in 1955, I found the industrial plant looking rather stale and here and there worn-out.

First ride through the town. New hotel, new technical school, new boulevard, and new mining school; a hospital, a workers' development club, another workers' development . . . Just a taxi ride through this city reveals that The Great Leap Forward was not a myth. Anshan has an urban population of a little less than a million, but there are another million and a half in the surrounding working-class suburbs and peasant villages. My guide tells me that since 1955 the building program has created room for 80,000 families. However, there are still hovels to be seen here and there. Behind the rows of solid brick public housing along the avenues one often catches sight of another row, one much poorer in appearance. It is only four in the afternoon and all around these buildings swarm children less than seven years old. All those above seven are in school and I can see thousands of them in the schoolyards. Which will be faster? Construction or reproduction?

Another ride, the factories this time. Here I am again suddenly plunged into that fascinating world of heavy industry coming into existence at the edge of Asia. Today one hundred thousand Chinese work in the vast panorama of factories, warehouses, chimneys, complexes of pipes, rails and ironwork that make up the installations of the Anshan Iron and Steel Company. And right off one sees that it all works—it's in the movement, the smells and the noise. This vast complex in every way indicates a new surge forward after the difficulties of the last few years.

I was shown the heavy rolling mills. Not very new, they date from 1953. And not so new to me either—I saw them in 1955. All the same I can make comparisons and discoveries. And one of them is that very little has changed. All the equipment is the same except that it's older and probably overworked. But the 1,500 workers in this section worked fast and well. I am told that in three eight-hour shifts they produce 30,000 tons of rails and girders per year.

The Steelworks No. 3, which is often shown to visitors, dates from 1958, the beginning of the Leap Forward; it contains open-hearth furnaces. There are twenty-five of them arranged in rows of five, but ten of them aren't fired. Around the other furnaces workers are tapping the molten steel or tamping sand into the mouths of furnaces to close them. They seem to me not too well protected from the flames. Safety regulations appear to be generally inferior to what they are in Europe. Straw hats and shabby clothing cannot hide the healthy appearances these workers have. Among them I catch sight of engineering students who in their fourth year have to spend a month as workers. I am told that certain furnaces yield as much as 10.63 tons of steel per square yard of furnace floor. The quality and variety of products from these mills and furnaces has increased since 1962. Twice as many sorts of alloy and special steels are made. In particular they are working for the installation of new fertilizer plants, or those which build tractors and trucks; for instance, the great automotive works, at Changchun, north of Mukden.

Next we visit Blast Furnace No. 10, the pride of Anshan and the glory of China. Why? Because its equipment is 100 percent Chinese, I'm told. And because of the tremendous speed with which this plant, entirely designed and executed by the Chinese during the first enthusiasm of the Great Leap, was brought to completion. "Four months and three days," my guides keep repeating. That such an enormous plant required only four months and three days for its installation disturbs me rather than astonishes me as they intend this record to do. However, I am assured that "it has always worked very well." It produces 2,700 tons of cast iron per day in nine pourings of 300 tons each. This is the newest and most efficient of the company's ten blast furnaces. Others, like No. 7, are at present being repaired, as are certain other plants dating from before the Great Leap.

Thus my impressions of Anshan, based on too short a tour I admit, aren't bad. But they aren't brilliant either, by no means as striking as in 1955. Perhaps this is because that was a period in which progress was exceptional on all fronts. In any event we are still at a stage that remains far behind the industrialization of America, Europe or Japan. Anshan appears to be several years behind those ultra-modern steelworks that I saw two years ago at Yawata-Kokura in the south of Japan. Certain faults appear so surprising and so obvious that one wonders what miracles China's engineers will dream up to get themselves out of hot water.

The most startling thing is the unbelievably short supply of motorized vehicles. Seeing few trucks in Peking, I said to myself, "They're up in Manchuria where they're really needed." But I was wrong, because here in Anshan, the most industrialized town in the country, they are still few and far between. Changchun is only a bit farther north and its factories began to produce a four-ton truck, the "Liberation" model, in 1955; but they are still rarely seen in Anshan. Just as elsewhere, and probably even more than elsewhere given the importance of transportation in this city of steel, we have returned to a world of human motor power: loads are manually pulled, pushed, and lifted. The height of mechanization remains the pedals of the delivery carts. Teams of animals are less frequent than teams of men and, as I noticed upon my arrival in China, most often the animals are badly matched. It should be evident that such a system of transportation must be terrifically prejudicial to the smooth workings of industry and cannot help slowing down its operations. My automobile remained motionless in a bottleneck for more than five minutes because a battalion of wagons and carts were being held up by two mules and a donkey. Neither the curses of their driver nor his whip could force them to budge a light cart too heavily loaded with a long metal framework. And this exactly duplicated something that had happened to me here nine years ago!

Another thing that distressed me about these factories was the obvious lack of means of maintenance, perhaps even of a sense of what "maintenance" means! One feels that they simply haven't any notion of what "paint" is, and that a little rust surprises no one, not even when it blots the enormous gas pipelines that have not been repainted since they were put in place. Communism has taught the Chinese that they must keep streets and sidewalks clean, but in many places no one seems to have any idea of what a well-run factory looks like. The confusion that reigns in their shops is appalling. Scattered ironwork, beams of wood left lying, broken ceramic pipe, fragments of former assemblages or previous manufactures—are they too busy to clean up? Why have carefully nailed crates, which appear to contain parts, been allowed to stand outdoors long enough for the wood to weather? When I see castings, or metal rollers, or machine parts or other working stock standing out in the open, is it finished material waiting to be moved or is it old material that has been condemned and thrown out? Aren't there enough workmen for some to be detailed to remove it? Are faulty means of transportation to be blamed? Is it rather that the former sloth that drove Europeans mad but never moved the Chinese themselves is not yet dead?

But there is another explanation that certainly plays a part in the situation: this disorder may be one of the traces of the crisis from which industry has just now recovered. Many other signs of that crisis remain in Anshan (and I shall run across the same ones in Fushun and Shenyang, and even later, in the cities of Central China. A great many factories had to shut down after The Great Leap Forward. They are easy to spot, as I had already noted during the stretch from Canton to Peking, because of their dead look, broken windows, deserted yards, and smokeless chimneys. And again it is striking that all those new factories that the foreigner is shown date from around 1958 and that with a very few exceptions, which I shall discuss later, there is nothing dating from the years after 1960. This gives some indication of the sudden stop, at about that date, to their previously feverish construction. It also indicates the slowness with which things have been picking up.

The visitor receives no figures. The 1960 law making statistics a state secret has not been rescinded. This makes a startling contrast with the situation in 1955. At the time of my last trip Anshan was the center for the publication of statistics designed to publicize the regime at home and abroad. Production graphs of these steelworks decorated walls all over the country. Today there is nothing of the kind. It is likely that if the present figures were given they would reveal levels of production below, even far below, the heights attained or pretended to in 1958. However, one important observation can be made by any visitor to Anshan or almost any other industrial town: in many factories and shops part of the machinery isn't working. The guides explain that it's being repaired, or idle, or merely in reserve. But since generally this amounts to 30 percent, and sometimes more, of the plant, it is obvious that such a mothballing must result necessarily from the overall state of the economy.

At Anshan a guide makes the customary talk, but its lack of precision is heartbreaking. I am not entitled to a single figure, neither local nor national. "In 1962 we produced 70 varieties of new products. In 1963, 120 types above the figure for 1962. Our technical abilities increase from day to day." But in this embarrassed modesty there is an honest admission that interests me: Anshan is still undergoing a "readjustment." Translated into plain English "readjustment" means the period of convalescence and slow reorganization following the total overthrow of the Plan. The improvement of quality and diversification seem to be the main efforts, and they are crowned with a certain success. But no one boasts of quantity, nor records, nor even increases in production. And the official slogans of Readjustment are "readjust, Consolidate, fill the gaps, and raise the standards." Evidently those gaps aren't always so easily filled. When I questioned my guide about the supply of raw material for Anshan, he answers with surprising frankness. The entire output of the mines cannot fill the demand. And he explains that the problem is not in finding sources of supply (deposits of ore are found just outside Anshan) but in developing them. "Construction and basic works still lag far behind the rest of industry." In other words, the minerals are there but their exploitation requires large-scale capital investments; in the meantime, many demands are unsatisfied.

Next I am shown Fushun, city of coal. This stop at least allows me one comforting visit—the refinery where more than fifty petroleum products are produced from the oil shale supplied by the famous open mine situated in the neighborhood. The petroleum industry is one of the few that has not been ordered to cease investments in its plant. Here all is modern and well kept. For the first time I am supplied with production figures: crude oil, 300,000 tons per year; diesel oil, 188,000; gasoline, 70,000; high octane, 55,000, etc. Yield: one ton of crude from twenty-five tons of shale. And also for the first time I am shown a plant that dates from 1964, the buildings new and clean, aluminum paint still bright on the tanks, automatic metering equipment (in part East German, although they tell me that the whole works is "Made in China"). This installation turns out from 500 to 700 tons of light kerosene and related products per day. For the first and, I think, only time I am told of the existence of a Plan that in three years' time will bring the whole installation up to date. In the meantime part of their equipment lies idle—a third of their crushers, for instance.

Another good impression. This time in one of the principal coal mines of Fushun, the *Dragon's Furnace,* where 11,000 miners turn out two million tons a year. A narrow hoist took me down as far as the main gallery, which was well ventilated and whose cement floor carried an electric railway. Among these workmen in decent work clothes, helmets and boots, I felt that for once what I was seeing was the simple reality undoctored for the visitor. Nearby, the *Victory Mine* has just opened another shaft, a rare example of expansion in 1964. This mine employs 7,000 workmen, and the third great mine, *Tiger Terrace,* has 10,000.

Next we see the extraordinary *West Mine,* one of the largest open mines in the world. Since 1959 it has been joined by the *East Mine,* which promises to grow as large. The former is now almost four miles long, almost one mile wide and 225 yards deep. The latter is not yet quite three miles long. The gigantic "stadium" of the *West Mine* is something one should see for himself from the top of an observation tower: the greenish cast to the upper parts comes from the shale, which in some places attains a depth of 190 yards. Farther down it is black from coal in seams that run in depth from 40 to 120 yards. Nineteen giant steps cut into the deposits form the steps of this "stadium," and the railways they bear look like toys. I am told that this mine employs 15,000 persons. It is clear that while the removal of the shale is continuous there is little work in the coal at the bottom. The briefing is scant, but I gather that here too "readjustment" reigns. I am not given a single production figure.

Riding through the city of Fushun leaves me with various images. Broad streets but little traffic. The former Japanese section can be recognized by the good shape it's in. At the hotel, I entered by a new "Great Leap Forward" wing, but was led through a labyrinth of corridors to my room in the older part built by the Japanese! The pipes they laid more than thirty years ago are still better than the plumbing in the new wing. In the center of town there are other new sights: the beautiful square in front of the station and many workers's quarters that look like red brick barracks. Just as my guide is speaking of the misery of the past our car passes a sad-looking row of old-fashioned mining villages whose overcrowding cries out that some of the people are still impoverished. Nearby the Hun washes down mud black with coal. In the shallows, women, children and old people gather it in baskets, and the dirty heaps dry in front of every door. "It's for the winter," say the guide. "It's free and it will burn." I am surprised that such is the case in a city where coal abounds.

The population (900,000 in the city, 1,200,000 counting the suburbs) has more than doubled since the Liberation of 1949, and between the modern pieces of this scene, as though bursting the seams, Asia appears, eternal Asia with her primitive misery. Out past the *West Mine*, across the river, a "Hooverville" has sprung up. Frightful little shanties, densely packed; their walls of brown or gray mud bear roofs of thin planking or any available tarred paper, and on top of these, large rocks protect the whole thing from blowing away when the wind comes down out of Siberia. Farther on we skirt a line of shops and tiny factories, dirty and pitiful shape—I'm told they are "sub-factories" connected with the refinery. Most of them look dead, victims of the crisis, evidently. But elsewhere new constructions are going up. A 1959 factory that produces generators is in the process of being doubled. Housing too is rising. I saw a girl of fifteen or sixteen surrounded by workmen. She is handing up bricks, to the men up on the scaffolding. . . .

On the train that takes me to Shenyang I notice a curious phenomenon that will be repeated somewhat less startlingly elsewhere in the north of China: the landscape is absolutely flooded with coal. Obviously no one knows quite what to do with it all. Mountains of it are heaped beside the tracks. Sometimes rails run along the mountain at right angles and transform it into a long wall of coal. Elsewhere, a sea of coal submerges a factory, fills its yards, breaks over the walls. The excess has begun to invade the countryside; it encroaches on the green tumuli of the Manchu tombs, their sleep so far respected, which suddenly disappear. How is this situation to be explained? Overproduction? Underconsumption? Reserves created for a possible upswing in production? Or is it simply that once it's a question of transporting all this coal away from the rail line the problem of trucking is run into? Whatever the cause, a disequilibrium in the economy could not be more obvious.

Shenyang. The old name, Mukden, was Manchu. But at the same time that Manchuria was rebaptized the Northeast, Mukden was given a Chinese name, to erase the last traces of particularism and to assert the national unity. Shenyang has a population of two and a half million. It is the capital of Liaoning Province—population 25 million. The whole Northeast has about 60 million inhabitants. In Liaoning, which contains Anshan and Fushun, also includes the great port of Dairen and the naval base of Port Arthur, which Russia returned to China in 1954 and which has been rebaptized Lushunkou.

Shenyang, no longer a "colonial" town of the Russians or the Japanese, is proud of its heavy industry, almost all of which dates from the Communist epoch. For example, there is an important plant for heavy stock which is often shown to visitors. Other factories produce tractors ("Red Orient," 28 horsepower), cable, electrical apparatus and transformers, equipment for metal and chemical plants, trucks, cars, etc. Light industry here runs to textiles (cotton and wool), pharmaceuticals and foodstuffs, paper, rubber goods. The working population: 600,000.

The revolution in society and in industry, I am told in the course of the customary briefing, owes its success to the complete overhaul of the school system after 1949. Mukden had only one college, Shenyang has sixteen. The disciplines taught are many: engineering, agriculture, humanities, physical education, medicine, etc. In addition to the colleges there are now 190 secondary schools, 30 technical schools and schools for teachers, 900 primary schools, and 400 night schools and schools for adult workers.

Here I omitted the tiring round of factories. I preferred to get an idea of the town, visit a distant commune, look into the situation of the Catholics, etc. In this city I am struck once more by the historical weight of poverty still resistant to progress and reconstruction. And once again I wonder: in the race between obsolescence and renewal, which side is winning? Certainly the race looks close! On the other hand the older is not necessarily always the worse. The former Japanese sections remain among the best constructed: the Japanese built with good materials and had a sense of how to lay out a city. I am happily surprised to once more find myself in the Japanese hotel in which I stayed more than a quarter of a century ago! Unchanged, it is excellent. But except for that hotel and a few public buildings, recognizable as dating from the days of the Japanese Empire by their placement on circles or broad avenues laid out in stars, these sections appear aged and to have never been repainted; and once we pass farther into the Chinese section the situation deteriorates. I imagine that at the end of the last century Lille or Roubaix, or at least their poorest neighborhoods, must have contained ancient, smoke-blackened brick that looked like this. The main street swarms with pedestrians and carts, but it is clean. The shops are full of customers, but everything seems worn down by a human erosion.

All the same, trees have appeared along all the principal arteries and the trams have been replaced by trolleybuses. The north-south avenues have been broadened and there are policemen in white stationed at important junctions. The road that leads to the ancient Imperial Tombs (which have been restored and surrounded by a very lovely park) brings us to a vast neighborhood where areas of green surround buildings which house many families. In addition, there are also dormitories, the university, a hospital, a gigantic hotel, etc. This is the new Socialist City, and streets lined with shops wouldn't make sense, so parks have replaced them. Purchases are made at state department stores or at cooperatives. But who lives here? A favored minority, assuredly. Indeed, returning to my hotel that evening I plunged through the poverty of the suburbs, through the poor. returning to their alleys, the eternal *hutungs*. The same old China changed very little, physically at any rate—only made healthier by a good cleanup. Humanity still swarms in this patched-up world. Beneath a decoration supplied by worn laundry that hangs in swags from one building to the next is a jumble of objects and people dispossessed by the heat and overcrowding of these quarters—and thousands of children bump into all of it! These children and their laughter somehow brighten the gray tones of the surrounding scene. Back in my hotel, close to midnight, from the park beneath my windows I hear the boisterous joy of children laughing and shouting.

One last visit before I leave Shenyang: the Industry Show in the Liaoning Exposition Hall. It will allow us to end our tour of the Northeast on a note of optimism. The presentation here of all the best and newest products of the province, both parts and finished goods, was impeccable. Machine tools, high precision lathes, heavy machinery, equipment for automobile works, machines for the production of tractors, parts for the plastic industry, etc. Here we were up to date for once, both as to the intended use of the material and as to date of fabrication—1962, 1963, 1964! Textile mill machinery, machines and parts for the electrical industry, high-frequency induction furnaces, electrical locomotives constructed at Dairen—no, just their pictures!—machinery for the pharmaceutical industry, agricultural insecticides, tractors, trucks, tires, nylon, plastics . . .

I'd like to be sure that all this wasn't made up of models, of prototypes that have never gone into production; I'd like to be sure that the assembly lines have started working; I'd like to see a few figures. . . . But whatever else is true these are a very modern group of products and the variety of machines marked "Made in China" is particularly striking. Here we are in the period known as the "readjustment," or just coming out of it. It certainly seems to end with one obvious success, the production by the Chinese, without any outside help, of designs perfected by themselves and at least in appearance workable.

My tour through the Northeast has come to an end without anyone ever having made more than a vague or implicit reference to the crisis that preceded this readjustment. Take the case of the two guides whom the authorities have detailed to show me the Northeast. One is a representative of the provincial Office of Foreign Affairs, the other is an interpreter supplied by the Chinese "Intourist." Both of them are men in their thirties, and both very probably typical of cadres formed since the Liberation by the Party. We get along quite well. They are as polite as they are efficient.

But if they are asked for information or to pass judgment on the recent past, they are unable to supply either one—unless "passing judgment" means total acquiescence, and "information" means an "everything's all right," that applies to both the past and present. They don't seem to realize that their powers of persuasion have lost their edge in this confrontation with a foreign visitor not totally devoid of critical abilities and armed with a certain amount of knowledge about recent Chinese history. Therefore, it would probably be best, before following my itinerary to the next industrial center on the list, Wuhan in Central China, to tell what I myself know about that period of crisis.

The crisis of those black years was much more than an

agricultural crisis that produced a shortage of foodstuffs; it was also a crisis in industry. The latter inflicted a terrible reverse on hopes fostered by The Great Leap Forward. Mao Tse-tung demanded "three years of uninterrupted labor" from the Chinese people in mid-1958, but promised in exchange a basic transformation of their country, an economic metamorphosis. The people were told that because the masses are capable of working miracles when directed by the Party, China was certain to cross the threshold of underdevelopment with a single "great leap." A new epoch would begin in which it would become possible to overtake older capitalist countries like Great Britain in a matter of fifteen years.

However, the three years having passed, the picture China presented in 1961 was considerably below expectations: she was in the middle of grave industrial disorganization. And the Occident was made well aware of both this crisis and the agricultural difficulties. Of primary importance among the mass of information available on the subject are the publications of the Chinese themselves—a wealth of official pamphlets, public announcements and government newspapers—although it is true that they have since maintained absolute silence about the statistics involved. Though it is true that the Great Leap often obtained significant results—in construction, in the records that were achieved in certain sectors of the economy, and in the production of certain key materials (steel, for example)—this progress was offset or even annulled by slowdowns, backsliding and failures in other economic sectors. The result was the overall production mixup that was one of the distinguishing marks of this particular crisis. There were indications everywhere of shortages or imbalances—"weak links" they were called in Communist publications—that paralyzed production. Shortages of electricity and fuels, shortages of raw materials, and irregularity in the deliveries of one factory to another. Slowdowns in the delivery of machine and parts led to a crisis in the mining industry (many mines had to lay off their forces—some closed completely). There was also a crisis, it now appears, in China's attempt to build its own atomic industry. The Chinese bomb could not avoid falling considerable behind schedule.

Light industry too found itself in serious difficulties. A general scarcity of consumer goods developed, particularly of textiles. Not only were the Chinese badly nourished, they lacked a variety of ordinary necessities: soap, fabrics, hardware, etc. There was even a scarcity of handcrafted articles made from bamboo, wood or wickerwork. Even when such items were to be seen in the showcases of state department stores, they were not available to the masses since they were only sold in exchange for ration coupons that had to be saved for more urgent needs.

These difficulties were due in part to the coincidence of the agricultural crisis with certain "grave natural calamities"—and the subsequent weakening of the work force. But it is also obvious that errors on the part of the planners and executors were an even more important cause. As in the case of agriculture, the regime allowed itself to be led astray by overinflated statistics received from below, where they had been made on the basis of flattering fictions. One paradoxical result of the Great Leap is the way in which, in a country heretofore absolutely under the spell of the Plan, it led to the abandon of any serious attempt at planning. A race for records led to imbalances and dislocations that are still making themselves felt. The Great Leap destroyed the coordination between the various sectors of the economy, particularly overstraining transportation, and causing certain industries to expand too rapidly—machine tools, for example, did not wait on a parallel expansion of those industries for which the machines were designed—while allowing other industries to languish—hydroelectric plants and mineral extraction.

Lack of quality was another plague that was often cited by the papers; another was the deterioration caused by worn-down, overburdened equipment and the tragic neglect of maintenance and repair. Here is an example from the Northeast, from the spring of 1961: a tremendous explosion in the largest mine in Fushun occurred, as the *Worker's Daily* in Peking reports, "at a time of deterioration in material conditions and of depressed morale." The wear and tear on the machinery was paralleled by the condition of the personnel, and by the serious labor difficulties indicated in the expression "depressed morale." One report mentions that at Anshan some of the workers were "out of step." They protested against impossible living conditions, onorous work, and the arbitrary changes in their shifts that followed as a result of arrests made among them.

In January, 1961, the planners in Peking finally decided to initiate a recovery program that consisted of a basic reorientation of the whole economy and that is known as the "readjustment." At a meeting in Peking the Central Committee of the Party published a text that contains passages betraying real alarm at "the extraordinarily great and difficult tasks" the country has in store for it. This text announces a Spartan cutback of industrial investment. It initiates reforms of the communes. It decided, in a first blow to the sacrosanct notion of industry's priority, that from now on agruculture be considered "the basis of the economy."

It was only a year late, in April, 1962, that the National Assembly met in Peking (the crisis had been such that a meeting could not be called) to take note of this change. Premier Chou En-lai proclaimed a new list of priorities that would henceforth determine China's planning. Heavy industry not only lost first place, it also lost second, which went to light industry, and ended up third on the new list of priorities.

Of the first importance now was agriculture, or more precisely, *saving* agriculture, and emergency measures were passed to this effect. The most spectacular was the order sent out to towns and factories to give up a certain percentage of their inhabitants or their surplus personnel, who were to be returned to the country. Heavy industry also received the command "to continue cutting down on investments"—a reemphasis of the retreat begun in 1961. Henceforth, all effort would be concentrated on supplying and protecting established industrialized areas such as the Northeast. Opening new factories or hiring more workers was forbidden. The severest cutback began. Factories were closed down or slowed down and many were cannibalized to the advantage of those that were better run. In this way light industry inherited some of the stock of heavy industry. Model factories that had formerly concentrated on competing for records and turning out ambitious products were directed to modify their layout for less exciting tasks such as supplying the factories that make plows, or bicycles, or tinware. To put an end to this emergency China returned to caution and to a slower rate of development.

In the absence of Peking statistics on the collapse of China's economy, experts in Hong Kong, Washington, London, and Tokyo have been forced to work out figures for at least certain important sectors. The sensational 18 million tons of steel announced in 1960 for that keystone of the economy were never produced. The real figure is 12 million tons, and even that wasn't reached until 1961. After that came a drastic fall in production: only seven or eight million tons in 1962. Western experts generally assume that the following figures in millions of tons are correct for coal production: in 1960, between 350 and 400; in 1961, 425; in 1962, a bad fall to 240. Electricity shows a descending curve in billions of kilowatts: 55 in 1965, 42 in 1961, 30 in 1962. Petroleum production was less disappointing and it rose to six million tons in 1962 after a slump in 1961. The chemical industry showed progress in 1962, but only in relation to 1961; it had not yet gotten back to the level of 1960.

It was only in 1963 that what Chou En-lai cautiously referred to during the October 1st celebrations as "a tendency toward a general improvement" made itself felt. (And notice that he did not say "a general improvement," he said a *tendency*.)

But now that hopes are beginning to rise again, will China simply dust off the old plans from before the crisis? To believe that would be to misunderstand the true situation. In reality the old plans no longer mean anything. The present demands an overall modification of the complex structure of Chineses industry. The most important reason for this is that when the Peking planners called for swift industrialization and accepted the breakneck speed required for it, they counted on agriculture financing the whole effort. They believed that in the new communes they had discovered a revolutionary recipe for obtaining an unprecedented return from the land and from the labor of peasants. They had expected to pay for China's new factories with the sharply increased revenues communes were to supply. With the failure of the communes, or at least of the first conception of them, came the collapse of the dream of a rapidly constructed, powerful industrial setup. The source of all this instant industrialization had dried up. The plan to "force" the soil and the peasants on a tremendous scale by bringing into play a revolutionary social organization did not work, and all industrial planning based on its success became pointless.

But there is another reason why all these plans have to return to the drawing board. Another fatal blow was dealt these plans by an event that long remained secret and that the outside world has not yet sufficiently explored: in July, 1961, Russia cut off all aid to China. For the next three years the Peking government never mentioned this fact. It did its best to hide a dispute with Russia. Thus China's industrial crisis, like the crisis in agriculture, was blamed in the first instance on natural disasters, and secondly on "some shortcomings and mistakes in our practical work"—read "errors." Only after July, 1963, when the great quarrel was exposed to the full view of the world, did Peking finally admit that there was another reason for the emergency: the withdrawal of Russia's aid and experts which caused—now they shout it at the top of their lungs—"incalculable damage" to the Chinese economy.

Let us return to the factories of the Northeast. Now we know enough to understand fairly accurately the situation we found there. If heavy industry is only slowly getting underway, if its present condition appears neither particularly brilliant nor even satisfactory, we must remember that the departure of the Russians placed it under a terrible handicap. It would have been more than enough just to answer the "S.O.S." of agriculture while ironing out the difficulties left from the Great Leap. In order to respond to the new order to "serve agriculture," it is necessary for industry to reorganize all its planning and all its products. Working directly or indirectly for the increased production of China's fields involves, for example, a changeover to producing basic equipment for tractor plants or plants producing chemical fertilizer.

But this upset, unsettling enough, was deepened by a second upset, the departure of the Russian specialists. At the very moment when their presence would have been most welcome, their sudden withdrawal left a vacuum and universal confusion. Indeed the first job of the "readjustment," even before the rescue of agriculture, was finding Chinese personnel for the necessary factories, producing Chinese machinery, and Chinese plans and blueprints. Everything Russian had to be replaced.

Throughout my travels I was told of the Soviet "betrayal." The first mention came in the three great industrial centers of the Northeast. But in that region there seemed to be instructions not to enter into detail. "Tremendous losses . . . All our plans modified . . . Aggravation of our difficulties . . ." The very words of the first communiques, and the guides must have learned them by heart. The same goes for these figures: "Two hundred and fifty enterprises affected by the withdrawal . . . 1390 specialists recalled by Moscow . . . 343 broken contracts . . . 257 cooperative undertakings scrapped . . ." And what do *they* think? Whom do my guides consider responsible? "The Soviet people remains bound by fraternal ties to the Chinese people. Those responsible for this betrayal are Khrushchev and his clique." I learned no more in Anshan, Fushun or Shenyang.

If such discretion is the rule in the Northeast, it may be because no other region benefited so much from Russia's aid and the presence of Soviet advisors, and thus no other suffered so dreadfully when they were recalled. It was here in 1955 that I had the surprise of my life, at least of my life in China, when I realized the extraordinary extent of the assistance Moscow gave China's first Five Year Plan.

I had arrived in the Northeast just when that assistance had gotten off the ground: straight off the Trans-Siberian and into Soviet-style new factories poured hundreds of ultra-modern machines bearing Cyrillic inscriptions. Today I begin to realize in the very same locale how terrible was the blow that Moscow struck. (In the two other industrial regions I visited next they were able to speak about this much more frankly.)

CHAPTER FIVE

CENTRAL CHINA: THE ACROBATICS OF INDUSTRY

BENEATH A LOWERING SKY FULL OF WARM MIST AND CURTAINED by summer rain, the muddy river stretches in a long avenue that separates gray towns dotted with factory chimneys. Given the absolute flatness of this melancholy terrain, it's difficult to see, at least from this distance, how the water is kept within its banks, since both water and banks appear level with each other. This is what the Chinese call the Long River. Foreigners call it the Yangtse, but the Chinese don't. The French call it the Blue River but it isn't; it's red whenever it isn't—as it is most of the year—café au lait or chocolate. . . .

Hankow, Hanyang, Wuchang: again three towns make up one of the principal industrial sites in China. But this time we are in the very heart of the country, and the three cities are so close together that the Chinese have found a single name for all three of them taken together: Wuhan. And today it really is one enormous city, cut in three by the Yangtse where the Hankiang runs into it to form a great horizontal Y on the map.

Hankow on the north bank is the principal town, and it was there that the "imperialists" had their concessions. Wuchang on the south bank is the town that grows fastest now. Hanyang in the middle, on the tongue of land between the rivers, was formerly a suburb but is now an industrial town.

The Wuhan Iron and Steel Company, which has several plants in Wuchang, is the most striking industrial layout in that metropolis of Central China. I passed through this region in 1955 when the work of staking out the terrain for future construction had only just begun. Five years later the steel poured abundantly in Wuchang, where, the Chinese say, not even a pig of iron had been produced before 1958, although ore abounds less than 70 miles away, at Tayeh. So here we are in the presence of an industrial group that owes its existence to the Great Leap. Construction, almost wholly dating from the three years between 1957 and 1960, was terminated two years ahead of schedule. Against the distant horizons of the plain it paints a landscape of gigantic installations. My guides point out the most important ones: plant for the treatment of ores, sinterization plant, cokery and chemical plant with five coke furnaces, foundry, three blast furnaces, steel works with batteries of open hearth furnaces, rolling mill, heavy rolling mill under construction, power plant, plant for the production of fireproof materials, etc. Not to mention an untold number of secondary factories and connected installations. The personnel of the whole complex comes to 70,000 workers, 40,000 belonging to Wuhan Iron and Steel while a sister company, Metal Construction of Wuhan, accounts for another 30,000. The total population around these factories comes to 200,000 in round numbers.

One fact worth remarking. When this enormous population was moved into an area which in 1955 had been nothing more than open fields, proper housing had been created for it at the same time as the factories. And more than mere barracks and lodging had been constructed. With the factories rose a whole working-class city: well-paved, tree-lined streets, schools, nurseries, parks, clubs and auditoriums, hospital, bus routes, etc. What I am aware of here and have already noticed in the Northeast can be seen wherever the Plan has brought forth its great complexes.

Chinese Communism does not seem to have imitated Stalin's Russia in this respect. When the first great Soviet factories for heavy industry were finished, too often a roof over the worker's head was forgotten. Or at least that is what I heard in those days.

On the whole, the Wuhan steel workers and other plants I visted in this region (the factory for heavy machine tools in Wuchang, for example, or the diesel motor works in the same locality) made a better impression than ones I saw in the Northeast. The factories here were better cared for, and my guides seemed much more willing to talk and to answer questions. For the first time I heard one ticklish subject frankly broached—Russia's leaving them in the lurch.

On July 16, 1960, news arrived from Moscow that her technicians, who numbered more than 1300, must return. A month later most of them were gone, and all those machines, plants and materials destined for China as part of Russian aid were held up in Siberia.

"Before 1960 our relations were excellent," Mr. Ni Shien-hwai, the public relations man of the heavy machine-tool plant in Wuchang, assured me. "We had respect for them and for the most part followed their instructions." (This was backed up by those Russians I talked to in Peking.) "We were careful of their well-being. They all lived at the Hotel Victory, where you're now staying, and it's still the best in town. We took them to the factories every day in chauffeur-driven cars. Often I went with them to the beach or to mountain lodges or resort hotels, to Tsingtao or Luchan. We even put rugs in their offices. They were paid between 400 and 600 yuan per month ($160–$240), which is two or three times more than the best Chinese technicians are paid, and they also received a supplement from their own government. In addition, we supplied them wth automobiles and theater tickets, and so on. When I saw them off on the train to Peking their wives cried, and they said that we would always be friends, that they had been better off here than they were in Soviet Russia. . . ."

How many of them had there been? At this particular factory there had been more than thirty between 1956 and 1960. At the time of the break there were four engineers. Twenty percent of their plant was of foreign origin, mostly Russian. In the Wuhan steel works there were "more than ten" Russian experts at the time of the break, and "more than thirty" had filled these positions since Russian aid began, I was told by another official in charge of public relations, Mr. Chou Yung-shou. The men who directed the installation of the open hearth furnaces had only remained a quarter of their scheduled stay. . . .

What were the results of the departure of these advisors? All of my informants, although they spoke with discretion, made it obvious that horrified surprise and complete confusion reigned in most factories. In the Wuhan ironworks a plant for the production of sheet steel which the Russians were to set up and equip has never seen the light of day, I'm told. The heavy rolling mill, under construction since 1960, is still unfinished four years later; before it is ready "more time" will be required. The Chinese have been forced to draw up their own plans and then do the building with their own resources. Although they appear to have finished, evidently all is not well, because the rolling mill isn't working. At the moment it's shut down "for cleaning."

Standing near the open hearth furnaces in the steelworks, my guide explains the two sorts of difficulties caused by the defection of the Russian experts. "Our workers generally discovered that they were unable to get the machinery working. They were not yet sufficiently trained. A whole world of problems came up for which they had no solutions. In addition, our engineers had difficulties with the machines themselves: expected deliveries never arrived, supplies of parts and machines gave out." I heard the same thing at the heavy machine-tool works in Wuchang. Here everything was designed, supplied and set up by Russian experts. "We had no experience whatsoever," my guide, Mr. Ni, told me, "and the departure of the Russians produced grave difficulties and losses. . . . Before they left they offered to resolve our immediate difficulties, but after that we would be on our own."

All these revelations were being made now, four years after the original drama, only to allow my informants to put their ultimate success in relief. They felt real satisfaction with their resourcefulness in filling the gap left by the defection of their advisors. In order to return thousands of factories all over the country to operation, they were forced to supply parts and replacements for thousands of machines, and not just Russian ones— many came from Czechoslovakia and East Germany. In many cases they had to draw up plans themselves because the Soviet experts had taken the blueprints with them! In order to replace Russian-made machinery with Chinese models, the Russian model had to be copied first, and then a Chinese model worked out, produced and improved. Quality, often low in the beginning, had to be improved. Many change-overs were necessary: shops had to be reorganized, manpower reassigned, various factories supplying parts for the same finished product redistributed. Even so the most serious problem still remained—the creation of Chinese technicians. The departure of the Russians emphasized the dramatic absence of qualified personnel and forced the Chinese to take recourse to any means whatsoever to attain their ends. For instance, an accelerated program promotes workers to the position of engineers after experience in the factory and study. Those are just a few of the problems of this "readjustment."

"We pushed our revolutionary spirit as far as it would go, just as though we were at war," I was told by a spokesman of the Wuhan Steelworks. "We had fought Chiang Kai-shek, and we had fought the Americans; now we were fighting these technical difficulties in the same spirit. So you see why our self-confidence is greater today than it was before. We used to think we were weak, and today we know we're strong!" One engineer told me, "Since we lacked technicians, we opened a technical school in the factory. Every qualified workman trained others at his own machine. Since we lacked material to build with, we built the factories that could produce it. Confronted with insoluble problems we called together engineers and workers and attacked the situation together. Together we conferred on what we had achieved and what remained to be achieved. We called on the workers to suggest technical innovations. Just think, when we started only 20 percent of our employees knew anything about metallurgy! Now they have all been trained. And we have arrived at the appreciation of a great principle: Do it all with your own

resources. From now on foreign aid is of secondary importance."
Another quoted Mao Tse-tung without naming him: "We have
tried and failed and tried and failed again, and at last we have
succeeded."

Is the "readjustment" over? One of my guides ventured this
frank reply: "Readjustment? That's what we're still in the middle
of." And besides, anyone with eyes could see that this is so.
In the heavy machine-tool plant, alongside Russian machinery
delivered before the break stands a Chinese copy of it. That they
are still in a period of transition is shown by the groups of workers
and technicians in conversation around their new models. This
machine or that—planing machine, vertical lathe, drilling ma-
cine, etc.—is undergoing a tryout, my guide tells me as we pass
it. He emphasizes that these are all new *Chinese* models. "The
Russians were helping us produce a planing machine that was
5 yards wide, 14 yards long and weighed 400 tons. They told us
to write to them after they'd gone and that they would solve our
problems by mail, but that hasn't been necessary. Oh, we had a
great many difficulties, but we have pulled through on our own
and now we've manufactured our own model. How long did it
take? A year or more . . ."

In another plant my guide told me, "We began with copies
of foreign models. Now we've arrived at the stage of designing
our own. Take our vertical lathe, diameter 6.30 m, height 2.20 m,
entirely Chinese and in production since 1963. Our designers
are young—one is just thirty. Quality, solidity, and efficiency
now meet required specifications. We have increased the number of prototypes: from the 5 m vertical lathe we advanced to
this 6.30 m and we're even making an 8 m. And all along we have
improved the quality, that's the important thing. At first we
were unable to maintain consistency. Machines worked well
during trial runs but had problems in the factory. And there
was the repeated experience of oil leakage. The makers of the
machines got together with their users and worked it out.

At Wuhan Steel, Mr. Chou told me, "On the whole we've gotten
over the shock now. We have reached the stage of mass-produc-
ing replacements and parts that we have designed ourselves.
Our production has finally reached an advanced stage."

But everywhere it is also obvious that victory has not been complete, and as at Anshan, a proof of the fact that "readjustment" is still the order of the day is supplied by the amount of machinery that stands idle. At Wuhan Steel four of the battery of six open hearth furnaces are out of commission the day of my visit. A mixture furnace is at the moment "stopped for inspection," my guide says, and not until it's working again will three or four open hearth furnaces be able to go back into production. The rolling mill isn't turning out large-dimensioned products; it's now confined to the production of 150 mm. "We have had to change over to other varieties of steel; for instance, to increase those types used in the manufacture of tractors."

Of the three blast furnaces at Wuhan one is dead: "being reconditioned" is my guide's laconic reply. In the machine factory in Wuchang at five in the afternoon a group of workmen are engaged in "tidying up the machinery." Tomorrow is Sunday, he explains, and work won't begin again until Monday morning. At the diesel motor works there is little activity on the assembly line and the yards are almost empty. The factory representative who showed me around said, "The end of the month is only four days off and we've already fulfilled our monthly quota. All we have to do at the moment is get ready for the first of next month."

But whatever difficulties may still remain, the answer now is confidence and this confidence seems to me neither unrealistic nor pretended. Once more the Chinese have something to be proud of. They have gotten out of trouble. And their pride is increased by the knowledge that at one point (and this they more than hint at) there was a good chance that their entire industrial effort would be torpedoed. "We were suddenly in the position of a child who is being taught to walk, and who is let go of too soon," my guide at Wuhan said. "But we didn't fall! We have kept on walking!" (Later on during my trip a Chinese economist told me, "We didn't sink.")

Not to have fallen and not to have sunk, sound like rather negative achievements, but they were great victories in the eyes of the Chinese. It does imply that they felt their situation to be a shipwreck. When they speak about this they give the

impression that one day they were suddenly as helpless as arm-
less men. Nothing but the extraordinary hold that the regime has
on the masses was able to galvanize them into action; otherwise
they would have given in to their discouragement. Reversing
the downward trend required exceptional efforts. In the end
one can say only that the "readjustment" was an extraordinary
acrobatic performance. At least one result of the success of
these juggling tricks is that the Chinese people have been given
a much needed boost in morale. To the workers, to the people,
and to foreign visitors the regime keeps repeating that from
now on China means to be self-sufficient—and that now the world
has the proof of her ability. In December Chou En-lai could
tell the National Assembly that the "readjustment" was now
"on the whole" completed and that the way was open to a new
upsurge of industry.

Now let's ride or walk through this triple city on the Yangtse.
Just as elsewhere, the contrasts will be numerous and there will
be the same mixture of improvements and sad holdovers. Obviously a large-scale effort has gone into the attempt to modernize
Hankow and her sister cities by cleaning, rebuilding and renovation. But the result leaves two easily differentiated decors.
Here—just as in Peking—the old city inherited from the old
regime gives the impression of having been touched up a bit or
merely glued back together.

But as soon as the former center is left behind we enter a different decor, new and recent—a whole garland of workers'
housing, factories and public buildings dating from the Liberation. Red brick and red tile produce a uniform color. The style
is monotonous. Green fields dotted with three- and four-story
workers' apartment houses that resemble barracks. Just as I
noticed in Shenyang, the idea of a street and little shops has
disappeared. The new sections are not yet completed, and
what has been finished appears scattered about without thought,
so that there are great empty spaces between groupings. But at
least things are on a large scale, and two or three times as much
land as is necessary for the present structures has been set
aside. And just as everywhere else, reforestation has been tre-

mendous, in the center of the city as well as along the roads and even in the middle of nowhere.

The main streets are particularly remarkable: a well-shaded, landscaped center strip often divides them into two separate roadways. Beautifully flagged sidewalks extend as far as the streets. A walk here barefoot wouldn't hurt or even dirty one's feet. Indeed when it rains, as it has during the last few days, a great many bare feet make their appearance, just as in the old days, probably to save shoes that are not of the highest quality. (On these excellent roads and sidewalks I could not help but think of the awful roads and sidewalks—where there are any at all—of Japan!) At important corners there are police to direct the traffic, but here too there is little besides carts and wagons. Along the main streets there are an unexpected number of absolutely new large public buildings. En route to the steel works by car I note the following: Railway Technical School, Institute of Iron and Steel Industries, Textile Plant No. 2, and College of Engineers for River Transport—a huge, splendid edifice that has just been finished. Here and there in the vicinity of these buildings are large, well-kept dormitories. Returning toward the center of town I note an impressive gymnasium, a pool, a hospital and medical school, a large and quite luxurious Department of Public Works, a park full of flower beds, a Moscow-style Palace of Sino-Soviet Friendship that has been rebaptized the Hall of Expositions, another park with flower beds, a new theater with a very respectable facade, etc.

And then there is the bridge, the celebrated giant bridge over the Yangtse. I rolled over it on my trip north by train and now I am, of course, taken to see it. This bridge is the only one in the world, as far as I know, that includes a reception room for tourists and a public relations man. Indeed no visitor can avoid the inevitable lecture the manager delivers over teacups while he stands in front of a plaster bust of Chairman Mao. This lecture passes over the essential collaboration of the Russians as swiftly as possible. We are told nothing more than that foreign experts made "technical verifications." The lecturer compensates with a rare abundance of statistics: total length, 1670 yards; length spanning water, 1156 yards; height, 80 yards; width of roadway,

22½ yards. It was the only bridge over the 3600 miles of rivers until the men who built it completed another in Chungking. . . . The largest steamers can pass beneath it; trains cross it on a lower level, and an upper level is used for automobiles, buses and pedestrians. All I can add to what he said is that little carts pushed and pulled by men and women make up most of the traffic and offer a distressing contrast to the magnificence of this structure.

Back in the older sections of the city, I am shown many improvements. The broad avenues of the recently constructed neighborhoods have thrust their way into the old city, and the network they create has been built up with new apartment houses that partially mask the buildings of the old sections. Most old streets have been repaved and cleaned. The crowd is for the most part suitably dressed. Most of them are barefoot because it's raining, but the majority are protected by raincoats, umbrellas or big straw hats. Shops are numerous and not too badly stocked, although the quality is lower than that in Peking. The customers are legion. At night the shops look picturesque under the electric lights, but in broad daylight their peeling fronts reveal the ravages of humidity and the years since the last painting.

As soon as I leave the principal arteries I come upon poverty-stricken ancient alleys of brick houses. The farther one goes the worse things get. Many of the houses are old wooden dwellings and consequently shaky and dilapidated. Their coating of red paint has just about weathered away. The roof tiles could use repairs. Along some mud-choked alleys there are even some recently constructed slums thrown together out of rejected planks, matting, cardboard and old sheet metal. Perhaps these are the huts built by refugees from flooded regions. Once again there are floods somewhere in central China. Even in Hankow there is a part of town where the water is knee-deep after three days of rain. The ground floors are flooded.

This town gives me the feeling that for the first time I am beginning to decipher a few of the enigmas of everyday-life in China. Little by little the true face of a Chinese city comes through to me. I have already pointed out the obvious differences between housing in the old and the new parts of town. But those were not the most important differences; I see now that there are others that concern the inhabitants more directly.

First let us look at a main street, Sun Yat-sen Boulevard, one of the principal arteries of Hankow. The setting is old and filthy, since it easily dates from 50 years ago: we are in the old city. And yet, if we look carefully, we will realize that after all something *is* new. What is new makes itself felt in the almost restless activity of everyone we see; they belong to the part of China that moves forward; they are on the go. The whole crowd hastens to and from offices, factories, and schools. This crowd is busy, restless, and relatively hurried. The shops lining the street are busy, the personnel excited. People catch the trolleybus, crowd in, look at their watches. Others continue on foot at quite a pace toward appointments or employment. Just like anywhere else in the world it's easy to spot the official headed for his office or the white-collar worker with his cardboard or leather portfolio. Obviously both people and things are directed toward a goal. The presence of the regime at work is felt.

Let's turn the corner off the boulevard into one of the narrower cross streets. The paving is much older and so is the rest of this section. It is immediately obvious that the people here are less "involved," so to speak. This is the world of piecework done at home, and it hasn't greatly changed although socialization has touched it. The lower orders who pass their days here differ from those seen in the main thoroughfares: these lack modernity, the brisk pace. Here they sit all day at their work, either at home or just next door. How different from the modern shop seen on the boulevard are these craftsmen's workrooms, where things are made but not sold. If anyone who lives in these alleys does not work at home or in the neighborhood, very likely he is part of the lowest class of workers—the unskilled pullers, pushers, pedalers, carriers, etc.

Thus two well-defined groups have appeared. On the one hand there are the activists of the new regime, those who are a living part of the changes of the last few years, who have contributed to their creation or even direct them, who are leaving the old to enter the new. On the other hand there are multitudes who are not directly caught up in the current of the times, who are still washed by China's past. This category includes those who are too slow, a little too old, unwilling to take a chance, docile, and unemployable. They are all condemned to disappear because they're behind the times, left behind by the continuing revolution and ill-placed to break loose from their circumstances. The people out there on Sun Yat-sen Boulevard do all the work and they're the ones who count as far as the government's concerned; they form an avant-garde, or the shock troops of production. And the others whom we see immobilized in the back alleys belong to that inherited delay and slow motion willed to China by her last government, the Empire, and Asia itself.

Without my guide I make my way into these alleys between sagging houses. Suddenly I am hundreds of miles from all those factories and modern industries I've visited. Here I am in the ancient world of craftsmen. Tinkers' shops where hammers noisily tap at iron or copper; the three-walled rooms where men saw and file and hammer also serve as dwellings. Ancient handicraft shops occupy the dark ground floors and turn out tin pots, molded metal spoons, and everything made of wood: buckets, handles, mallets, chests, old-fashioned household wares. Farther on I see cradles painted red and decorated with flowers in the ancient manner, and simple baskets for new-born babies. Next door hammers beat against brass or tin. Another racket comes from the shop of a maker of gongs: to test the tone of the finished product he beats as hard as he can. Six boys, naked to the waist, assemble barrels and circle them with iron. Weavers of straw manufacture matting of all sorts. A man saws wood, holding it in place with his toes. Unidentifiable jobs are lost in the darkness at the back of shops.

In these rooms whose only light comes through the opening onto the street all these familiar objects appear crusted, worn, chipped—even the picture on the wall or the family photograph —everything dipped in the brown lacquer of age and poverty. On nails in the wall hang clothing, peaked hats, straw coats for rainy weather. Yellowed newspapers have been pasted to the walls. On brick that was once whitewashed, red paper has been glued and then written on with brushes. Workbenches, saw horses, wooden benches, everything is polished and varnished by service. Chickens and children avoid grown-up legs. Just like children the poultry divides its time between dwelling and alley. Brats in ripped pants, little girls, their hair done like Chinese dolls, chase one another with shouts. They run barefoot because it's raining.

And the street continues with never a turn. Shops for repairs, for patch-ups of all sorts; lumberyards where all the wood is secondhand; old rags in bales. Suddenly a prosperous-looking grocery clashes with its surroundings—but it is also the only grocery in all this long, long street. A public bath with blackened front. A hydrant for drinking water: a man oversees the operation as a long line waits to fill buckets balanced in two's on a bamboo pole. A market: vegetables, duck eggs, misshapen peaches (very Chinese). A peasant sells red eggs from a great wrought iron basin. From windows high in the wall he leans against fall the voices of children singing in chorus. At portable stalls vendors offer an assortment of brightly colored hanks of silk, thimbles, necklaces, plastic combs and barrettes.

A family eats dinner on the doorstep at five; metal mess gear has replaced the traditional crockery. In a boilermaker's shop everything is covered with rust, including the family. A dyeworks floods the street with bright anilines.

The narrow and straight alley is paved with stone slabs of various sizes on which are often cut half-effaced inscriptions. A peasant is selling vegetables I can't identify: polebeans 16 inches long, bunches of sweet herbs, and Chinese cabbage, very cheap. In a workshop a team surrounded by children, umbrellas spread open to dry and thin chickens discusses the quota for the coming month. The walls that line this street are scratched, worn, and eroded to the height of a man by the human sea pouring through them. The bottoms of the walls crumble and split. The wood in windows and doors weathers, and anything of iron rusts. Paint has been forgotten here for many years. All the same the street can be said to be clean. A sewer has been installed and there are no puddles after the rain. Just as in Peking there is a long list of NO's: no flies, no rats, no beggars, no whores, and no vermin, as far as I could judge. No bad smell, and it's summer. Also no motorized vehicles, or very few, and very little else: from time to time a bicycle; a few carts; delivery carts transporting pellets of pressed anthracite and streaked with black dust. And no foreigners either, for that matter.

My stroll causes a little astonishment but no "incidents" until five o'clock, when the children of less than six are reinforced by the "big kids" returned from school. They really are surprised! Little by little the crowd of them increases and they surround me when I stop. Suddenly the cry spreads, "A Russian! A Russian!" They say the word without hostility but with a sort of disbelief. They must know that "Russians" are a vanished breed. They point at me and grown-ups begin to pay attention. So I leave their long alley and after making a zigzag down several smaller ones, I'm back on the boulevard that was never far away, beyond Old China, in the New China of the trolleybus.

CHAPTER SIX

SHANGHAI, OR COMMUNIST FLEXIBILITY

HERE ARE SOME NOTES I TOOK MY FIRST NIGHT IN SHANGHAI. "GOT in at 10 PM by plane from Hankow—Russian two-engine. First impressions of Shanghai by night: extraordinarily good! A splendid boulevard runs right in from the airport. We cut through no grimy suburbs but came right into the city, where the streets were well-lighted, crowded, full of shops and clean. You wouldn't know it was Shanghai."

A day or two later my notes say: "This town has been put in order, cleansed, disinfected and healed. It is replanted and green once more, and everything has been fixed up. Impeccable roadways and not just on the great avenues—they were always well kept—but in those little *Chinese* streets that were formerly often breathtakingly filthy and poor. The fronts of the older buildings have been spruced up—different from Wuhan and elsewhere. The Bund (main quay along the Whampou River) has been completely transformed. The great avenues: shops by the hundreds and very well stocked for a large clientele. The people look spruce and there are thousands of clean, happy children. No flies, no smell, no vermin! My refrain. Feeling that most people must be holding their own or even on the way up. Everything seems organized and oriented. Wide areas of achievement."

And a more careful investigation did not on the whole turn up anything to contradict this. (It is also true that I saw awful enough alleys in Shanghai and suburbs that were extraordinarily overcrowded and terribly poor—for example in the industrial area beyond the former Japanese concession. There the impoverished proletariat swarms over a landscape of warehouses and factories with walls of tired brick, and a veritable flood of pedestrians invades streets and cinder-strewn byways to mix with humans in harness pulling the usual carts.) Here and there an island of hovels remains, and I know of a squalid string of shanties along a road that branches off the one to the airport. But these horrors are relatively rare. I knew the old Shanghai as a city *full* of such things, and the Shanghai of today, although its background has not been greatly changed since then, is a totally different place.

I have to go as far back as 1937 to find a Shanghai that was well administered and prosperous looking—and in memory even more beautiful, at least from a certain point of view. There was mad activity in its shops with their thousands of signs, and there was the traffic of all those fine foreign cars. In those days France had its own little colony in the very heart of Shanghai, the French Concession*, and the International Concession next door was as carefully managed as any town in England or America. Foreigners were at home there—how those times have changed! And yet next door to all that was well-kept, the abyss of physical and moral misery yawned and Japanese aggression (which I watched in the summer of 1937) would only increase it.

I saw Japanese bombs rain on Shanghai—on the *Chinese* parts of Shanghai—and refugees from burned-out sections living under matting in the streets of the rich. I was there when a patriot threw a bomb into the Japanese victory parade while another

* France more or less maintained her prestige here until 1949.

threw himself from the top of a building, with the cry "Long live China!" Long afterward the surrounding countryside stank with the corpses of Chiang Kai-shek's soldiers—until the dogs finished. And all the while, in town, on the green lawns of the race course, Chinese and foreign racing fans, won and lost millions. At night, behind the racetrack along the Avenue Joffre the professional *mamas* sold pretty Chinese girls, their protegées, "two dollars, all night." In winter, at dawn you often found dead babies in the trash cans.

They were still to be found there eight years later during the winter of 1945–1946, although the Shanghai that I visited then was an American Shanghai this time. It had been liberated by General MacArthur. That contrast between the squalor inherited from the war and the riches of the few who had benefited materially from the victory was as shocking as ever. There was a flourishing traffic in everything imaginable—and terrible unemployment. Corruption seemed to deepen as dollar aid rose. Merchandise from the PX and American aid from powdered milk to blood plasma went straight to the black market.

Three years later, at the beginning of 1949, when I next saw Shanghai it was at its absolute nadir of confusion and filth. Outside, the Communists lay siege. Inside, galloping inflation worked harder for Mao Tse-tung than any Fifth Column of "Reds." The face of Chiang Kai-shek danced about in the gutter—on his banknotes! Instead of a wallet, people left home in the morning with a potato sack stuffed with paper money in bundles of 100,000 "dollars" just to cover the day's purchases. The rich literally flew away, to Hong Kong, and took their gold bars with them. Poor devils, rumored to be Communists, were executed in the middle of the streets. Of the besiegers the people said, "Let them come! They can never be worse than those we have."

And then "they" were inside. Early one morning the silent army of peasant soldiers in cloth shoes entered without murder, pillage or rape. But they inherited a city that was broken-winded and dilapidated, eaten up with vices, ruined. The army brought with it only a tiny minority of Communist cadres whose dispiriting job it was to bring order into this chaos. The masses surrounding them were indifferent and apathetic. Wouldn't this small minority lose itself in the mass, the fundamental mercantilism of the Chinese, in the prevailing individualism and hunger for money?

Well, six years later when I returned to Shanghai for the fourth time, in 1955, I saw that just the opposite had taken place. The masses had not contaminated the purists. The purists, armed with the germs of Communism, had succeeded in infecting the masses. Perhaps they had not really conquered the minds of the populace, but every arm was theirs, at work, obedient and orderly. A physical and moral cleansing of the city had been accomplished. The beggars had disappeared. The prostitutes were all in rehabilitation centers. There wasn't any more prostitution. There wasn't any more race course. Mah-Jongg was no longer played in Shanghai. People had even lost a little habit particularly dear to them, clearing the throat and spitting—no one spits any longer anywhere in China. The streets were clean. The most commonplace objects' had become broom and fly-swatter. . . .

Nevertheless, repression and coercion weighed heavily on this city. Shanghai experienced the throes of socialization in fear. Property, commerce, industry and labor were socialized—and so was thinking. Shanghai resisted. The majority did everything in their power to stave off Party-line thought.

Have they ever accepted it? I'm not so sure, but I am aware of a sense of relaxation and contentment on their part. Compared with what I saw in 1955 there has been considerable progress in the look of the city and the bearing of its inhabitants. And if I compare what I see here with what this summer has shown me in other cities, Shanghai clearly belongs in a higher category. There is a striking difference, for instance, in city planning. Here at last is one Chinese city that has not allowed its older section to fall into decay and disrepair as the newer portions were built—and as we shall see, these are considerable. Shanghai has not been content with mere growth; effort has also been expended on problems inherited from the previous regime.

The older city has for the most part been renovated. Whole streets of old buildings have had their faces lifted. Other streets I saw were covered with bamboo scaffolding on which whole tribes of masons bustled. The roadways have been asphalted. Buses here as elsewhere have replaced the trolleys. Here and there the sidewalks or the streets have been broadened. Open sewers or those gulleys that differed only in name have all been replaced by underground pipes. Take the little stream called Zikkawei in the western part of the city. In 1937 I saw the Japanese engage the Chinese on its banks. Where this nauseous stream once flowed a beautiful road runs now, bordered with grass and flowers: fuchsia, gladioli, dahlias and hollyhocks—for two miles.

The city planners responsible for the growth of Shanghai have chosen an intelligent means of dealing with satellite towns. The latter form part of Shanghai administratively, although they are from 12 to 25 miles away. Each town boasts its own distinctive industry. Minghao produces electrical equipment, Wuchang chemicals, Wusung iron and steel, Pengpu machine-tools. I have visited Minghao, the one that is considered to have turned out best. People here are probably even better off than in Shanghai. For once the apartment houses don't resemble barracks. They equal the better public housing in France.

Although the town was constructed as recently as 1958–59, the landscaping is green. There are many flowers. The population of workers lives close to factories that produce electrical equipment, turbogenerators, hydraulic pumps, ball bearings, etc. Minghao lies about 25 miles southwest of Shanghai on the Hwang-p'u River. The ancient village of the same name still exists. This little Chinese market town with its narrow alleys has been brightened up and "revolutionized" by the changes so nearby. It enjoys a visible prosperity. Its mended facades have just been brushed with whitewash and the shops are full of foodstuffs and consumer goods. Minghao used to have a population of 5000; now the new city and the village together come to 70,000. However, overpopulation has become a grave problem, and every new apartment houses two or three families. I'm told that the population of Greater Shanghai, satellite cities included, amounts to 6,500,000. But Shanghai administers all the surrounding countryside, so the total figure would be about ten million; of those, three million peasants.

But let us return to the city itself. Of all those cities open to foreigners, Shanghai and Peking are decidedly the best that the Communists have to show. They have not merely "touched the place up," they have spent a great deal of energy trying to beautify it. The celebrated Bund, for example, has become a green park. In the old days here the banks of the Hwang-p'u saw two estranged worlds pass among the picturesque but noisy confusion: capitalists in their foreign cars and barefoot coolies unloading steamers; bankers and businessmen from the proud buildings that hugged the quai, and all the homeless of the harbors—the dockside thieves, the beggars, the poor fishermen living in sampans.

Today the Bund is no longer a place of business. It serves as a thoroughfare and a place to take walks. Everything is orderly and clean. There are benches on which one can sit and look at the river. The jade waters bear junks with three black, rectangular sails, floats of logs pulled by small craft, and crowded ferries. Sail-less junks today outnumber those whose bamboo-ribbed sails used to remind me of bats' wings. Diesels are the order of the day.

Nanking Road runs nearby. The principal commercial street and center of a famous quarter, it has once again achieved great animation on its sidewalks and in numerous shops crowded with buyers. The only thing missing is the traffic of a great city. Except for the buses loading and unloading a well-dressed crowd, there is almost nothing. Parked cars are almost unknown. Yet there are certainly more motorized vehicles than in either Wuhan or Shenyang. Little three-wheeled trucks and larger ones built in Shanghai pass occasionally. The city must keep them jealously to herself, because they are seen nowhere else.

Although Bubbling Wells Avenue has kept up its buildings, which date from the capitalist epoch, it has changed its name, and the celebrated race course has become a People's Park. When I saw this transformation begin in 1955 I thought that all those beds of roses and banked chrysanthemums would be too luxurious a decor to have more than an ephemeral existence. Not at all. The park that fills the oval of the former track has even more flowers now and boasts groves of tall trees. People stroll on shaded paths. They swim in a pool. There is even an artificial stream for canoeing. . . .

Are the people of Shanghai better off? Not all of them, by any means; many of them lived very well in the old days and they have now had their standard of living depressed to that of the mass of the population. The masses, however, are appreciably better off. Just boarding the trolleybus will prove this to anyone who knows what Shanghai was like. The passengers are dressed simply but well. For the most part they will be men in blue trousers and white shirts that don't tuck in; no hats. Sitting next to me is a woman who wears a well-ironed jacket with a stiff military collar. She chats with her daughter, who wears barrettes and pigtails and holds a plastic shopping basket. One worker has a watch on his wrist and is wearing a cloth cap; glasses and a pen are visible in a pocket of his coveralls. An old woman gets on and several passengers get up to offer her their seats. That's new! The conductor sells tickets without ever leaving his seat at the entrance. That too was unheard of in the old days.

Let's walk back down Nanking Road. Practically anything one wants is on sale there, from a photographic enlarger to a nylon toothbrush, with radios, watches, clothing, and lipstick in between—but who buys lipstick? (I've never seen any lips that were rouged. . . .) As everywhere else in China there are two scales of prices: very cheap for necessities and very, very expensive for the rest. But shoppers are many and they're buying. Obviously "there's money there," as the saying goes. And enough of it for a certain amount to go for purchases that are not utilitarian. A really fine art shop sells painted scrolls, woodcuts, artist's supplies and paper for calligraphy, books of Chinese art in reproduction.

In Shanghai commerce has been socialized of course and all shops belong in one of the following categories: state department stores, cooperative stores or stores with mixed management ("state-private," they're called here). I have the feeling that the socialized personnel of today are every bit as eager to make a sale and to tote up their profits as the capitalist shopkeepers of the past. In any event they seem as happy to make their fingers fly over the abacus. No adding machines here . . . In the streets here and there billboards advertise various products of Shanghai: electric fans, glassware, lighting fixtures, insulation and plastics, foam rubber, etc. For the last year or two the regime has tried to spur light industries—after their neglect—and thus to put on the market a greater variety and quantity of consumer goods.

Besides this upswing in light industry, another change has taken place since my visit of 1955, the development of heavy industry. Heavy industry made up a mere 13 percent of Shanghai's production at the beginning of the first Five Year Plan (1953)—I was told by a spokesman for the city government during the regulation introductory briefing. Today heavy industry accounts for 50 percent. Shanghai has built steel works, chemical plants and factories for machine tools. The one I visited in Yangpu has 5200 workers and manufactures about forty different types of machines; special pride is taken in the various models of grinding machines, some of which attain very great precision. The equipment with which the workshops have been outfitted appears very mixed in origin and age, but the factory functions and looks alive.

Shanghai produces equipment for the mining industry, steel industry, chemical fertilizer industry, etc. At the Exhibition Hall (until recently the House of Sino-Soviet Friendship), I was shown the prototypes of machines and installations dating from 1963 and 1964: high-precision lathes, grinding machines, milling machines, vertical lathes for large dimension work, giant diesel engines, giant compressors, a 25,000-kilowatt turbogenerator made in Minghao, etc. From the Shanghai tractor works there were the seven-horsepower cultivator with a great many uses, a light tractor, and a heavy (35-horsepower) tractor called "Good Harvest" (*Fungse*)—vintage 1964. Here I saw that truck I'd noticed in the city: four tons, 80 horsepower—which gets eleven miles to the gallon. Next came the Phoenix, an impressive blood-red automobile, six cylinders, 90 horsepower. It dates from 1960. But this is one phoenix that has not been able to be reborn from the ashes of The Great Leap Forward. Or so I hear. This luxurious car is no longer in production. And according to rumor (foreign) no one can lift the hood on this model; it's been sealed tight to conceal the fact that the motor has been removed. This beautiful piece of machinery is just for show.

The factory built most recently is the one in Wuching, another satellite city on the Hwang-p'u. It is devoted to China's most recent industry, chemical fertilizer, and is one of Shanghai's proudest achievements. Right off, my guides announced that this factory is one hundred percent Chinese, which means "built without Russian help." Begun in the second half of 1960, it was near completion two years later; then after a year of tryouts it started regular production in September, 1963. Production: 100,-000 tons of ammonium sulfate annually. The plant was scheduled to be enlarged in order to produce urea. There are 2400 workers and other employees, as well as about thirty engineers. There is a fair amount of automation.

"It was one tour de force after another," a guide said to me during the visit. "Of our thirty engineers at the start, only three were qualified chemical engineers. Our training program had to take all sorts of people, from delivery boys on up. We put them into a night school. In addition to working, they also visited other plants. We ran into many problems and often made them worse with our faulty solutions. For instance, since we didn't keep track of the types of piping we installed, it was necessary to test them all to discover which could stand a pressure greater than 300 kg per square centimeter. All that would have been unnecessary if we had only gone about the installation properly, since the manufacturer had tested them in the factory."

Ninety different concerns in Shanghai and elsewhere collaborated on the production of high-pressure alloys, converters, and other pieces of heavy machinery that would formerly have had to be imported. I was shown gigantic compressors assembled from 1400 parts—all of which had been produced by a factory in Shanghai, a factory already famous for having equipped an entire steel works with Chinese machinery in 1958. A Shanghai factory that makes boilers has produced a converter that is as tall as a five-story building and that attains a pressure of 320 kg per square centimeter. Such things had never before been done in China. For this project experts were brought in from everywhere.

The railroad did not reach this far then and all this heavy material had to be brought in by road—for example, an 85-foot, 80-ton scrubber manufactured in Harbin. It arrived on a special forty-five transport. The ammonium sulfate "isn't of the first quality," an official tells me. This factory also supplies canned and bottled ammonia to the surrounding area.

As I walk through the plant I notice that only a third of the machinery is in use. But three new compressors to be installed will double the plant in size, and new installations are already under construction. A nearby coking plant supplies the coke for synthesizing ammonia. The coal comes from the provinces of Shantung and Anhwei. The iron sulfate for the production of sulfuric acid arrives by train or by boat on the Hwang-p'u. The impression given is that of a going concern. Wuching is the pilot plant for the rapid development of the Chinese chemical fertilizer industry. It is the model for new factories springing up elsewhere —in Canton, for example.

"It was one tour de force after another," they repeat at Wuching. But surely the greatest feat is the way Shanghai has been able to assert itself, to remain true to its own genius, that mixture of open-mindedness and common sense—under Communism! I will go even further. I believe that an important part of the genius of modern China found in the Shanghai of the past a soil favorable to its development. The China that closed itself behind walls and rebelled against the "foreign devils" was not the only China. There was another China, one that followed the example of Japan. Turned toward the ocean and the outside world, this China called for changes and asked for an encounter between East and West. From the turn of the century on, this spirit guaranteed Shanghai's prosperity. It also gave her a lasting head-start on the rest of the country. Shanghai still has that head-start working for her. For instance, if there is no other city in China where city planning shows, it is because in the past Shanghai was almost the only city in which capable architects worked with good material under strict local legislation.

Today Shanghai tries passionately to establish in a China now free from foreign encroachments her place as a modern metropolis. After having cleansed herself of all her former sins, Shanghai can give full rein to her many abilities: a spirit of enterprise unique in China, and an equally unique experience of modern administrative techniques, economic methods and technology.

On the other hand the regime must make its peace with Shanghai. The sin of having been the base of the imperialists, a capitalist paradise, was atoned for by years of suffering and fear. In the first years of the new regime, Shanghai was the theater of a thorough purge of bourgeois and reactionary elements. During these campaigns, the "Three Antis" and the "Five Antis," the number of suicides caused by "political desperation" was considerable. Next followed that difficult period of socialization during which I saw Shanghai in 1955: private production, private commerce and private ownership were abolished, and the state took over all businesses. The Party also proceeded to "re-educate" the intellectuals, and literature and the arts were recast in the Communist mold. At the same time the most important Catholic community in China was deprived of its leaders and placed under the surveillance of the Party. In addition, Shanghai was a victim of economic planning. The regime had made up its mind to displace the country's center of gravity northwestward and westward—to turn its back to the ocean for a time, in order to face central Asia. The idea was that in so doing China would become more closely connected with Soviet Russia. In addition, the development and peopling of backward regions, and the decentralization of industry (which was felt to be too concentrated in regions vulnerable to attack) would be stimulated. This new orientation of the country fit in very well with the vengeance of the regime. Here was yet another means to humble the citizens of this city, still suspected of harboring an incurable nostalgia for capitalism.

But even before the Great Leap the planners in Peking began to see that they were injuring themselves when they penalized this metropolis by not making full use of her resources. Besides, the destruction of the former social structure was nearly complete and the resistance of the affected classes was broken. Little by little, the regime and Shanghai—which had been "re-educated" after a fashion—arrived at a separate peace, an understanding based on the advantages to both parties of their collaboration.

Thus Shanghai had an important role in The Great Leap Forward: it is from that epoch her heavy industry dates. The crisis of the three black years gave Shanghai another opportunity to demonstrate her indispensability. Her factories became absolutely essential. It turned out that they had been less hard hit: more intelligent, more experienced men had been in charge here. Dependence on Russian aid had been less servile, so there was less of a sense of having been left in the lurch by Khrushchev.

Shanghai was able to recover from the crisis faster than Wuhan or the towns of the Northeast. In 1961–1962 Shanghai's rehabilitation—and revenge—began. Shanghai has become the city whose upward trends come in for preferential treatment. Her plants are cited everywhere as examples. From all over China thousands of workers and engineers come on visits to study methods and organization, to observe the birth of new industries—plastics and electronics, for example.

Such a reconciliation was worth making a few concessions for. And the most surprising of these, the one that the regime devoted the most publicity to, was the reintegration into the socialist system of a residue of repentant capitalists who had been pardoned —provided they remained faithful to their "conversion" into obedient servants of the regime. The state entered into partnership with them, turning their corporations into "corporations with mixed capital." Only theoretically can the state be considered a partner; in reality it is the master. But since the state had need of them, it made an offer. In substance something like this might have been said: "You will continue in my service, and receive more than a simple salary. Interest will continue to be paid on your capital. Refractory capitalists and others I have rejected have lost their civil rights. You retain yours. In exchange you will continue to work and to apply your experience in managing factories and businesses. And in all things you will behave as good socialists, disciplined but enthusiastic."

One of these "converts" received me in his home. Mr. Liu Tsing-keu is the director of a large textile concern. This visit, of course, was arranged by the authorities in Shanghai. In addition, they also recalled (their files are good!) that nine years before I had been introduced to another tame capitalist. They invited him also to meet me at Mr. Liu's. He is Mr. Tseng Ming-shen, whose company manufactures pharmaceuticals.

At Mr. Liu's, for the first time since I arrived in China, or at least since I left Hong Kong, I was in a decor such as I remembered from the old days: luxurious salon hung with paintings by masters of the Ming Dynasty, silk-cushioned chairs and couches, waxed parquet, and flowers in vases of antique porcelain. A maid serves tea. A chauffeur waits for orders in the garden. To hear the praises of Communism sung in such surroundings is laughable! Has his position in the company been downgraded? "I used to be a self-appointed director. Now I am the director appointed by the state," he says jovially. Has his salary been reduced? "Not at all, the pay is the same: 670 yuan per month," (equivalent to $275) he says, fanning himself with an ivory fan. Has his capital been attacked? "On the contrary, the state has been extremely honest and often very generous too; this vase, for example, which bears a valuation of five in my catalog they've assessed at eight, and my factories, reckoned at 3,600,000 on my balance sheet, they have allowed me at 7,400,000." And his interest? "I receive 5 percent in cash, and I spend it as I please. No deductions. No taxes of any kind."

But of course I am not in the home of just any "convert" to socialism; I have been sent (because of course the visit was "arranged") to interview a most unusual subject (habitual error in Chinese propaganda), a man who manages five textile mills employing more than 11,000 workers. He is the president of the Federation of Commercial and Industrial Companies of Shanghai. In other words he is at the very head of similar repentant capitalists. And last of all he is a delegate to the National Assembly and member of a party expressly created for him and his kind, the Association for the Democratic Construction of the Fatherland.

In 1955 I refused to take this system of mixed capital seriously. It had just begun and affected only a very small number of concerns. I could believe neither in the regime's sincerity nor the system's durability. I was wrong. It's still going strong and has spread to 90,000 Shanghai capitalists. Many of them were formerly shopkeepers and have been regrouped into larger outfits, less numerous and more strategically located in the city. Later an official in Peking told me that in the whole of China there are about two million capitalists who receive interest payments fixed by the state. This sum amounts to between 120 and 130 million yuan annually (49 to 53 million dollars). Out of the total only 100,000 are "big time," the remainder for the most part being "small fry." Many of them are not strictly speaking "capitalists," but former professors, former small land-owners, etc.

Mr. Liu is decidedly "big time." Still jovial and enthusiastic, he describes his new life under Communism, and I have to admit that it isn't without a certain piquant quality—when I think of the way seven hundred million other Chinese live. "Cars? One is enough for me," he says. "Clothes? I could have as many suits as I want—but all I need is ten or so. . . . Travel? I've been to the Congress for World Peace, to Vienna, to Moscow . . . I no longer have any worries about my children. Every one of them is set for life as an engineer, professor, etc. When I die they will continue to receive my 5 percent, and although they cannot inherit the factories they do get the house. In the old days what a torment children were!" Mr. Liu laughs loudly as he calls up that not so distant past with all its evils. He paints a picture of rich children being kidnapped when they were little, seduced by women when they were older, and soon ruined by opium. And all the while their mother spent a fortune on extravagant clothes and their father lost his factories at the gambling table. "Oh, life is far better today!" Mr. Liu exclaims with the earnest voice of the repentant sinner.

I am flabbergasted. The extraordinary pliability of the Chinese character was certainly the deciding factor in the working agreement made by repentant capital with the regime. Mr. Liu himself is an example and a proof. He knows an ancient recipe from the book of Eastern Wisdom: in the face of angry power, behave as in the face of angry nature—and bow. The poor have always done this. Now it is the turn of the rich, and they know it very well. And they have succeeded: a flattened capitalist has the right to survive. That this survival continues depends on a corresponding attitude of those in power. Intolerance is the rule of the new regime, but in this country even intolerance has patience. Communists know how to wait, how to call the shots. But all the same I wonder who will win this match between the non-violence of the basically violent at the top and the non-resistance of the basically resistant at the bottom. . . .

Just how long will the capitalist converts continue to clip their 5 percent coupons? Mr. Liu goes into this. At the beginning they were told until 1962. Then there was an extension until 1965. And after 1965? Mr. Liu indicates that he believes that the present deadline will again be moved forward. There is assurance in his voice when he adds, "We'll talk it over." That phrase tells a great deal. Obviously Mr. Liu and Mr. Tseng feel themselves to be in a position of power. They, their experience, and their willingness to collaborate are still needed. That is one trump and they have another, their solidarity, which is reminiscent of freemasonry. The rehabilitation of Shanghai and its rise to importance in the eyes of the regime also give them an opportunity to make themselves heard. Men from Shanghai have found their way into government everywhere in China. They are numerous in Peking, for instance. While Canton must take the trouble to speak Mandarin, which is the dialect of Peking and theoretically the national language, the people of Shanghai are almost alone in being free to use their native dialect in public—even in Peking itself.

About ten years ago Shanghai had the reputation of being the one city in Communist China that was not "right-thinking." I took down the admission of a Communist who judged in 1955 that the number of people truly won over by the new regime could not be greater than 20 percent. I am of the opinion that this is no longer the case. Would I go so far as to claim that in Shanghai the majority are now right-thinking? It is possible, but I believe that they are engaged rather in a far subtler game, that of maintaining an opposition in the midst of conformity, a sort of resistance by success. The ideas of the regime are not what interests them, but the practical results obtainable within it and almost in spite of it. In Shanghai, capital construction is on the increase and economic recovery in every sector has been ahead of the rest of the country. Business volume and consumption are greater here. Prosperity exceeds anything to be seen elsewhere in China. Those are the exhibits for the case Shanghai wishes to prove: the town that is the least severe in its Communism is precisely the one that runs most smoothly. If Shanghai can prove her case, perhaps the regime will be persuaded to institute a general softening of the Party line.

This gambit is skillful, but it is also dangerous. The close surveillance of this former capitalist center continues. The Party suspects that the liberal spirit might flare up again after lying some time beneath the ashes. Before the revolution Shanghai was one of those cities in which a true middle class developed. There was a confluence of many things that could not help but endow Shanghai's inhabitants with minds more open than those elsewhere in China: material and intellectual contacts with the West, the presence of a large foreign colony, Western science and logic, and the attainment of a certain level of comfort. The legacy of history and the hazards of geography have prevented the regime from eliminating all these influences completely. Just the presence of 90,000 former capitalists who have been able to survive after the defeat of their class is enough to maintain a steady will to Revisionism.

Still, as I have already noted, Shanghai is a city in which one feels money on the move again, or at least enough of it to raise the level of commerce above the simple purchase of absolute necessities. It is hard for Shanghai to believe in the virtues of the Spartan life. A citizen of this city will abandon discomfort at the first opportunity—and comfort has never been a favorable climate for conformity. Artists and writers are better off here than anywhere else in China; they are numerous and enjoy a cultivated public. But it is in just such a climate as this that it is most difficult to maintain the sort of isolationist culture that the Party wishes for China. Here there are still artists and intellectuals who resist the guidance of Marxism: an offensive which I shall describe later on has been launched against them.

There is a parallel lack of compatibility between management and politics. In the factories the bourgeois directors who have stayed on often lock horns with the Party cadres sent to supervise them. Not all these former capitalists are as docile as Mr.

Liu. And there is friction between religion and politics. The power of the Catholics has been broken and the churches placed under the guidance of a Catholic Patriotic Association, a group owing complete allegiance to the authorities. But suddenly the faithful no longer go to mass except in very reduced numbers, and paradoxically the authorities are enraged because they know the reason: not that religion is dead but that the flock no longer trusts the shepherds.

Shanghai, along with Peking, remains one of the few towns that is still exposed to the physical presence of foreigners, thus to possible "contamination." Freighters from almost everywhere in the Free World drop anchor here and give their crews shore leave. Tourism has developed, especially since Air Pakistan began its flights to Shanghai. A few foreign businessmen reside here permanently, brave and patient representatives of companies like Shell and banks like the Hong Kong and Shanghai Banking Corporation. Three foreign consulates—the British is one—are still in operation.

In 1963 Shanghai was placed under the direct control of the Peking government, and the Central Committee of the Party has established one of its six regional offices there. Since these offices are designed to increase the control of the Party over the area, these steps are significant. The Party may agree to allow certain advantages to the great metropolis, to refer Shanghai as a model to the other cities of China and to show her off proudly to foreigners, but secretly the Party suspects this city of being potentially dangerous. Shanghai's success could lead other Chinese to risk the thought that two sorts of Communism are possible, the comfortable, money-making Communism of Shanghai, and the Communism of austerity that reigns practically everywhere else in China. And this is a suggestion that Peking will not and cannot tolerate. For many reasons, the most important of which are that as a whole China cannot afford this way and that it is the loathesome way of Revisionism, Peking cannot depart from the dogmatic formulations of Chinese Communism, the Communism of austerity.

CHAPTER SEVEN

THE PEOPLE'S COMMUNES CONTINUE

I HAVE VISITED FOUR PEOPLE'S COMMUNES: TWO NEAR PEKING, ONE near Shanghai, and another in Manchuria. Three of the four struck me as being exceptions rather than the rule—for reasons that I will go into in this chapter. But I am hardly able to project the generally favorable impressions that these four visits left me with, into a certainty that the communes have everywhere been successful. There are 74,000 of them throughout China. Of course no one visits any but the ones that the authorities wish to show. There are vast stretches under cultivation that have not had a foreign visitor in years and years. I had hoped to see, as I have already mentioned, one of the richest and most beautiful of the agricultural provinces, Szechuan in the west of China, but I did not receive the necessary authorization.

In spite of these limitations, the observer can still make a few generalizations. And the observations made during the course of arranged visits to showplaces can be filled out by keeping one's eyes open all the time the train or car passes through the country-side on those long trips that the visitor is obliged to take.

First and most importantly, the communes continue to exist and to exist everywhere. Even though it is true that subdivisions of the commune built up around the village have added the concepts of "brigade" and "team," it is still within the framework of the peasant commune that they operate. Nor has this framework been so emptied of content as I had believed before I returned to China. In other words, the Chinese peasant remains strenuously subjected to an artificial social organism of a socialist character, larger and more demanding than the Soviet kolkhoz, and much broader than either of the former natural organisms out of which Chinese society was formed, the family and the village. In addition, this new organism is much more powerful, thanks to the close control exercised over all the peasant's activities.

The visitor can also see that hardly a trace remains of the foolhardy novelties that the regime experimented with when it launched the communes in 1958. The communal meals that were to replace family meals have disappeared. Now a second generation of communes has replaced the first generation that the Great Leap gave birth to. These new organizations have apparently discovered stability in a less revolutionary stance and by aiming at more modest goals. Where there was once a single giant commune there are now three and their dimensions differ. The average commune must contain between four and ten thousand inhabitants, but often there are more—twenty thousand or even higher.

It is obvious (and this was repeated to me in the country as often as it was in Peking) that the regime, rightly or wrongly, considers the communes a success. They are here to stay. The communes are one of the means by which Chinese Communism intends to reaffirm its originality. In China the revolutionary movement has been faced with the problem of "revolutionizing" (as they say in Peking) and "communizing" the most enormous mass of peasants our planet knows. In the thought of Mao Tsetung the people's communes are the instrument for that revolution, an instrument that permits change in the course of a revolution that will necessarily take a long time.

Thus one can predict that as soon as the argicultural situation allows, the communes will once again be the scene of the most daring new experiments. A third generation of communes will then be called into existence, and once again the regime will set out in a direction that was attempted too hastily with the sudden innovations of 1958.

The road's green lines of poplars run across an absolutely horizontal plain. The blank light of a Manchurian summer colors these fields gray and blue. Ten miles from Shenyang is "The People's Commune of Sino-Korean Friendship." I am welcomed in a friendly fashion and taken around by a little man whose face hardly ever breaks into a smile, Li Cheng, the manager. If I am to believe him, the labors in irrigation, reforestation and farming undertaken by ten. former villages consolidated into a single commune with seven thousand inhabitants has deeply changed the poverty of soil and life that once kept these peasants wretched. He tells me of the three plagues from which they formerly suffered: floods, moving dunes, landlords. The landlords have disappeared, an irrigation project serves a third of the 5250 acres under cultivation and protects the rest from floods, and the dunes have been stabilized.

None of this would have been possible, he explains, without large numbers of laborers and large-scale planning. It would not have been possible in the kolkhozes for instance (called "co-operatives" in China) because they were too small. Incidentally, in speaking of the past my guide lets slip that out of 1400 families only 80 were initially in favor of the neighborhood cooperatives, and of ten villages only two volunteered later for consolidation into kolkhozes of "a higher order"—which doesn't square at all with the official version in which socialization is an irresistible momentum created by "the broad masses of the people."

Not a word from Li Cheng about the first generation of communes. In answer to my question he says nothing more than that he has been manager here since 1961, which was probably the date of the return to a modified and more modest idea of the commune. The most obvious change that took place at that time was the parceling out of individual plots to the peasant families. In this village these were little kitchen gardens around each peasant cottage, a much better solution of the problem that I was to see in many other places where the plots were placed in odd corners and poor soils. Moreover, here the individual plots from 10 percent of the cultivated area, while the average is only 5 percent. Another change, but one that does not meet the eye is a cutback in the size of the group each peasant works with. In 1958 he was lost in the tremendous sea of commune members; now he belongs to a "production team" of about 80 workers. This is the lowest level and above it comes an intermediate grouping, the brigade. In this commune there are ten brigades. And there are exactly ten villages. This means that the village, which had been dissolved in the communes, has been at least partially rehabilitated.

When I visit the principal village, the small capital of this commune, it is obvious to me that the regime has supplied this backwoods settlement with a homogeneous collection of organizations previously unthinkable in such a place. I am shown a primary school—there are ten for the 1200 schoolchildren in this commune. A small ten-bed hospital was built in 1962 and there's a first-aid station for each brigade. There was a well-kept "old folks home" where live the two dozen old men and women who have no families to look after them. The state cooperative store was amply stocked—there are three in all. The agricultural school has 130 students, four veterinaries care for sick animals and experiment with the raising of improved breeds; there is a station for agricultural experimentation. Here the selection of seed has been much improved, my guide tells me. The average yield of the harvest per acre rose from more than 1600 pounds in 1962 to more than 2200 in 1963. He will say no more.

Decent cottages. A good number seemed to have been repaired or improved at a fairly recent date. Swarms of children bursting with health. The average yearly income of the workers has almost tripled in a decade, the manager tells me. There was an increase of from 130 yuan to 340. This boils down to only $8.40 a month, but we must remember that this is China and that in this People's Republic the prices for basic commodities are very very low. A household can earn about 100 yuan annually ($40) from the sale of produce from the family plot.

All this represents, says the guide, a standard of living higher than the peasant has ever known—but not a word about the scarcities of 1959–1961. The proof, he adds, is that in this commune there are now 350 watches, 380 bicycles, 750 radios, 110 sewing machines, and 440 new houses built in 1963. Each of the 1400 families has at least one pig. Over cups of green tea, while a secretary takes down our conversation, I am treated to a few statistics: 500 head of livestock (including 80 horses and 14 cows), 200 modern plows or other pieces of modern agricultural equipment, a repair shop, and 60 pumps or other sorts of irrigation equipment . . .

And how many tractors are there? To this the manager responds with a curious "About nine." That "about" explained itself when I was taken to the repair shop. Of the seven tractors I saw there (I take it the other two were in the field) three were rusting in the open air. They were obviously not in working order and were being cannibalized. Parts could be had in no other way. There must have been half a dozen lathes in the shop. I saw two mechanized sowers, but all around them were various fragments of older machinery. Census of the automobile population: one.

On a visit to a brigade center I was equally struck by the disappointingly primitive nature of their equipment. Except for a few carts with rubber tires, there wasn't any modern equipment and everything looked very worn. That was particularly true of the twenty-odd animals I saw, horses and donkeys, which, like most of those I was to see on my trip, were worn-out and unhealthy. One last question: what about fertilizers? This time the answer I receive is even vaguer. The manager has nothing to tell me about this subject, except that when there is any at all they use 40 pounds per *mu* (approximately ⅙ of an acre), but there generally is none.

This commune in the Northeast near Shenyang is probably the most representative of the four I visited. I believe that it is fairly normal, not larger than average and obtaining average results. The next I saw was just the opposite: the model commune in Danhwei about 20 miles from Shanghai in a fairly rich countryside. It has one exceptional advantage: its 4500 acres under cultivation received 3300 pounds of ammonium sulfate last year, liquid and powder. The commune's proximity to the plant in Wuching that produces this chemical accounts for its privilege. In 1963 an acre planted in rice yielded 4675 pounds; in 1950 hardly 2700 pounds was reached and only a little more than 3500 pounds in 1957. Cotton, the commune's secondary crop, has almost quadrupled its yield—1850 pounds per acre in 1963.

This commune is larger than most. There are 20,000 inhabitants divided among 12 brigades and 128 teams of unusual size (100 to 200 members). As everywhere much labor has gone into irrigation. They have opened a new canal that runs all the way to the Hwang-p'u and allows them a novel enterprise: they carry their produce to market in wooden boats of their own making and fish in their canals and reservoirs. They are very sparsely mechanized: five tractors, three of them Czech (thus without new parts since the break with Moscow), a single truck, 32 electric hulling machines (those worked by hand are twice as numerous), and three motorized cultivators; a repair shop and a woodworking shop are both supplied with a modern plant. I am told that in this commune near Shanghai the average monthly earnings are in the neighborhood of 45 yuan ($18)—a figure that seems unusual when compared with what I heard elsewhere: $12.

Each of the communes that I am shown in the country near Peking is exceptional in its own way. One of them, the "Commune of Sino-Vietnamese Friendship," is of unusual size (16,000 acres under cultivation, 32,000 inhabitants, 35 villages) and stands out in another way that is absolutely sensational in China, completely modern equipment. The combines and threshers look like ultramodern ones from Canada, but they were built in China. The whole ragtag and bobtail of foreign correspondents in Peking were taken out here on a visit by a group from the Information Office of the Foreign Ministry. As they stood in front of these machines in action they were filmed by government cameramen. All this was doubtless destined for propaganda uses. The average monthly earnings of a worker in this commune: $10.

There are an even greater number of exceptional features about the "Red Star," commune near Peking: gigantic dimensions (25,000 acres under cultivation, 55,000 inhabitants, 110 villages) and even more extraordinary mechanization (64 tractors, says

the manager, and 11 combines; 35 trucks) and the unusual mixture within the commune of agriculture and factories, villages and
workers housing. This is due to the proximity of the capital. I
am taken to the tractor garage. Unfortunately the 64 tractors I'd
been told of were not there. I was not even shown half a dozen.
And my guide is very vague about their whereabouts: "In the
field, with the brigades." What are they doing there with the
grain harvest a week away?

Some of the shops in this garage look quite good, almost like
small workrooms in a factory—lathes, milling machines, etc., all
made in China. Others are not so good. And everywhere around
them there reigns the most unutterable messiness. Bands for cater-
pillar tractors rust on the ground where they were thrown.
Large-scale harvesters rust unpainted as though they had been
abandoned, and in any case sit out in the open. A great deal of
material has been left out in spite of an overcast sky and yesterday's several downpours. Certainly, at least if I judge by what
I've been shown, agricultural mechanization has not gotten off
to a good start.

Be that as it may, if I am to believe the manager of this
commune, the poor soil of what was once an imperial hunting
preserve has been profoundly improved since 1950, and since
1958 in particular, by quadrupling the area under irrigation. The
return for grains was 3300 pounds per acre in 1963. This commune raises 1100 horses, 5300 head of cattle—2300 of which
are dairy cows—and more than 100,000 ducks. The average
worker's wage is $11.

The grave food shortage of 1959–1961 certainly had as primary
cause a series of natural calamities. But it is also certain that the
haste and overconfidence in the creation of the first generation
of communes played an equal part. It is only fair then that I
emphasize that the recovery of the years 1962–1964 owes a great
deal to this second generation of communes. According to Western estimates in 1960, China harvested 150 to 160 million tons
of basic foodstuffs (we include in this category, as do the Chinese,
cereals, plus dry beans and potatoes at one quarter their weight).
Only 165 million tons or a bit more were raised in 1961. These

figures are well below China's minimum need of about 180 million tons—a total reached again in 1962, thanks to more favorable skies and the reform of the communes. In 1963 about 185 million tons were harvested, and the 1964 harvest is expected to surpass it—they say that it will reach 200 million tons.

Throughout my trip I had repeated proof that the food shortage had ended. I visited the dining halls of factories, where the meals look nourishing, very simple but ample. Families seemed to have enough, although foodstuffs continue to be rationed. Vegetables were in overproduction, as I have mentioned. There were sufficient markets, groceries and restaurants everywhere. The Chinese look healthy. And never before have I seen the Chinese countryside appear so well worked, so beautiful.

But what equipment did the peasants have at their disposal to work this miracle? There is a surprise in store for any specialist who, like myself, devoured texts published by the Chinese during this period of readjustment.

In the books, the Chinese repeatedly announced three innovations: mechanization, chemical fertilizer, and electrification. These modern methods had previously been lacking, these texts say, and now they are making their contribution thanks to the regime's new policy of "placing industry at the service of agriculture." Unfortunately, in this case, reality differs greatly from the printed page. . . . It is more than obvious that help from industry is slow in coming.

As for mechanization: the use of tractors is still a rarity. Certainly they are not completely absent, as we have seen on our visits to a few communes, but they are scarce in relation to the tremendous area of China. In 1963 there were 100,000 "on the basis of 13 horsepower per tractor," say the official texts. In reality there are probably something like 70,000 machines of one type or another. That is what the experts believe. In China I saw a 58-horsepower "Red Orient" made in Loyang, a 28-horsepower model of the same make, and the 35-horsepower "Good Harvest" from Shanghai.

But only once did I see a tractor working in the field. All the others were not in use. And again, the only communes I visited were close to large cities. It would appear that these, rather than the more distant communes, are the ones that have a priority for the allocation of tractors. There is also preferential distribution of tractors to "state farms," a special sort of agricultural collective, different from the communes. State farms are generally situated in the underdeveloped regions on China's frontiers— Sinkiang, for instance, or the far north of Manchuria—and practice farming on a very large scale with a partially military work force.

Though it has made the tractor a glorious symbol of the new agriculture, perhaps the regime is not really in such a hurry to spread its utilization. Overpopulated China is above all a country of intensive cultivation where the earth is gardened rather than farmed, and there are millions of arms to accomplish this. If tractors spread and mechanization develops, a time will soon come when the problem of what the millions of arms thus liberated can turn to must be solved. It is clear that at the present time industry would not be able to grow fast enough to find a place for all these peasants thrown into unemployment.

Unlike China, the Soviet Union has need of machines for its large-scale agricultural enterprises because the density of peasants per square mile is so much less than China's. Thus the building of tractors and a plan for agricultural mechanization date from the first Five Year Plan. China, on the contrary, from the very beginning, waited until the third Five Year Plan (1963–1964— but the whole plan was not in operation in 1964) to commence a broad mechanization of agriculture. In so doing, China departed sharply from the Soviet model and even from orthodox Marxism, in which the socialization of the land follows upon the mechanization of agriculture.

In proper Marxist economics, political organization follows the modification of the economic basis, is its consequence, instead of the reverse. But it is characteristic of Mao Tse-tung and his comrades that the political revolution must come first and economic revolution later.

Be this as it may, the slowdown in the delivery of tractors results in part from the difficulties industry must be having in producing them. Tractor plants were among those hardest hit by the "perfidy" of the Russians in the summer of 1960. At the same time, the partial drying up of Russian petroleum products seems to have condemned China to a period of very severe fuel rationing, and thus put a temporary halt to many of the tractors. In Peking one of the economic planners, Mr. Yung Lung-kwei, explained quite frankly that until the break with the Russians the manufacture of tractors depended almost totally on imports of Russian steel.

Thus it has been necessary for the Chinese to learn the art of manufacturing the proper alloys and parts. Of the 460 items that are necessary, 430 were in production in December, 1963, Mr. Yung told me. The remainder were expected in 1964. The industrial readjustment that began in 1961 had as its objects the modification and the increase of production. For example, there is the case of the great tractor factory at Loyang, in Honan, the province south of Peking, The texts tell that in 1963 production was up 30 percent. Aid was given in the construction of a factory of equal size—probably the one in Tientsin. Training was supplied to qualify workers for positions in other factories in the Northeast (Shenyang) and the East (Shanghai). Since the break with Russia forced China into a path of technological independence, 130 factories in other parts of China have begun to work for Loyang. In short, four years have been necessary in this sector as in many others to heal the effects of the quarrel with the Russians and the difficulties of the bad years.

As for heavy agricultural machinery or any other machinery besides tractors, here China is even further behind. They have gotten no further than prototypes and tryouts. Such combines and heavy harvesters as I saw outside Peking seem even rarer than tractors. On the other hand, what I did see just about everywhere, except for the specially privileged communes, were scenes of rural life that are as old as the world and China. Mechanization was almost completely lacking. Teams of peasants were cutting wheat or rice with sickles, others threshed by hand or with wooden flails, donkeys trod in circles over the straw, boys and girls armed with wooden shovels threw grain into the air above the piles so that the breeze would husk it, etc. Although motorized cultivators and plows appeared in the industrial exhibition in Shanghai, I never saw even one in the field—but once

I did see six brand-new mechanized plows unloaded on a platform as the train approached Wuhan.

The real task that faces the regime should be increasing and improving the simple basic tools, rather than aiming at the mechanization of agriculture. They might replace the ancient wooden plows with metal ones and create a battery of small machines made almost entirely of wood and worked by hand, machines such as the Japanese peasants have used to thresh with since the thirties. China appears at the moment to be aiming again at these modest and realistic goals. After having believed in dreams about the possibility of instant mechanization, the planners seem to have renounced their excessive ambitions in favor of much more reasonable goals.

A new expression has been born: "semi-mechanization." This describes all sorts of small agricultural devices whose elementary technology puts them within the powers of manufacture of small local enterprises or even village shops. The *People's Daily* has even explained recently how "semi-mechanization" can be preferable to mechanization: the equipment is simpler than modern agricultural machinery and thus more easily repaired and more economical. And besides they are "better adapted to the level of economic and cultural development found in the majority of rural areas." The Party newspaper indicated (October 15, 1964) that this was the conclusion of a national conference recently held to discuss the problems of equipping agriculture. It admits that Chinese industry cannot yet "deliver a sufficient supply of agricultural machinery." It adds that the collective resources of the communes at time of writing is "not yet substantial enough" and that in any case very few production teams or brigades have the means to purchase such machinery.

There was however at least one category of equipment that seemed to be rather widespread: power pumps. They are worked either by small electric motors or diesel engines—economical both of them, and equally easy to keep in repair. My trips through the countryside confirmed the impressions of the Canton-Peking stretch, namely the progress of rural electrification, which is one of those happy surprises reserved for the visitor who returns to China after an absence of several years. Electrification blankets the environs of large cities, and then follows the main arteries of communication from which it has begun to penetrate into the farthest villages.

In most communes there is no question of bringing light into each peasant cottage. This is the exception rather than the rule. Except in the neighborhood of the larger towns, peasants in the millions are still using kerosene lamps—and since kerosene is severely rationed they must be most economical. As evening deepens around the villages lights are rare and dim. The real importance of rural electrification lies in the powering of those little shops like the ones I visited near Shanghai or Shenyang which supply the most elementary industrial and mechanical needs.

Of all these installations that electricity has made possible, the most valuable are very probably the power pumps. More and more it is they. that protect the fields against natural calamities. Near the lower reaches of the Yangtse in the Province of Anhwei pumping stations form a real network. More than 617,000 acres under cultivation are protected by this network from water-logging or drought. Here the rice harvest was saved during the summer of 1963 at a time when a flood threatened the paddies. In the great rice-growing region of the delta, 80 percent of the 6,200,000 acres under cultivation are pumped by a network supplied with electric or diesel power.

And what about the third factor in that mecahnization of agriculture which the regime speaks of so often, chemical fertilizer? Indeed, this great innovation of which China is so proud *is* China's hope, but as in the case of tractors we must be aware of one thing: the battle has hardly more than begun. Only once, as I have already said, did I see peasants spreading chemical fertilizer in the rice paddies; it was in Hunan. Of the four communes that I visited, only one, in the neighborhood of Shanghai, received an ample supply. In the three others, when I broached this subject the only reply was a complaint that they did not receive more. "We just don't get enough," I was told on the "Red Star" near Peking, a commune otherwise very favored—it received 3000 tons in 1963. "Deliveries are on the increase," was the laconic reply of the manager of the "Commune of Sino-Vietnamese Friendship"—but no details. And in the Ministry of Agriculture in Peking I was astonished to hear a high official dwell at great length on the virtues of *natural* fertilizers without being able to answer any of my importunate questions about artificial fertilizer—he was the man who never mentioned tractors.

It is strange, given the extraordinary farmers the Chinese have always been, that ten years of Communism and the three black years passed by before any important effort was made to provide China with large works for the production of chemical fertilizer. Except for the superphosphate works that were set up with Russian help in 1956 at Nanking, the plans provided for nothing at first but small-scale operations. Only after 1958 did the Chinese begin producing installations that turn out nitrogenous fertilizer, the fertilizer that best takes into consideration China's possibilities and needs.

Not until 1961, when the reversal of priorities put industry at the service of agriculture, did the chemical industry begin to expand. At once this industry attained a high priority rating for the limited funds available to invest in capital construction. At the same time China disbursed part of her treasury of foreign currencies in order to purchase in Japan and in Europe fertilizer and equipment for chemical plants.

Large factories are now the order of the day and the main goal is the production of nitrogenous fertilizers. This is responsible for the fine factory at Wuching, near Shanghai. As I have already noted, this plant is still expanding, in order to produce urea. In April, 1964, after a year of tryouts, a large factory in Canton, which seems to be a copy of the one in Wuching, went into production. It also has a capacity of 100,000 tons of ammonium sulfate and the manufacturing process is highly automated. It is only the second important producer of artificial fertilizers which the Chinese themselves have designed and equipped with their own machinery.

In South China, in Kwangtung Province, another great factory going up at Chankiang, on the Luichow Peninsula, will yield 100,000 tons of superphosphates. A factory at Kaifeng, in Honan, has already begun to deliver ammonium phosphate. If we can believe the reports of the Reuters correspondent in Peking, the plan for the chemical industry calls for the construction of six large factories: in 1964 the experts in Shanghai had already designed three of them and the fourth was on the drawing board.

Then again all the smaller factories built before or during The Great Leap Forward are being enlarged. For instance, the Nanking plant that I have already mentioned now employs 1800 technicians and includes a setup for the production of nitrates as well as superphosphates. Five other factories in this category are located at Kirin and Dairen in Manchuria; at Lanchow in the Northwest; at Taiyuan (southwest of Peking); and Tsinan (in Shantung, south of Peking).

But the requirements of China's tired soil—if artificial fertilizers are to allow it to deliver all it's capable of—are enormous! Taking various estimates into account, China's minimum falls between 30 to 40 million tons of nitrogenous fertilizer per annum. Now in 1963 China produced about 3 million tons and only 2 million were nitrates. And China's imports of fertilizers for that year came to $2\frac{1}{4}$ million tons, two thirds from Europe and the rest from Japan. Thus the peasants had a mere $5\frac{1}{4}$ million tons at their disposal, and that is far from enough. According to the *Far Eastern Economic Review* (Hong Kong, June 11, 1964), an acre in China receives an average 55 pounds of fertilizer, while an acre in Japan receives an average 477 pounds. However, in the communes I visited they told me that they allowed 266 pounds per acre—when they had any fertilizer.

In the end only a small part of the glory for getting China out of an agricultural crisis in 1962 can go to the two touted programs: the inauguration of modern methods and industry's aid to agriculture. What got China out of this mess were the peasants themselves, for the most part using their time-honored tools and their own strong arms. But it is also certain that the success obtained with these limited means owes a great deal to the communal system as it now operates. The communes had as their special task the practice of what the official propaganda calls the "eight-point charter of agriculture."

The eight points are "irrigation, improvement of the soil, selection of seeds, close planting, protection of plants, organization of field work, modernizing equipment, and fertilizers." It is significant that neither mechanization nor electrification are listed. Fertilizers aside, the other seven points have little to do with the promised aid from industry. Irrigation, first on the list, certainly benefited greatly from the communal system that allows the application of a greater labor force and more thorough planning over a wider area. The communes have contributed heavily to the development of what René Dumont (*Révolution dans les campagnes chinoises*, Editions du Seuil, 1956) calls "small-scale hydraulic engineering." M. Dumont, a leading expert in this field who has visited China several times, believes that the efforts of the Chinese peasant in this area have resulted in far and away the greatest irrigation system produced by any country at any time. To this continuing effort is due that hallmark of Chinese agriculture, the way every field has the look of a garden. The intensive cultivation on which such truck-farming depends is possible over vast spaces whenever the source of water is assured.

Other "points" such as "improvement of the soil, organization of field work," etc., have been equally stimulated by the communal system. A commune introduces the ferment of continual change into the countryside. The commune will not leave the peasant alone as soon as it's a question of getting him out of a rut and switched over to new methods of proven worth. And thus even now, in spite of the growing role of the lower ranks (brigades and production teams), it is the upper ranks of planners and managers who are the real organization of the communes and who determine the countryside's present look. Instead of simply being a geographical grouping, the commune turns into a tremendous estate so to speak, all under the planning and watchfulness of a veritable general staff and its hierarchy. The commune gives form to collective undertakings—from canals and reservoirs to shops, kilns, quarries, silos, new housing, old people's homes, nurseries, etc. And all these have deeply modified the rural economy and the rural life. One of the commune's merits has been to realize considerable investments at the lowest possible cost. Perhaps this has been onorous for the peasants, but it has been profitable to agriculture and, insofar as it contributes capital, to industry, too.

Just how much of the recovery in agriculture has been due to a return to the individualism of the peasants and to a partial setting aside of rural collectivization caused by the crisis of 1959–1960? Much has been made of this by foreigners who have not taken into consideration the fact that if there was any retreat it was only half a retreat. There was no fundamental questioning of the principles of the system and surely the state of agriculture after the crisis is not the one it was in before collectivization.

Nevertheless very little of the "communization" of peasant life attempted in the second half of 1958 remains today. That was the time when an attempt was made to explode the limits of the village and of the family. They were both felt to have lost their validity and to have become too narrow. Meals were no longer allowed at the family table: there were communal dining halls. Wives were expected to join their husbands in the fields while the very young and the very old were taken in charge by nurseries or old-age homes. This was the beginning, all the announcements said, of "mass living." The peasant had become a mere atom in a huge collective composed of tens of thousands of human beings. He was thought of as a sort of worker-soldier of the soil, nourished and clothed by the state, and good for any of its interchangeable tasks, whether sowing and reaping or the production of steel in the village foundry.

In reality this unprecedented revolution never succeeded in becoming anything more than a poorly ordered and often half-hearted experiment. After six months the tide turned and the years 1959–1960 show the progressive abandonment of revolutionary innovations, a "de-communization" of rural life, so to speak. The peasant was returned to his village and the family to its hearth. In 1961 came the allotment of the much-publicized "individual plots" that each household is allowed to cultivate after its hours of employment on the collectivized fields. Peasants are authorized to possess certain tools of their own, to raise certain animals (a pig and chickens, for instance) and carry on certain small handicrafts in their own cottages—all this on their own time. At the same time free markets were opened throughout the country, and in these markets, at the risk of competition with the socialized trade in rural areas, peasants could sell for

their private profit the vegetables, poultry or handicrafts produced during their leisure.

Throughout my trip I was careful not to exaggerate the importance of these "little liberties" as they are called, nor to regard the individual plots as a vindication of the peasant's
property rights. As I have several times remarked, these plots
account for only about 5 percent of the commune's cultivated
area, and they often lie in poor soils. Whatever income these
plots and household handicrafts bring the peasants, it is small.
I was given almost the same figure everywhere and suppose that
it is a ceiling set by the regime: about 100 yuan ($40) *per year,*
per household. These plots probably saved the peasants from
dying of starvation during the black years. They have contributed to improvement in the provisioning of towns, especially
in vegetables and eggs. But the regime sees to it that they are
not enlarged. They have not been allowed to become rivals of
collective farming. The open markets are under strict control to
prevent speculation. Thus I find it difficult to attribute a very
important economic role to any of these non-communal activities.

The real retreat from the first formula that dissolved the
individual peasant in a gigantic organization was to transfer the
principal role from the brigade of from 200 to 300 members to
the production team of from 50 to 80 peasants, itself a subdivision
of the brigade. Villagers were once more among their own neighbors, and recovered a certain amount of autonomy in their labor.
Working in smaller numbers and among themselves, they were
able to operate more efficiently as well as to keep the books to
distribute the fruit of their toil more easily. They are assigned
draft animals, larger pieces of equipment, and the specific area
they are responsible for. All this is the collective property of the
peasants—if "collective property" still has any meaning. To encourage production, a quota is set with the understanding that
anything over it will be paid for and the proceeds will be theirs.
On the other hand, if they do not meet the quota they will be
penalized. The "team" keeps its own books and pays it members
in money or in kind.

But even while bringing the team to the fore the regime has
not shown any misgivings about the commune as a system. The

peasant in China has not returned to independence, and these "little liberties" have little to do with Liberty. The right to property has not been allowed him and his personal efforts are strictly limited. He is nothing more than a part, a fragment of the collectivity, team, brigade or commune, which is all that really exists. He is an employee of the earth so to speak, and his salary is fixed according to an extremely complex system of "work points" which takes into account hours, types of work, level of return, etc. He is a mere performer. There are still superiors to whom he owes obedience, for the Party is behind them and its cadres and secretaries retain control of the countryside. And the presence of the Party means that the authorities continually intervene in the peasant's work and, more important, in his opinions, his political beliefs and his very thoughts.

We have touched on a most important subject, the political role of the commune. If the regime persists in seeing such capital importance in the commune, the explanation of this attitude is political. The communes may suffer disappointments on an economic level but the regime seems to consider them to have been a success—politically. In reality the commune is the state's lowest rural echelon. It is in the form of the commune that the state exerts its presence among the lowest and broadest orders of the population. In this form the state asserts the omnipresence of its control and political leadership. There is a characteristic of the Chinese commune which differs totally from the Soviet Kolkhoze: on the communal level political leadership and economic management reside in the hands of the same personnel, instead of residing in two different groups.

And finally the commune is the means by which the Party maintains its hold on the country and organizes its plan of action there. In the rural areas the Party forms its committees and spreads the lowest subdivisions of its network: its own cells first of all and then its satellite organizations, most important of which are the Youth League and the League of Women. For example, in the commune that I visited near Shanghai the Party had less than 400 members, but there were a thousand in the Youth League, while the League of Women included every adult woman. The entire hierachy of cadres (in this case all officials and responsible parties) on whatever level, whether communal, brigade or team, forms a system of faithful agents assigned to communicate Party orders to the masses and to inform the Party of the mass's reaction. In the above-mentioned commune there is a fifteen-member communal committee with a chairman and assistant chairman. Each brigade committee has from seven to nine members and there are from five to seven on the team committee.

The presence and the labors of the Party at this level remain almost invisible to the visitor or chance inquirer. Very little is said about it to him. This or that undertaking on the commune is explained as being the idea of the people, or "the masses" which "decided to go ahead with it." But the power that really plans and executes everything is never mentioned. Its action is kept a secret, at least from strangers. And yet it has always been on the greatest importance, from the beginning of the movement, to socialize the countryside by creating the cooperatives that were the Chinese equivalent of the Soviet kolkhozes, and that preceded the communes. What the Party was doing in the days of the agricultural cooperatives it is doing now on the communes— only doing it with more system.

Documents relative to this hidden effort are very rare, as one might guess. During the course of my trip I had the good fortune to run across a pamphlet which, while known to the experts, is not very widely distributed, and least of all in the English translation that I possess. It is nothing more nor less than a collection of reports made within the Party itself, that is to say, something we do not often have a chance to read. The title is *Socialist Upsurge in the Countryside,* and it was published in Peking in 1957. It is a work compiled for the use of rural cadres by the General Office of the Central Committee. That Mao Tse-tung himself saw to the preface proves its importance. The subtitle might read "How to win over the rural masses."

Let me quote from this pamphlet. Here is the report that heads the list; dated 1955 it deals with the activities of the Party in the rural areas of Hopeh, the home province, in 1952–1953. At that date there were still very few Communists in the villages. The administrative cadres of the regime were almost as hostile to socialization as the peasants were. For a long time the Party got nowhere because it tried to work indirectly by pulling strings. One day the secretary of the local committee of the Communist Party finally decided on simply taking control of the cooperative and installing Party members in every post of any consequence. From that moment everything began to work and the movement went forward. This story was given as an example.

Another report recounts the progress of the Party on three co-operatives in the far-off province of Kweichow in the Southwest. Here too socialization got off to a slow start. There were very few Communists, but they began an intensified training pro-gram for ideological education among themselves and the Youth League. In the second stage, these carefully educated zealots attempted to set up cell groups among the populace, which they divided up among themselves: young people, women, this village for you, that one for me. In this way they could scout out for the Party what people were thinking and saying, and especially their criticism and dissatisfactions.

Next the Party selected "activists" from the minority that ac-cepted its leadership. First they were subjected to a thorough training in politics and propaganda, then they received responsi-bilities. The best were called upon to swell the ranks of the Party and the League. Fourth stage: With increased personnel the Party attempts to assume leadership of the masses in order to persuade the peasants to form cooperatives and to accept col-lectivization. Instructions sent out to committees suggest a series of methods. Here are a few: seize every opportunity to publicize the collective system, saying "Look, this point or that has been responsible for such and such an improvement;" point out that those peasants who favor cooperatives have the support of state and Party (and let them understand that those who do not will run the risk of the wrath of the regime); announce the arrival of fertilizer and machinery that will bring prosperity; give public praise to good teams and good elements, isolate and attack the recalcitrant in order to force them back into line, etc.

How a few resolute men, lost in a mass of peasants who were suspicious when not downright hostile, applied themselves to

mastering this mass; how to accomplish this they first of all in-
filtrated this mass and then began a tireless propagandizing, so
that their ideas would catch and cell groups could be formed;
how they recruited new agents and trained them, laid siege to
the resistance and broke it, and finally began the organization
of a submissive multitude—all that is to be found in these pages.
Although written with reference to the cooperatives of 1955–
1958 they apply equally to the first generation of communes or
the second. I find the reading of this document fascinating!
Never before in history has a single group of men taken such
pains, brought to bear a will so obstinate, a method so carefully
worked out, strength and cunning so great, for the transformation and the conquest of a group more attached to its own way
of life, its traditions of independence and individualism, the
peasants of China.

Has this transformation ended? Is the mass of peasants finally
submissive? All my official guides, whether in Peking or out in
the country, replied that the job was not yet done and that
socialization still runs up against stiff resistance from a reactionary minority in the countryside. . . . Some people may find
such a confession a surprise. It is easily enough explained. Not
only is such resistance a fact, but the Party has reason to encourage it to a very limited extent and announce it to the country
at large because in so doing arms are put into the Party's hands
and reprisals against recalcitrant peasants justified. Its most
powerful weapon remains "class struggle." Class struggle legiti-
mates the dictatorship of the Party. The Party will never allow
class struggle to rest. The Party has even announced this thesis
as fundamental doctrine: that for a long time, that time which
must elapse before Socialism can become true Communism, the
advances of socialization will never be absolute, they will always
be exposed to counterattacks from reactionary elements.

Once out of the bad years the Party began to work (and it
was at this time that I took my trip to China) toward rekindling
and intensifying the class struggle in the communes. This was
necessitated by the fact that the bad years have encouraged the
rebirth of a right-wing opposition among the peasants. The
opposition has not been able to organize itself into anything

consistent because of the difficulties and dangers that confront resistance, but the regime has become concerned; this opposition believes that the allotment of individual plots and other "little liberties" conceded during the crisis point to a retreat of socialism from the countryside. Later Chou En-lai was to say that enlargement of the individual plots and an increase in the private control of trade were two demands often made by the reactionaries. Thus, after the black years the regime found that it had to take the peasants in hand, especially since the raised standard of living itself secretes a poison which official doctrine refers to as "the peasant's innate tendency toward capitalism."

"Capitalist tendencies reappear constantly and sometimes become very serious, particularly in the case of moderately well-off peasants," wrote *Red Flag,* the monthly review of the Central Committee, in April, 1964 (reproduced in *Peking Information,* April 13, 1964) in the article that announced the new hard line for rural areas. For the last five years socialization had been warmly welcomed "by the broad mass of poorer peasants and the better-off peasants of the lower stratum." On the other hand there are two categories of peasants—and here we have the official terminology that stems from Mao Tse-tung himself—"the formerly rich and the feudal ex-proprietors," who "became involved in acts of sabotage." Between the two, those peasants who are better off than the vast majority have "attempted by various means to weaken the collectivist economy by trying to give a capitalistic turn to all undertakings."

Red Flag thus announced to the countryside the commencement of a tremendous new program for socialist education, a program based on the "implacable and ineluctable" class struggle. The task is the education and reindoctrination of the peasants, with special reference to creating class consciousness in the lower categories, the poorer peasants and low-middle group. It is upon these that the Party must particularly depend, by organizing a "powerful class force." Thus it will be possible to obtain the allegiance of the middle category of the better-off peasants and even more important "to unmask and wipe out the sabotage of all class enemies." The Party publication goes on to say that "the dictatorship of the proletariat must be reinforced in the countryside"—a classic formula for the announcement of hardening the line and hunting down the opposition. The article congratulates the regime in the possession for this purpose of "a powerful weapon," the people's commune. I do not believe that a better formulation of the basically political role of the commune can be found, nor a better statement defining the importance that this organization has in the eyes of the regime.

But how is class struggle manifested in the life of the commune? Who are the enemies and why? What measures are taken against them? These are all questions for which it is difficult to obtain answers, even—or especially—in those communes that I visited. "Explain to me," I asked the manager of a commune, "just what class struggle means here." He let out a surprised "Ah!" in a tone of voice that suggested "Now you have touched on a delicate subject. . . ." But he recovered and recited chapter and verse from *Red Flag*, only adding for himself that "the battle has its ups and downs. It remains hidden, or it bursts out, according to the situation." When I asked, "At the moment it has burst out, hasn't it?" he evaded the issue with "Here we have the very lords of creation and the rich alongside the well-off and the poor." But I had him there: "Do you mean to tell me that the commune has not changed things from the way they were before the agrarian reforms? Inequalities have not been abolished? If there are still poor and rich how has the system been a success?" He was terribly embarrassed. "Those are the old social categories that we have maintained from before the reforms." That answer is very interesting—if it means anything, and I believe it does. It means that the formerly rich even after they have been stripped of their possessions still bear the infamous name that prevents them rallying to the poor even should they wish to. The Party must have someone it can label "enemies" in order to keep its own people on their toes—and that's all the class struggle on the village level is.

I kept up my questions. "Thanks to the communes life is better for a great many peasants, isn't it?" Yes, that is the case I was told. "But suppose peasants who were formerly poor become well-off or even work very hard and very well and become rich. What do you do then? Do you *struggle* against them?"

More embarrassment! In spite of contradicting himself the manager goes into another explanation of the social categories in the commune. "If 'rich' and 'poor' can be said to exist here it is because some families have many small children while others have many members of working age, or again because the quality of the soil differs from one team to another."

I decided not to cross-examine him further: it is clear that the subject stings and that the answers are mere evasions. What I feel I have established is that in the communes there *are* poor peasants, that social inequalities have *not* been totally abolished, in fact that social classes are still very well defined and social harmony doesn't reign yet in the countryside because, far from it, the Party wishes to maintain the opposite and call its faithful to struggle "ineluctably and implacably."

The visiting journalist should be prudent in forming conclusions, especially on the peasant question. He can say for certain that the fields are beautiful, that the harvest is rich and that villages are well cared for. But he must realize how much he misses, how many secrets can exist behind doors closed to him—without his even being aware that something is being hidden! I have only seen a very few communes. Each one was picked out for me, and I met only the officials. I was allowed hardly any contact with the peasants themselves and never without witnesses or a translator, of course. I was never allowed to simply spend twenty-four hours in a village. . . .

CHAPTER EIGHT

THE BOMB AND THE BICYCLE-CART

A LOADING ZONE BESIDE THE YANGTSE IN HANKOW. THE GRAY SKY that covers this place assembles everything into scenery for a melodrama. Backdrop: the coffee-and-cream river slices the horizon. To the right a peeling house, alone on the bank, lapped by the rising water. Through the broken windows that pockmark its front, the interior shows through with its laundry and rags and general grime. Families are crowded together around boxes that serve as furniture. Stage-center, three beautiful river junks with their sleek black hulls. One of them has hoisted a tall gray sail, all full of holes and as transparent as an autumn leaf; light and yet thanks to its bamboo ribbing solid enough, the sail dries after a cloudburst, motionless in the heavy air, beautiful. To the left some sort of warehouse from which the stevedores made their entrance over a vast expanse of mud.

One after the other I watch them leave the warehouse, all of them pulling or pushing at dissimilar burdens. Two aged men with nothing on but trousers rolled high on their knock-kneed legs, their sandals vanishing into the mud, sadly tow a cart that is heavy with two great metal drums. Four men follow, carrying an enormous tree trunk. They are yoked two and two to heavy beams by ropes passing under the tree trunk, but one rope has slipped, and although the labor of all four men is concentrated on getting it back under the trunk, they don't seem to be getting anywhere. After them come teams of men yoked between the shafts of various carts and wagons, mostly ancient—but some have bicycle wheels and are obviously the last word in mechanization here. Next appear a couple, man and wife, both wearing washed-out and patched mauve sacking and yoked by a rope over their shoulders. Then the coolies in rain-soaked straw hats, bronze chests glistening with sweat, their legs working to push forward bicycle-carts piled high with boxes. Certain more athletic fellows effortlessly carry huge burdens on their backs. An ancient with runny eyes, wearing sandals made of old automobile tires and string, sweats and pants as he pulls almost on the diagonal between the shafts, to move a pyramid of crates and baskets. From the junks, as from a warehouse, come strange collections of freight: bales and wickerwork, things bundled together in wrappings of straw, and used crates badly tacked together again—all of it borne away in wagons and carts pulled by men.

Then suddenly the song of the stevedores reaches me. Four coolies begin it as they carry along roped trees of crushing weight. What a great distance this song comes from! It is one I remember. More of a cry than a song it gives rhythm to hard work gasping for breath. This poignant song reaches me from the very beginning of life in China, from the depths of an Old World, the old world of sorrow, part of which goes right on existing in the New China. . . . but here again there is a touch of this new China: on the edge of the loading zone a man doles out drinking water, thanks to the union. The water comes from a sort of wooden tub mounted on an ancient bicycle, and the teams and coolies, pushers, pullers, and porters stop a minute for several mouthfuls of cool water from a bamboo ladle. Do they pay? No, it is free. And the man in charge watches his customers, his cold, sphinx-like eyes set in the shaved head of a Caesar sculpted in brown marble. Once on the street the stevedores divide their burdens among a squadron of waiting bicycle-carts.

The cargo is stowed—tied not without a few mishaps—and then the pedalers mount and set off hunched over their handlebars—rather like ancient Mongol cavalry. The tarpaulin flutters behind their naked shoulders like a cape.

The sight of a "rickshaw boy" who trots along between the shafts while his customer lolls behind him on the cushions has been banished from China by Communism. Men are no longer *hitched* to other men whom they transport. The new regime has absolutely put a stop to this humiliating job, but it has also almost completely disappeared from all other Far Eastern countries. However, although the bicycle-cart that resulted from the mating of rickshaw and bicycle is motorized in Bangkok and Djakarta, in China it is still powered by a pair of human legs. While it is true that the number of bicycle-carts devoted to the transportation of human beings has greatly diminished, I don't believe I have ever seen so many pressed into the transportation of merchandise. And never before have I seen so many men between the shafts of wagons loaded with goods. *That* job, rather than disappearing, seems very much on the increase. Everywhere one sees proof of the fact that the regime, lacking not only trucks but even wagons and draft animals, has hit on the idea of yoking millions of men and women to millions of economical little carts. Besides these there are the millions of bicycle-carts. All of these workers have been organized into a vast corporation. They belong to groups, which are further subdivided into teams, all of them part of the Plan.

And even this, for poor backward China, is progress. If you have lived, as I have, in the old China, and can call up that past, you will suddenly become aware that another character is missing from a scene in which there used to be millions of them. Perhaps you will see one or two today: the Chinese who carries over his shoulder a bamboo pole with two little baskets at either end. Such a laborer was not yielding all the work of which he was capable. As soon as he was given a cart, often a metal cart with bicycle wheels, his economic return was greatly increased. China is rich in unskilled labor. Fifty men, a hundred men, are probably capable of doing the same work as one six-ton truck.

Nevertheless, where are the trucks and why are they so few?

And if there are still only a few trucks, why are there so few draft animals? I will not attempt to answer these questions here. I merely note this shortage to illustrate another startling weakness from which China still suffers. It is another striking proof of the lack of balance and the contradictions that still affect China's economy. Because China is not weak in every sector —there's the atomic bomb!

The Chinese bomb had not yet been exploded when I was in China. I left three months too soon. Quite a few travelers and foreign residents whom I saw in Peking expressed grave doubts about China's ability to produce one, given the state of affairs that they had seen. "In the end," said one Frenchman who had been in the provinces, "how can they manufacture an atomic bomb when the only means of transportation in their newest factories is the mule-cart?" But he showed insufficient acquaintance with this new China's incredible ability to keep secrets, its sometimes stupefying contradictions, and its ambitious will. The truth that we must grasp is just this—the country of mule-carts and bicycle-carts wanted the bomb and got it. Here again we have an example of what I said about the "black" and the "brilliant" which co-exist in this new China where reality consists of adding the two. And another truth that needs emphasis is that no matter how much the traveler learns about a multitude of subjects, even if he sees all that is to be seen on a tour of more than five thousand miles, *he cannot have seen anything but what he was shown.* He must realize that if he is forbidden by the authorities to visit this town or that the reason is not necessarily that they are having difficulties there—it might be the opposite. There might very well be defenses or successes that they wish to develop in secret.

Now I understand why I was not allowed to revisit Lanchow on the very edge of Central Asia: the fascinatingly medieval city that I saw when the shock of the industrial and political revolution reached it in 1955 has in a mere ten years become one of the great atomic centers in China. And perhaps the same reason is behind their refusal to allow me to revisit Chungking, from which I had hoped to leave again for the fantastic descent on the Yangtse gorges. And again if these was one subject never touched on during any of the briefings I received it was "the bomb." The Chinese said nothing about it and showed me nothing that had any connection with it. As far as I know there has not been a single visitor over the last few years to whom the Chinese have ever shown any installation that could be connected with the creation of nuclear energy, nor has any information been forthcoming which would allow a judgment on where China stood in this area. Silence and a "Great Wall" surrounded the topic.

Could there be any place on this planet as shut away and distant as the one China chose for the explosion of this ball of fire, brighter than Hiroshima's terrifying mushroom. The very depths of Sinkiang, the most remote province in China, probably the spot on this globe farthest from the sea, saw these atomic tests. Although Sinkiang contains steppes that flower in the spring and oases through which the Silk Route once passed, there are also deserts there at the very end of the world, and one of them is the Taklamakan, in the basin south of the Tarim River which disappears into Lake Lob Nor. More than 175,000 square miles of sand, gravel and clay are closed in on the north and south by treeless mountains rising in some places to more than 18,000 feet. This is one of the most inaccessible places in the whole world and even more of a desert than the Gobi itself. It was here on the 16th of October, 1964, that China exploded her first bomb. Incidentally, Khrushchev fell the day before. . . .

And yet the secret of China's nuclear preparations had been sniffed out. Well before the explosion spies had warned the outside world and they were American spies—but of a very modern variety: Formosa-based U-2's and perhaps even satellites. Thus America was prepared. And the Japanese knew of it too. Secretary of State Dean Rusk predicted the event shortly before it took place. If there was little surprise as to the date of the explosion, there was a great deal about its nature. In the West the explosion of a rather primitive "device" (as it was called in Washington) was expected. It would be something like the very first bomb that was set off in New Mexico in 1945, or at the very best the equal of the bomb dropped on Hiroshima. It would be "dirty," which is to say that the radioactive fallout would be considerable, because it would not be technologically developed. We were told too that it would doubtless be a plutonium bomb since a uranium bomb is more difficult to manufacture.

But a week later the world had another surprise in store for it: the Atomic Energy Commission in Washington after an analysis of radioactive debris in the atmosphere announced that the Chinese device, far from being the plutonium bomb that the entire world had been led to expect, was in reality an enriched uranium bomb. This produced a sensation in scientific circles. The picture was changed. The facts demand a China far more advanced in atomic technology than anyone had been willing to believe. China may very well be ahead of France, which at the same date had been producing enriched uranium for five years without having accumulated enough to manufacture a bomb. All the experts began to ask how it was that China, considered too poor and backward to make progress this swiftly, could have gone about the production of uranium 235, a substance that demands heavier investments and a higher technological level than the production of plutonium.

China's secret goes back a good ten years—it seems that her atomic industry began as soon as the Korean War ended. The Russians, who were later to become particularly hostile to Chinese efforts in this domain, began by aiding them in research for peaceful uses of atomic energy, as detailed in the Sino-Soviet agreement of April, 1955, which was made public at the time. The Russians helped the Chinese set up their first reactor, which began operation in June, 1958. It is situated near Peking and is believed to be an experimental reactor for uranium 235 and heavy water with a thermal power of from five to ten megawatts. Aided by the Russians the Chinese also put into operation at about the same time a 25-million electrovolt cyclotron and an acclerator with high-electrostatic pressure. If the Japanese news services are to be believed, at least three more reactors have joined the first, although Russian aid was suddenly interrupted in 1960. They are located at Shenyang in Manchuria (some sources say Harbin), at Chungking in the West, and at Sian in the Northwest. Other sources, American this time, mentioned in October, 1964, that a plutonium reactor under construction or just recently operative, had been observed near Paotow, a new industrial center that has sprung up in the last ten years at the edge of Inner Mongolia on the Yellow River.*

In the province of Kansu, not too far from Paotow, there is supposed to be a plant for gaseous diffusion which must have been begun shortly before the bomb of October 16th. The location is Lanchow or the nearby town of Kao Lan, and it receives electricity from a station at Liuchia Gorge on the Yellow River. There is said to be yet another factory somewhere in Sinkiang for the extraction of plutonium from uranium bars. Besides, let me add that China has made great strides since 1950 in mapping her mineral resources and in so doing has discovered important reserves of uranium ores in her extensive territory, particularly in Sinkiang and on the island of Hainan which faces North Vietnam across the Gulf of Tonkin.

Are we obliged to believe that China has succeeded without foreign aid in perfecting a method of producing enriched uranium, an extremely involved process, and that the gaesous diffusion plant at Lanchow was further along than anyone supposed and already producing uranium 235? Or the next best hypothesis, that China had created and was operating a whole series of plants of various kinds leading to the production of this same uranium 235? Such a hypothesis supposes achievements in the production of special alloys that are not easily manufactured and in the delivery of large quantities of special materials. If either of these hypotheses is true, we can expect China to follow America and Russia in serial testing of nuclear devices, numerous tests relatively close together. And a Chinese hydrogen bomb shouldn't be too far off. But there is another line of thinking that yields less spectacular results. Perhaps the Chinese have simply made use of the enriched uranium that was furnished by the Russians in experimental reactors, and subjected it to some added enriching. Such an operation is less complicated than the one that starts off with the simple metal, and it can be accom-

* Cf *Le Monde*, October 18–19, 1964, "An Impressive First Step," by Nicholas Vochney; and *Bulletin of Atomic Scientists*, Chicago, February, 1965, "Ten Years of Secret," by Robert Guillain.

plished by several methods: gaseous diffusion, ultra-centrifugation, or electromagnetic separation by means of accelerators. If this hypothesis is true then China will only be able to explode a few bombs. Thus it will be the actual unfolding of China's nuclear tests that will allow us to form a more precise motion of the state of atomic industries in China. But whatever processes were utilized in the production of her first bomb, China is obviously considerably ahead of where the West supposed she was in October of 1964.

Even after foreign aid stopped in 1960, China had a certain number of atomic scientists who had been trained abroad, particularly in America, Russia and France. And it is not unthinkable that foreign scientists came to work in China. Unverifiable reports maintained that the British scientist Bruno Pontecorvo, who went over to the Communist camp in 1950 had spent some time in China. The head of atomic research in China, probably the father of the Chinese bomb, is a scientist who received part of his training in France before the war, Professor Tsien San-kiang, director of the Chinese Institute of Atomic Energy. He was born in 1910 in the province of Chekiang and received a degree in 1936 from the University of Peking. In 1937 he came to France to work on nuclear physics in the laboratories of Frédéric Joliot-Curie. He is said to have been such an unusual assistant that the great scientist and his wife Irene turned over part of the laboratory to him. His wife, Ho Za-wei, aided him in his experiments. When he returned to Peking in 1948, he put his capacities at the disposal of the new regime—when it was absolutely new—and aided by the Russians he laid the foundations for China's atomic industries. He became their leading spirit when he was named chief of the above-mentioned institute in August, 1958.

Another great atomic physicist, of the Russian school this time, Wang Kan-chang, is associate director of the same institute. He is in his forties. In 1956 when Russia and China and other East-block countries contributed to the financing of a center for nuclear research at Dubna, north of Moscow, Professor Wang was the associate director—the director being, we hear, Pontecorvo. A great many Chinese researchers made the trip to Dubna between 1956 and 1960, at which time Wang Kan-chang was recalled to devote himself to the creation of China's bomb. Let me mention a figure cited by Suslov in his report of February 14, 1964: since 1949 a million Chinese scientists had worked in their various specialties in the Soviet Union.

As for the many scientists trained in America, one of them is an associate director of the institute, Professor Chao Chung-yao, a graduate of the California Institute of Technology. There is another man with a degree from Caltech whose work, although unconnected with atomic physics, has a connection with the Chinese bomb, Professor Tsien Hsueh-sen, who taught in California until he returned to China in 1955 and who is considered the world's leading authority on rockets (*U.S. News and World Report*, December 28, 1964). Upon his return to China, Dr. Tsien was named director of the newly created Institute of Dynamics. He was born in 1912. Let us mention two more scientists who are often cited as deans of atomic physicists: Li Su-kuang, born in 1889, minister of geology and vice-president of the Chinese Academy of Sciences, and Wu Yu-sun, born in 1897, who has negotiated most of the scientific agreements between China and East-block countries. The former has a degree from the University of Birmingham, the latter from the University of Chicago.

In China perhaps more than in any other country research is carried on by teams rather than by individuals. If the Chinese bomb has Tsien San-kiang for its father, it is also the child of numerous scientists in collaboration. Who are they? The same secrecy that surrounds atomic installations surrounds the names of China's atomic physicists. All we know is that under that sprinkling of deans of science in China there has arisen a new crowd of very young physicists recruited from among the approximately two hundred thousand per year who graduate from universities and institutes. In 1960 General Electric published a report on Chinese science and technology which estimated that in order to create an atomic industry five hundred scientists of a high caliber and eight hundred engineers would be required. American sources believe that at the time of the explosion of China's first bomb there were in China about a thousand atomic physics specialists.

It is clear that however limited the objectives of the Chinese atomic program may be, it must mobilize scientific personnel, equipment and capital in enormous amounts in a country poor in all three. Several times recently, the *People's Daily* has allowed the cares of the regime on this account to show through. "The technological strength of our country is far from being able to meet the demands of socialist construction," I read in this paper while I was in the capital in June, 1964. The author of this article went on to complain that too often technical work was hampered by the bureaucracy, closed down by political meetings, and bothered by the shifting around of specialists who were taken off their specialties. Two months before the explosion of the bomb Professor Tsien, its father, took to the pages of the same newspapers to warn the regime of the breadth of planning required by what he called "large-scale scientific experiments," which means, obviously, atomic testing. There are branches of science, he writes, that call for tremendous investments, massive construction, and thousands of tons of steel. A great center for research is an expense and dare not remain incomplete. Naturally it uses enormous quantities of electricity. If the Western nations have made the effort necessary for the creation of scientific organizations, there is all the more reason that a socialist country should possess "centers for research of tremendous size and powerfully directed." Such a plan could absorb as much as a third of the available technicians, a number that might some day exceed that of all experts involved in industry and agriculture. Such experimental centers might call for thousands of specialists, continues Professor Tsien, who adds (which makes me shiver) that it might be necessary to protect the secrecy of these undertakings by forbidding any of the personnel to leave these installations at any point in their lives. A few days later the *People's Daily* returned to this subject in an editorial entitled "Let's Look Deeper into our Future," which called on industry to remedy this lack of qualified personnel by training them: a certain number of technicians must be taken off the assembly line to join in research in the laboratories.°

Thus the training of technicians and scientists will for the

° *People's Daily*, June 6, August 20, and September 7, 1964.

next twenty or thirty years remain one of China's gravest problems, and perhaps a bottleneck in her economic development. Although about 330,000 to 350,000 engineers have received degrees between 1949 and 1963, according to American estimates, this will not be enough. The same thing goes, it is believed, for the present rhythm in the training of engineers. In 1957 the planners calculated a need by 1967 for more than 10,000 Ph.D's in science and two million engineers and set up the "Twelve Year Plan for Science" accordingly. These objectives will not be met according to schedule, not by a long shot. The shortage will be felt for a long time and most of all in the field of pure science, which in a backward country was sacrificed to fields where an immediate result in industry would be forthcoming. And furthermore, although the quantity of young scientists from the younger generation is much greater than in the past, there seems to be a serious difference in quality between most of them and their elders, the 150 or so great scientists of the older generation who were trained abroad. The younger ones lack their experience, they lack their international viewpoint.

Nuclear experiments and the development of atomic weaponry, especially if China aims at a hydrogen bomb and rockets, will weigh heavily on the rest of her industry, affecting the development of consumer goods and generally slowing the rise of the standard of living.

An atomic industry stimulates some forms of production and sectors of the economy while it causes others to atrophy or slow down; it diverts tremendous resources into nonproductive channels and imposes grave sacrifices on the population. Indeed, one might ask if the gravity of the recent crisis didn't result in part from China's decision to have the bomb at any price! I do not believe that it has often enough been pointed out and emphasized that the success of a bomb in 1964 requires preparations and tremendous investments that must have coincided exactly with the very bottom of the depression in China's economy, with a time when the people didn't have a thing. Won't the atomic bomb eventually have to be added to the other causes of the privations the black years imposed, along with "grave natural calamities" and "the perfidy of Khrushchev revisionists"?

It seems obvious that it has put a brake on "readjustment." And it supposes a terrific distortion of this readjustment in the direction of a military and political objective that will give power and prestige rather than improve the people's standard of living. To decide in the middle of such a crisis and in spite of that crisis to continue without foreign aid all those manufactures that lead to a bomb is a piece of audacity that only a dictatorship can allow itself.

The atomic bomb may give us a clue to certain of the enigmas and paradoxes of present-day China. When a visitor to the An-shan steel works notes that transportation is often by means of mule-carts, and that so many carts are pulled by human beings, isn't it because the atomic bomb has set up a system of priorities more urgent than the replacement of animals and human legs by motors? If the factories that turn out trucks at Changchun in Manchuria continue to disappoint, aren't there those secret plants in Sinkiang or Kansu which skim off the best personnel and material? And again if there are few trucks in the cities a foreigner visits, couldn't it be that a greater number are to be found in cities with atomic centers?

A visitor often finds the installations that he is shown rather poor and badly kept, but mightn't there be ultramodern installations, carefully kept up and the concern of a superior personnel, but in forbidden localities? In the same way if agricultural mechanization proceeds so slowly, if tractors are still rare and the supply of chemical fertilizers insufficient, isn't it that the priority officially in the hands of agriculture is nullified by a "superpriority" that is kept secret, the priority of the atom?

"The bomb and bicycle-cart"—that isn't just an easy formula, it corresponds to a basic reality of the new China. Now it would be dishonest, as I've said and as I'll say once more, to attribute to Communism all the economic weaknesses from which the country still suffers. For the most part they are all to be found in the age-old heritage of previous Chinas. They were there in the past and much worse then than now. The Party has done wonders to find remedies. But in the end such liabilities as this underdevelopment remain an awful dead weight. In the very year that China entered the Atomic Age—as though all the progress which I had registered on this trip only emphasized all that hadn't "leaped forward"—it seemed to me that I was more aware than ever before of all that the debit side of China's books carries under the headings of poverty, backwardness and overpopulation.

Under the heading of poverty I discovered an economic phenomenon that I have often observed in Japan and which the Japanese call "double structure." The foreign industrialist who visits Japan will be taken by his hosts to steelworks that rival the most modern in America, will visit dockyards that are busier than any in the world, or factories for electronic equipment that have no equals anywhere. But the Japanese do everything possible to keep the foreigner from seeing into the ground floor of their "two-story economy." There is a whole world of tiny workshops and very small concerns of the old-fashioned sort. The upper floor is right in the twentieth century or even entering an Americanized twenty-first century while the ground floor drags its feet in the feudal world of Japan's middle ages.

China too suffers from this double structure. What was the use of destroying as much as possible of social feudalism when her economy rests on a sprawling ground floor of Asiatic poverty and backwardness? China has already begun the construction of the upper story of modern technology and fine plants that form the avant-garde of the forces of production and that mobilize the more advanced elements of the populace. Below them this whole Asiatic universe carries on, and there are many trades and many workmen who have not been rescued from it. More than distance separates the employee of the great iron and steel group in Wuhan from the craftsman turning out wooden bowls in his little shop in Hankow. Ten years ago in Lanchow I saw workmen pouring the foundations of what was to be China's first petrochemical plant while other workmen crossed the Yellow River on little rafts made of inflated skins—the oldest boat in the world! Today those same swollen skins are very likely to be transporting personnel—while China's atomic installations grow.

How many Chinese are employed in industry today? An official spokesman in Peking of whom I asked this question was kind enough to supply me with figures—which is rare. Roughly thirty million all told, he replied, and that includes transportation and maintenance. He broke the figures down further: of these thirty million, ten million are industrial workers properly speaking. It is these ten million workers who make up the population of the "second story" of China's economy. They are the working-class elite of the new China, laboring in the great factories created in the past fifteen years by the state and by the Plan. Wherever modern industry springs up a whole sector of the population springs up with it into this second story and a privileged existence in the workers' developments that are built at the same time as the factories. But on the lower floor remain workers in small concerns, with a poorer and aging lay-out most of them, craftsmen at work in cooperatives, and those stuck in old-fashioned trades; and beyond even that, the ranks of the unskilled, a multitude engaged in hard labor as pullers of wagons and pushers of carts—and all those who carry, shove, dig and toil with their arms. . . . And I shall no more than mention here a whole population: 500 million peasants.

Under the heading of backwardness one of the newspapers in Peking recently had the audacity to indicate a few of China's more important needs (*Kwangming Jipao* [Light], April 27, 1964). China needs a million tractors, says this editorial—ten times more than it actually has. China needs 400,000 trucks—this figure is too low although probably less than a third that number are currently in operation. China needs forty million tons of chemical fertilizer—but production has only reached a tenth of that. These examples only illustrate China's deficiencies in relation to her needs. But what can we say about China's deficiencies in comparison with the rest of the world? Even in the field of China's greatest advance, the manufacture of an atomic bomb, she lags far behind the United States and Soviet Russia. And yet I was continually reminded during my trip that the average Chinese hasn't the haziest notion of the tremendous "leap forward" of technology in the developed nations—and I'm not so sure that all their rulers in Peking are aware of it either.

It is under another heading, overpopulation, that the causes of a good many of China's weaknesses must be entered. Demographic inflation—which I will deal with in the next chapter—

compels every sector of the economy to overstrain itself. Every solution to the most basic problems—housing, food—is superseded before it is realized. In Shanghai an official had this to say about housing: "Since the liberation here in Shanghai we have constructed housing for one million families. But as things have worked out even those families in new buildings are living in very close quarters. Every new one–family apartment contains two families—if there aren't really three families piled in there on top of one another." I have often felt that if China's rulers don't seem to pay much attention to what is going on in the outside world, and thus are not fully aware of just how far behind China is in the international competition, it is because they are so totally immersed in their internal problems and believe that they already have enough to keep them busy in the race between production and reproduction. Their attitude toward this human inflation has become more competitive, as I will explain. They no longer regard it passively. But in the meantime the problem remains. China would be a great power if the population had remained where it was under Chiang Kai-shek: 400 million. With 600 million or 700 million, that power has diminished. China risks total powerlessness when that figure reaches or passes one billion. In this breakneck race between the production of goods and the reproduction of consumers, it is frighteningly possible that in many sectors production is losing. And it is by no means certain that in a quarter of a century China will be producing enough to feed her billion inhabitants.

The regime has made considerable propaganda out of the recovery in agriculture and foodstuffs since 1962. And I have remarked à propos the communes that I believe the propaganda corresponds for the most part with reality. Nonetheless one subject of deep concern remains. The harvest of cereals in 1962 and 1963 has been estimated in the West (since China refuses to release any statistics) at between 180 and 185 million tons. This is what China consumed eight years ago when the population stood at 600 million. Since that date the population has increased a great deal, probably between 70 and 100 million, and the production of grains has not kept up with this demographic inflation. In 1964 a figure of 200 million tons may have finally been reached. But even with their vaunted "three beautiful harvests" China has only just managed to feed her people. She could hardly have set aside any reserves. There has even been reason these last three years for this country, which is not rich in foreign exchange, to buy significant quantities of grain on the international market. Purchases have averaged five million tons per year, an amount that would hardly nourish any large segment of the population but which nevertheless allows a little play and cushions a position that would otherwise be rather tight. If, as statistical extrapolation suggests, China reaches the billion mark in the next twenty-five years and her consumption of grain reaches 300 million tons, then her production of cereals must increase ten million tons every two years.

In a few years from now the intensified effort that China has finally begun in the realm of chemical fertilizers will begin to show increased returns from agriculture. But China should discover—if she has not yet found out—that it will be another twenty-five years before the production of chemical fertilizers catches up with demand. Thus there will be a growing need for imported fertilizers and foodstuffs. If the demographic inflation continues at its present rate, by the time the Chinese do produce thirty or forty million tons of fertilizer and give their fields a chance to yield at a maximum, the progress made will be completely lost and one might even say canceled out by the concurrent increase in population. And China then will be no more certain of her supply of food than she is today. Any slackening in the work force or any natural calamities repeated for two or three years will put China right back in the midst of a dangerous scarcity. It is known that the recent scarcities were the factor responsible for persuading China's rulers to step up production—and use birth control to slow down the population growth rate.

Thus China's economic successes may be considered only marginal—by which I mean that the margin between the real progress made and the danger of being overtaken by disaster remains very narrow. It is certain that many more people are much better off, but their situation is not out of danger. The margin is narrow and will remain narrow between needs and the goods that satisfy those needs, between a minimal standard of living and a slip back into real poverty. While the Chinese are no longer hungry, hunger is still close behind them: it caught up with them only yesterday; who can say that it will not do so tomorrow?

These questions are all the more disturbing when we stop to consider that as it readjusts after the three black years China's economic growth rate has declined. After the wild full-speed-ahead of the years prior to the crisis, a period of slower progress began. At the same time that the Chinese discovered that there are no shortcuts out of underdevelopment, they also discovered that there are no shortcuts to Communism. When the first Plan was launched in 1953 they promised themselves a totally developed heavy industry in fifteen years. They did not allow themselves enough time. Although the new schedule is not yet clear in all its particulars, and will not be until the third Five Year Plan is announced in 1966, it seems certain that the time allowed will be increased. The decision to put industry at the service of agriculture has already necessitated a setback for China's real hope, the creation of a complete modern economy. China's adventure into atomic weaponry will accelerate the growth of certain key industries but slow down the economy as a whole. And finally, the schedule will have to slow down even more if, after the pull-out of Russian assistance, China presumes that she must go it alone and refuses all future foreign aid.

The most important of all these factors determining a slow-down is the sudden about-face that the entire economy underwent in April, 1962, when China's rulers withdrew the priority that heavy industry had previously enjoyed and gave it to agriculture. In so doing they turned their backs on orthodox Marxism and the practice of the entire socialist world. Is Marxist methodology at fault or is the manner in which it was employed in China to blame? Even if we grant that Marxism is universally valid, it must be said that those who applied the method in China certainly asked too much of a poor country, still overwhelmingly rural, and overcrowded to boot. In order to succeed, this plan assumed not simple good harvests, but continuous successes, those "sputnik harvests" erroneously announced in the papers when the communes first began. The basis of the economy was incapable of supporting the rest. Agriculture could not "leap" like industry. On the contrary, agriculture had already reached some sort of ceiling, because except for one exceptional year, 1958, the grain harvest remained below 180 million tons until 1963.

But, you may say, isn't this situation only temporary? As soon as the recovery of agriculture has been definitely assured, won't these priorities be reversed? It is possible, of course, but all the same let's not fool ourselves: all the official statements indicate that a basic change has taken place which is destined to last. And this change amounts to saying that even should industry return to first place on the list, its development would be tied to just how much Chinese argiculture can carry, because it is upon the shoulders of Chinese agriculture, as it were, that the whole modern industrial superstructure rests. For twelve whole years everything seemed to depend on a state of mind in Peking which allowed the regime to say, "We have to have this or that industry—ask agriculture to raise its quotas so and so much!" But this formula has been reversed and now their calculations go more like this: "The land brings in so and so much —we can thus allow ourselves this much for industry." This reversal of doctrine can be culled from a whole series of publications which, dry as they may seem, are fascinating to anyone who follows the evolution of Chinese Communism.

"Agriculture is the foundation for the growth of the national economy," *Red Flag* wrote in June, 1962. "In other words the development of industry can not exceed the capacity of agriculture to deliver commercializable grain, raw materials and secondary products. . . . Since the level of production in Chinese agriculture is still very low, the role it plays in setting the speed and magnitude of industrialization is striking." Other texts explain that first the yield of agriculture must be determined and then on that basis the dimensions of the industrial effort that China can afford can be determined.

Considerations such as these would be taken for granted in a capitalist country. That they do not go without saying under Communism is proven by the history of that system in Russia.

And there is no better way to illuminate the scope of the present slowdown in China than to recall what happened in Stalinist Russia at an analogous moment in the development of the economy. When Stalin decided that Russia must have heavy industry he decided that it would be had at any cost, even at the cost of many human lives. And this is what happened: since the land had to pay for the factories, millions of peasants were quite literally sacrificed to heavy industry. And this was a path that China decided not to take. After three awful years the regime finally realized that it had exceeded the limits of what the peasant and the land could legitimately be asked to accomplish. It did not want to bring about bloodshed. So even if the motto "Heavy Industry First!" has only temporarily been set aside, we can be almost certain that its exaggeration into the Stalinist motto par excellence—"Heavy Industry at any Cost!" —will never be applied in China. Thus China, no matter how Stalinist it may remain in most matters, refuses to follow Stalin on this point. Mao remains in the end no Stalinist in that area in which he is an expert, agriculture. He pushed his methods of compulsion as far as they would go against those who form the foundation of his regime, the peasants. But peasant that he is himself, he finally took the peasants' side and announced this important decision: the future growth of China depends on the peasants, and so much the worst if all the original ambitious plans and impressive schedules must be scrapped.

That the goal has become much more distant is now admitted by all official spokesmen. Only recently the whole country repeated Chairman Mao's motto "Twenty years in a single day!" Today the words that were repeated throughout my travels were, "This will go on for a very long time." In 1958 they proclaimed, "We will overtake Great Britain in fifteen years!" This year in Peking a Chinese economist did not hesitate to correct this with rare frankness: "Listen, that was a slogan for the workers. Don't take it literally. It was ony an aspiration. . . ." In Shanghai an official spokesman confided, "In order to accomplish our undertaking we need several more decades, perhaps more. . . ." And that is a phrase that frequently turns up in the papers. And since it is difficult to give up a slogan like "The Great Leap Forward" after it has been publicized so heavily, and particularly since it really is still believed in, it has been redefined. The "leap" covers quite a large span of time, they explain, and it is only at the *end* of that time one can become aware of the magnitude of that leap, by making a comparison between where one started and where one has got to. This is an idea that Chou En-lai himself went into when he gave his report to the National Assembly in December, 1964. "Early this century, Dr. Sun Yat-sen, the great Chinese revolutionary and our precursor, said that China would make a great leap forward." (Note incidently that rather prudent attribution of paternity: Sun Yat-sen rather than Chairman Mao is father of the Leap.) And Premier Chou goes on to say, "His prediction will certainly come true *within several decades.*" Without departing from Chou En-lai's meaning or that of China's other rulers, I believe I can say that it will take thirty years as a minimum, and possibly more, to build this new China . . .*

China thirty years from now . . . Oh, we won't have to wait thirty years before we feel her presence on the international scene; we already do. And we won't have to wait thirty years —perhaps not even fifteen—to see China provided with nuclear arms. But we shall have to wait at least thirty years before China has completed her metamorphosis, before she has arrived at a well-balanced and consistent economy, before the power of her industrialization will correspond with the atomic age, before she has been able to check her galloping demographic inflation. But in thirty years the new China should be visible. And that giant will be among us in the full bloom of its maturity, one of the marvels of the year 2000. . . .

But in the decision to spread her effort over a longer period of time, China must be careful to avoid the opposite excess and allow her effort to slow down too much. I am afraid that this is at present the case. For the first time in years and years it seemed to me that the Chinese, although back at work again, are in no hurry and working somewhat listlessly! This was something I often noticed on my travels. In the fields there were teams of

---

* See the speech by Chou En-lai in *Peking Review*, January 1, 1965.

peasants taking it easy, some of them working while others frankly rested in the shade. At a construction site I saw workers sitting around chatting—an hour later when I drove by in the opposite direction they were still chatting. In a park in Shanghai more than one hundred grown men sat playing cards at three in the afternoon. In Peking's parks the strollers are numerous. Is there an unemployment problem, as I have heard? I don't believe there really is, although I did see too many workmen for some machines, personnel was in oversupply everywhere, women hold fewer jobs . . .

And isn't another cause of the slowdown a classical result of socialism? Socialism diminishes initiative and remains unable to interest workers sufficiently in production. Can peasants now herded together like sheep and working in teams under the command of a leader be expected to really produce when instead of grain from their own fields filling their own barns, nothing other than a column of "work points" appears abstractly in the commune's ledgers? I asked the manager of a commune how he interested his charges in increased production. "First of all I make use of intellectual means," he replied. "I use socialist education." Perhaps his response gives us a clue to a disturbing fact, the present contradiction between the tremendous labor of mobilizing the peasants into communes and the slow progress of agriculture itself.

Although there is no reason to push it as far as the excesses of The Great Leap Forward, a speedup seems absolutely necessary. And it is expected. This speedup will doubtless be a part of the new economic plan, the third Five Year Plan. By the time this long-promised plan is announced China will have waited some time. The first two plans covered the years 1953–1957 and 1958–1962. The third should have begun in 1963 and run through 1967. But for two years, 1963 and 1964, nothing was said—people began to wonder if China wasn't going to give up Five Year Plans and announce some other system. At last, in December, 1964, Premier Chou En-lai revealed to the National Assembly that the third plan was under consideration—but he gave no details. The only other piece of information was that it would begin in 1966. Thus the country will have gotten along for three years on annual plans. With a view to preparing the way for this new beginning, Premier Chou asked that 1965 see an energetic effort to create "an upsurge in industrial and agricultural production." And it was to prepare for these preparations that in 1964 the regime set off the great new movement of socialist education, which I will deal with later.

Will the Party succeed by means of the new Plan to revive the people's enthusiasm for breaking economic records? Will it once again present the Chinese with charts and graphs projected into the future, as it did ten years ago when the future was attached to every wall in the form of statistics and rising production curves? Meanwhile, one thing that struck me throughout my travels was the way the regime asks the people to look at their past—as though it were not yet certain about the future. Everywhere, the Chinese are busy looking backward, and dredging up a distasteful past under the direction of their leaders. "Compare today with the past" was the number-one theme for 1964, announced on the first of January in *Red Flag*. In factories, communes and offices, not a week passes that hasn't seen workers called together to discuss in detail the horrors of the former society and the happiness of the new.

But the future? In place of an actual schedule they are given a slogan that does not offer a particularly smiling prospect: "Simple life and strenuous work." *Red Flag* gives this as the indispensable second theme. Since its announcement, every Party operative has drummed it into the ears of the Chinese. They are warned that the Spartan austerity of today will continue tomorrow. It will be a long time before the standard of living can be raised appreciably and a new program call for well-being and abundance. If a small percentage of the people claim a few comforts and a better life, the rest won't have enough. If a little overconsumption were permitted, there would not be enough to go around. And if the spirit of sacrifice falls off by the least little bit, Socialist Construction will be in danger.

"China is poor and empty," Mao Tse-tung said several years ago. He went on to specify: "China is poor and blank, blank as a sheet of paper that hasn't yet been written on." This remark—which Liu Shao-chi used in concluding the great report in which he announced the Great Leap in 1958—is still famous. It comes up all the time now in Peking—perhaps because of its healthy realism. Indeed, China still is poor, even now that she has exploded her first atomic bomb. But this remark contains more. Mao finished it thus: "This may appear to be an evil when in reality it is a good. Poor people wish to change everything, wish to work hard, wish to make a revolution." These few words contain much of the regime's philosophy. Elsewhere poverty is something no one admits; it's a weakness. Here it is displayed and expected to become a positive force. Elsewhere a low standard of living is a state of affairs that a Communist government wishes to remedy immediately. In China, it is considered a normal state of affairs and an advantage to the country.

Perhaps one can go so far as to suggest that the atomic bomb is made possible by all those carts and bicycle-carts. Poverty allows a regime to assign a maximum to capital construction and a minimum to consumption, to remain stable at the absolutely lowest level the populace will stand for; and, besides that, to keep the people contented at a minimum expense, because the slightest rise in the standard of living will satisfy them when they recollect the wretchedness and suffering of the past. In each of these stands there is something else perceptible: an anti-Russian theme. Let Khrushchev's Russia go to hell in its own sweet way thanks to comforts and profits; in China poverty remains the guardian of the great socialist virtues: energy for work, revolutionary ardor and ideological intransigence.

CHAPTER NINE

SOMETHING NEW: BIRTH CONTROL

NEVER BEFORE DURING THE COURSE OF MY TRAVELS THROUGH China have I been struck so continuously by the flood of children; China's overpopulation never seemed as obvious to me as it did on this trip. The impression that remains is of rivers of children, tides of children, waves and whirlpools of children lost in an ocean of children! And that is one of the most important impressions the new China has left me with. Naturally, the "old" China was also full of children, but today they are even more numerous and they make their presence felt as never before. They take up more room, it seems to me, because of the importance now given to schools, because of the obvious concern of the regime in the formation of this new crop of citizens, and because of the almost continuous and always well-organized parades to and from school as well as to games and sports during hours of recreation. And never before have they behaved so joyously nor appeared to be so absolutely bursting with health, both girls and boys.

When I am asked if the Chinese of today are happier than those of the past there is at least one answer I can give with certainty: that never before have Chinese children been as happy as they are now, nor so clean either for that matter, nor so well groomed and well behaved, nor such a pleasure to see. But their numbers are even more impressive than any of that. At certain hours, especially four in the afternoon, big cities, Hankow or Shenyang, seem to belong to the children. Adults are at work and older children are in school, so all that is to be seen in the streets is a tide of children, a flood of humanity, between two and three feet high, bearing along thousands of little round heads. They appear to form a great commonwealth whose citizens are all between four and six years old. They all seem to date from The Great Leap Forward, to have been born between 1958 and 1960. There must have been a more successful "leap" in the production of Chinese babies.

But if you ask the Chinese, private citizen or official, just what the annual increase in population is, or simply for the number of inhabitants, you will hardly ever receive an answer. Beside the fact that statistics are a state secret, there is also the fact that the most recent census was taken in 1953 and that there have been no scientific studies of the whole of this problem. I suspect that the government in Peking is also uncertain of exactly how many citizens it rules today, much less what their number will be in five, ten or fifteen years. The census of 1953, whose figures, on the whole, have won the acceptance of Western experts, yielded a much higher total than was expected: more than 600 million Chinese, 574 million of them in China itself. The rate of increase was taken to be approximately 2 percent per annum. If that rate has remained steady, then today's population is in the neighborhood, or even above, of 700 million. But it would appear that in reality there were certain ups and downs in the course of the last decade. The rate probably went up in 1958 and 1959, to fall below average during the three black years, after which it climbed back to 2 percent or better. "An average of 2 percent since the liberation," I was told by an official spokesman in Shanghai. He was the only person who gave me any figures.

Western experts in Hong Kong calculated (*China News Analysis,* Hong Kong, July 31, 1964) that at the present rate China's population could reach 960 million in 1980, then one billion two or three years later; by the year 2000 China might have as many as 1,400,000,000 inhabitants! And no one has suggested that the curve would drop after that date. It will continue to climb. These figures are frightening, though hard to believe. However, there are indications that the Chinese government plans a China whose population will surpass the billion mark. And one of them, Tan Chen-lin, vice-premier in the present government, spoke recently of *two* billion inhabitants! As far as I know this is the first time such a figure had been made public, and it is important that the responsible position of the man making this pronouncement be remembered. I believe his words are important enough to warrant being quoted here as they were taken down in an interview (*Politique Étrangère,* April, 1964) with a great expert on the world's agricultural problems, René Dumont, during his visit to China in April, 1964.

"Today China has 264 million acres under cultivation," the vice-premier said. "Soon there will be 272 million acres under cultivation. But we will also have two billion inhabitants. . . . The most important thing is that they arrive as late as possible." But this official was not really disturbed. He added that actually since an increased yield could be counted on in agriculture, one *mu* (⅙ of an acre) would feed one Chinese, with the implication that China would thus be out of hot water because 272 million acres will make the two billion *mu* necessary to feed two billion Chinese. He also counted on an elevated cultural standard putting a brake on the population, and thus it would be a long time before that two billion arrived. . . .

Such optimism seems for the most part a mere display for the foreign visitor. It certainly is not shared without reservation by all members of the government. There is every indication to the contrary. The shortages of the black years seem to have been decisive in forcing some people to take stock of the dangers of demographic inflation and of the immediate necessity for putting on the brakes.

Something new, of great importance for China and for the world at large, has recently begun to appear: China's energetic policy of birth control. During my previous trip in 1955, when I broached the subject I met with stony silence. It was spoken of as little as possible. That state of mind has disappeared and today wherever I sought information on the subject, especially in Peking and Shanghai, I found officials willing or even impatient to talk about it and to arrange interviews with experts who could go into the matter more deeply. "This is a problem that has the particular attention of the Party and of the government," I was told right off by the head of one of the largest hospitals in Peking.

Actually, the official line, as I heard it expressed by functionaries of the Board of Public Health in Shanghai, for example, denies that there is any *economic* disadvantage in the size or growth rate of the population. For them the problem remains social and medical. The Chinese people are told the same thing. Not a word is said about the risk of hunger which China runs because of her increasing population, nor that her government risks being literally overwhelmed by the problems of finding work for the increasing multitude, room for it to simply exist in, and something for it to wear! All they are told is that the regime watches out for their health and their standard of living. If a family is too large, the budget will be strained, the mother's health undermined, the education of the children made more difficult, etc. In the same spirit, the phrase "birth control" is being systematically outlawed, while "planned parenthood" replaces it. But newspapers do not always take all the precautions they are supposed to, and many articles that have appeared since the days of the shortages have allowed us to surmise that the real preoccupations of the regime are economic, and on an even simpler level have to do with *food*. "Agriculture is the foundation of the national economy," editorialized a paper in commenting on the change of priority which placed agriculture ahead of industry, "but the foundation's foundation is food."

It is a good idea to recall an earlier and unsuccessful campaign for birth control. In 1956 Premier Chou En-lai spoke of it to the Seventh Party Congress. The following year abortions were legalized. Mrs. Li Teh-chuan, minister of public health, said in the spring of 1957 that China's population was growing by 15 million a year.* But these first experiments, conducted without much energy, were completely upset by the Leap and its philoso-

* *Le Monde,* March 9, 1957, and April 25, 1957.

phy of runaway production. The order of the day was "The more Chinese the better!" and there was Mao Tse-tung to back it up. "It is a good thing that China has such a large population. Even if this figure were doubled or tripled, China would be perfectly capable of finding a solution, and the solution is production." These words which date from the take-over in 1949 (Mao Tse-tung: *On the U. S. White Paper,* September 16, 1949) are no longer quoted. The crisis of several years ago made it glaringly obvious that "the solution, production" might be beaten in its race with a galloping population.

The new campaign on the other hand is being managed vigorously. Every organization in contact with the masses is actively involved—street committees, for example, and women's associations, unions, and the Young Communist League. Committees or information groups "have been formed by the masses themselves," I was told in Shanghai—which means that they were formed under the agitation of trained propagandists detailed to accomplish a task for which they were specially selected and carefully trained. Information circles have been organized where one can hear men and women who have been invited to explain to others the results they have obtained with various contraceptive methods. Pamphlets have been printed and circulated, contraceptive devices have been distributed or put on sale. The whole medical profession has been mobilized for this campaign. Each region has for its Planned Parenthood Center a hospital; there consultations—and operations—take place. Pharmacies have various means of contraception on sale—they're in the windows. Public Health watches over the production and distribution of all of them. The press contributes to the campaign with a flow of new articles in favor of birth control. Book stores sell manuals and pamphlets and even posters. A typical poster which I saw in a hospital depicts "the happy family"—and it's a family with only two children. Another which I saw in the hospital demonstrated in pictures the relevant parts of the anatomy and the relevant devices. Another showed how a man can be sterilized safely. . . .

Although both sterilization and abortion are now legalized,

there is no way of knowing to what extent they are practiced. The officials assured me that these methods were very little used and professed much prudence. I believe that this is indeed the case, for the time being. However, abortions are performed in the initial stages of pregnancy if both wife and husband desire it. In practice it seems to be resorted to after the third child and only in the larger towns: there women can find experienced doctors in the hospitals and clinics they are referred to. In Peking I was assured that this was "not often the case." In Shanghai it was "the exception." But in Manchuria, according to a Japanese nurse who was repatriated and whose story appeared in the papers in 1963, three days out of every week were set aside for abortions in Shenyang's big maternity hospital for the Northeast.

Sterilization is also legal, for men as well as women, if the couple agree to it and there are already too many children. Here again, it seems to be advised only after the third child. Refugees arriving in Hong Kong have testified to the truth of this. The authorities appear to view sterilization rather favorably, particularly for men, and articles in the press, in the April, 1963, issue of *Women of China,* for instance, have tried to justify this point of view and remove the various prejudices of those concerned.

But current propaganda certainly prefers the distribution of simple contraceptive devices to the above-mentioned surgery. Have the Chinese made any discoveries in this realm? Are they engaged in original research? If we can believe a doctor in Peking whom I asked about these matters, the answer is no. "We do not wish to make use of any methods that are not of proven value," he told me. "We want nothing that has not been tested and that is not easy for the people to learn to use." From non-Chinese sources I have heard that foreign pharmaceutical houses have approached the medical authorities in Peking with various contraceptive pills. The Chinese purchased enough for experiments that are now under way. But for the time being the pills are of only academic interest. They are far too expensive to be within the reach of the masses.

Although at the moment China's birth-control program lacks

the most modern methods, it still has a powerful weapon in the unique hold that official propaganda has over the masses. They seem disposed to follow whatever "advice" they are given. Thus Planned Parenthood can take advantage of the repeated opportunities offered by those meetings for political education to which the entire population is subjected. I believe that we are now touching on the major difference between this campaign and the previous one. Those in official capacities have always been at pains to point out to me that in order for their system of limiting births to function, the parties involved must be *willing*. And if there was ever a country in which this particular brand of "willingness" was widespread, it is this new China where a good citizen is one whose will is the will of the group, who has "given his heart to the Party"—which means simply that in large measure he has abdicated his right to manage his own life in favor of collective management from above. And it is the country in which the authorities have the world's most irresistible arsenal of "persuasives." It seems apparent that if there is any reason for the limited nature of the birth-control campaign, besides a laudable caution at the outset, it is the delay in manufacturing contraceptive devices and in training the necessary personnel. As soon as these problems have been solved China will be able to begin a psychological campaign such as the world has never seen.

At the present time the authorities have such a grip on the life of each individual, and especially on the youth of China, that they can produce a slowdown in the birthrate by means that have no equivalent anywhere in the world, which make use of no material devices, and which might even be termed "intellectual," *i.e.,* social and political persuasion. In this category the most important is the nationwide movement begun in 1957 against early marriages. It was stepped up in 1962 and 1963. The noisiest sort of propaganda filled town and countryside with the "advice" that a man should not marry before thirty, a woman before twenty-five. This is certainly part of the birth-control program, but no one ever says so. The reasons given invoke the comfort and convenience of the future couple who will have reached a more mature point of view, will have finished their schooling, found jobs, and have healthier children—if they can just wait a bit. There can be exceptions to such a rule of course because it is only "advice." But the whole of society exerts force on the young to follow this advice. The Party or its agents have become even more powerful than parents ever were in "old" China, and for young people who are in too much of a hurry they can create a long wait, like the old-fashioned engagement, or if the young continue to resist, they can create difficulties and penalties at school, in the factories or in the commune—and even go so far as separating them by imposing assignments to places at opposite ends of the country.

That couples are separated is something so typical of the People's China that it must be part of some governmental program, although no one ever suggests this. Households broken up by the assignment of the husband to one post and the wife to another are too numerous to be accidental. In a certain number of cases the reason is simply that the husband is unable to find in the new city quarters that could accommodate his wife. But it is clear even in these cases that the authorities make no effort to find suitable accommodations and do not feel hesitant about creating these separations. What usually happens could lead one to suppose that an effort is actually being made to put the whole breadth and length of China between married couples.

There are a great many reasons for the new regime to move people around and then leave them far apart. For one thing every post and position in China is handed out by the state or by public authorities. And again the regime wants to homogenize China as it were, and a good way is to send a Northerner south and vice versa. There are wide stretches of western China which are underpopulated. Almost everyone is subjected to work-periods in a factory or commune. And last of all being shipped off can be the punishment imposed for faulty political thinking. In all these cases the person affected must go even if it means leaving a family behind him. If he pleads the cruelty of a long separation, this age of socialist construction would accuse him of showing "a bourgeois attitude." Any good citizen will place collective well-being above personal happiness. And there's another separated couple—and for three or four years or even more. They write. They wait. And the husband can be just as certain of his wife's fidelity as a Japanese soldier in the old days could be of his: society and the family watch over her. But in this country the faithfulness of the husband is as much assured by these same social forces.

In reality the separation of husband and wife remains nothing more than a special case in a general situation. I mean that young people in China are expected by the regime (and that expectation implemented by society) to maintain a chastity as complete and as prolonged as possible. Abroad one hears of birth control and planned parenthood but I do not believe that this particularly startling aspect of the program is sufficiently known: the silent but powerful effort on the part of Chinese Communism to impose a maximum separation of the sexes.

More than one hundred million young Chinese men and women in their prime live in a rigorous chastity demanded by the rules of a morality more severe than that in a Catholic seminary, policed by the far-flung agents of the collective life, by mutual surveillance, by required tale-bearing to the authorities, and by life itself in a community that allows no privacy. To be a good Chinese citizen today one must forget that love exists—at least until thirty, for a man, or until twenty-five, for a woman. Love is neither a subject of conversation nor of thought. Obviously enforced abstinence on such a scale must have as its object the lowering of the birthrate. But no one ever mentions this. Indeed the reason cited is moral and, more strange, political. Political censure strikes any young couple foolish enough to abandon themselves to their feelings before the authorized age—or even married people who parade their affections in public. Such behavior rouses the ire of the authorities, who feel that it shows blameworthy tendencies toward bourgeois attitudes and Revisionism. A good Communist places love after the necessities of economic production and knows that in reality the two are not reconcilable. Love is a nuisance because it disturbs production, makes a worker irregular, takes away available energy and robs him of political zeal.

It is a paradox that the regime which demands such unfaltering chastity makes it particularly heroic by the practice of coeducation. Every high school and every university has its dormitories. In labor there is an almost absolute equality of the sexes which mixes men and women in workshops, offices, and in the fields. The regime favors all kinds of sports. Boys and girls live under the same roof while they are studying, but they must behave as though they had no instincts and as though any show of affection were unthinkable—until they reach the authorized age. At the university everyone keeps watch on everyone else, and besides there are always the watchful eyes of members of the Party, of the Youth League and of innumerable activists. The slightest objection is noted down and reported. It can lead to the disciplinary committee, to sentencing, to public confession, to being expelled. But breaking any rules is made difficult by the overall discipline of life in dormitories. Tracking down minor infractions has sometimes gone so far, a well-placed informant told me, that "a climate of sexual repression" has been produced which has led to terrible scenes and even suicide.

But that is exceptional. Millions of young Chinese have courageously accepted and approved a morality that recalls in its austerity the faith of the early centuries of Christianity. And the dormitory system actually allows the regime to preach and to maintain this morality. If millions of unmarried workers are housed in dormitories it is because they are at an age when the regime must keep an eye on them and keep them constantly occupied. To keep them out of temptation they have been turned into boarding-school boys, as it were, and they spend their evenings in the healthy perusal, in pious groups, of the works of Mao Tse-tung. Puritanism weighs heavily on China. As any occidental visitor or resident can tell you, the often suffocating psychological climate in this country owes a certain part of its weight to widespread repression.

What are the results so far obtained by the extraordinary attempt to apply the demographic brakes? One important object has certainly already been achieved, the sudden awareness on the part of the nation's avant-garde of this problem's existence. By that I mean the urban population in general; workers in the great modern plants, in the socialized businesses and government offices;

Communist cadres everywhere; and the "ruling class" taken in the broadest sense—intellectuals and all that remains of the former middle class. Planned Parenthood is more or less current in that whole group. An ideal family today includes two children, or three at the outside. In Peking or Shanghai the large family is the exception. An awareness of the problem and the resultant action in this relatively evolved segment of the population resembles rather closely what was to be observed in Japan right after the war, when the Japanese people realized that the demographic inflation from which they had suffered before the war had begun all over again; they began the practice of birth control with a determination and unanimity never before seen anywhere. The urban Chinese too, during the three black years especially, discovered that their numbers were swelling at a rate that production and employment could never keep ahead of. Overcrowded housing, half-empty plates, arms without work—these evils would be more easily combated if each family limited its size.

But in Japan what was most surprising and without a precedent anywhere in the world was the way the rural population too accepted and practiced birth control. In China this stage has not yet been reached. In the country, propaganda advising fewer children is ignored. The causes for this are obvious: the rural population in question is not only far larger than the urban population, but poorer and less cultivated. Thus the tradition of the large family as something admirable has been harder to eradicate. Also, the larger the family the more "work points" the household can accumulate. Partly illiterate, the peasants are uninformed and difficult to persuade; to reach this vast audience therefore requires millions of propagandists. I was told that since July, 1962 the 3000 villages in the neighborhood of Shanghai each have their special agent for birth control propaganda. In Kwangtung Province, 1400 midwives and 20,000 assistants were trained in birth control techniques. A similar network of agents will eventually spread over the entire country, but this hasn't been done yet; even when the network is complete it will still take time to distribute the necessary articles and make their usage general.

Premier Chou En-lai disclosed to the American writer Edgar Snow, in January, 1964, that the object of the Chinese authorities was to force a decline in the annual increase of population to below 2 percent. Since then he has chosen a more exacting figure for their aspirations: less than 1 percent—the present rate in Japan—by the end of the century. The premier boasted that the rate for Shanghai at the beginning of 1964 had dropped to 1.7 percent, but he admitted that this figure was an exception and that the figures for China as a whole indicated an upward curve. The rural population's negative attitude toward birth control, and the increase in the standard of living of the population as a whole, are to blame, he said in substance, for the growth of the rate of increase to—again he gave statistics—a yearly rate of 2.5 percent. In publishing these facts, the *Far Eastern Economic Review* (Hong Kong, July 9, 1964) added that this represents a yearly increase of much more than 15 million, possibly even as high as 17 million, if, as it is generally supposed, China already had 700 million inhabitants. If this rate continues unchanged, it will only be 1980 before China has a population of one billion.

The new demographic policies of the Peking government suggest that China will do anything within reason to avoid that catastrophic inflation. Will it adopt policies more energetic than those presently in practice? One way is already open to the authorities: they could intensify the means of forcing households to limit their size by societal pressure and a system of punishments and rewards. While in some countries fertility is rewarded, in China the prolific might be penalized. Since the middle of 1963 an experiment of that sort seems to have been in operation. Information has leaked out from Canton, Shanghai and even Peking, according to which ration coupons for food were being withheld from the fourth child—some sources even said from the third. When an attempt was made to verify these rumors it turned out that ration coupons for food were not being withheld, it was a matter of clothing coupons—and the third or fourth child can easily dress in hand-me-downs. It is said that in certain places after the third child a mother is refused certain of the normal benefits awarded mothers, such as bonuses or leave-of-absence. It has been difficult to get more precise information since the Chinese do not allow many questions, but it would appear that such methods of applying the brakes are quite general and indicate a significant trend. Perhaps this will be a concrete and immediate way to make the will of the authorities clear to the peasants.

Another way would be to discover and put into practice scientific methods of birth control newer and more daring than anything now known. According to what I was able to learn in Peking and Tokyo, Japanese specialists on population problems were called in for consultation in the Chinese capital. There they met with the Chinese authorities responsible for the program and with the premier himself. "How did you do it?" they were asked. They answered that the extraordinary slowdown in the birthrate which Japan was able to achieve in a mere fifteen years, thus allowing the country to pass from a population expansion of Asiatic proportions to that of the nations of the West with the lowest rates of growth, had been due more than anything else to the enormous spread of surgical abortion. Abortion was legalized and millions of young Japanese women made use of it. The Chinese wanted to know if this hadn't caused terrible situations, numerous death, and innumerable incurable injuries and sickness. The Japanese answer seems to have been that it did in the beginning, but that after the first few years the accidents have decreased. Little by little Japanese specialists experienced in surgical abortion evolved. Abortion has become "popular," less expensive, less dangerous, and practised even in rural areas.

This line of reasoning does not seem to have been accepted by the Chinese—at least for the moment. The Japanese solution not only fails to square with Peking's puritanism, but is inapplicable in present-day China. Such a program requires the training of an army of doctors and surgeons such as China cannot possibly have for a great many years. But it is also clear that as far as is consistent with China's present resources, surgical abortion is increasingly practiced. One indication of this is the visit to China, only a few months before my own, of the great Japanese specialist in this field, Dr. Kan Majima, who on the invitation of the Minister of Health made a three-month tour through Peking and the provinces to perform demonstration operations and lecture to his Chinese colleagues.

In the meantime, Chinese experts watch closely those experiments taking place in the United States, Great Britain, Germany, Israel and India. If the most recently discovered contraceptive methods, from coils to vaccination, turn out to be acceptable and capable of widespread use, they will start a revolution in the limitation of populations. The Chinese have been carefully following the experiments now under way abroad—such as a study of a sterilizing vaccine used in 1961 on more than 2000 men and women in India, Holland and the United States. They also keep up with the learned journals and congresses, such as the Seventh International Conference for Planned Parenthood, which was held in February, 1963. Although not given much publicity, this conference attracted about 200 delegates from more than thirty countries to a city, and this is significant, that can be considered Chinese—Singapore.

No one can make a prediction as to whether China will one day adopt a vaccine against pregnancy. But we may be allowed to believe that in the near future science will provide humanity with some unheard-of advance in this realm at precisely the time when the entire planet is threatened by a population explosion unequaled in history. And if there is any country in the world where we can expect to see whatever means are discovered adopted frankly and practiced on a large scale, it is China. The reasons for this are overwhelming. The political and psychological weapons in the hands of the regime are equally overwhelming. China is perhaps the only country in which the regime has sufficient hold on the populace to allow it to plan the production of human beings in a true relation to what can be produced in the line of foodstuffs and consumer goods. It is imaginable that in the future each commune will receive a quota for babies with the instructions that it not be surpassed and that it be divided among the villages and families under the commune's administration. And the inevitability of this birth control is perhaps another reason for assuming that the Chinese are in for a very long siege of Spartan discipline.

CHAPTER TEN

"DE-RUSSIFICATION" — AND THE NEW CHAUVINISM

THE MOMENT I ARRIVED IN COMMUNIST CHINA THE AUTHORITIES gave me a most useful gift. I held in my hands a bundle of pamphlets and tracts denouncing Khrushchev's Russia and its Revisionism. An employee of the smoking car brought me this reading matter. Perhaps he wished to see the leisure that long train rides force upon the traveler occupied with such edifying material. Those well-known articles that flow down the pages in rivers of type, continuing on page after page, were collected together here, complete, to offer me the chance of hearing every word of the Central Committee's accusations against Moscow.

Before my arrival I had often wondered to just what extent the regime kept the people informed of its quarrel with Russia. My question was immediately answered. China today persists in a totally anti-Russian stance. The break with Moscow is everywhere obvious and everywhere loudly announced. It has changed everything. It is reorienting the entire country. I was to find the entire dossier available everywhere as a series of pocketbooks.

It waited for me in the rooms and corridors of hotels, in public places, waiting rooms, trains and planes. . . . The whole collection is free. It is available in fourteen languages besides Chinese—Javanese, Sanskrit and Swahili, for instance. Finding a readable book in China is a difficult business: accompanied by one's interpreter, you have to go to the one book store in every city which caters to foreigners and which naturally has nothing that is not either Communist or tending frankly toward that philosophy. On the other hand, the visitor will be so inundated by the mass of anti-Russian tracts that he ends by believing that there is really nothing else to read—at least, nothing for him—in the whole country.

The Chinese are also fed on this diet. And they are given an opportunity by their press to enjoy a privilege that the opposing camp does not allow its followers: reading the fulminations of the enemy. Those of the Moscow Central Committee against Peking appear in the *People's Daily,* which selects passages most likely to inflame the chauvinism of the Chinese.

Thus, on the 13th of July, the paper devoted four whole pages to "the most representative anti-Chinese calumnies," as the headlines described it, gleaned from the speeches of Khrushchev and the Soviet press. This selection begins with the Soviet premier advising Mao Tse-tung "to see a psychiatrist," and runs to the accusation that China is attempting to foment a revolutionary internationale of underdeveloped nations. Every Russian complaint is made known to the Chinese people. They read of their "adventurism," that they are "neo-Trotskyite," that they "deify the individual"—meaning Mao—and "make a fetish of violence," that they have "usurped the leadership or international Communism" and that they are engaged in "repression of the arts and letters," etc.

It is certain that China's animosity against the Moscow "revisionists" is equalled only by Russia's loathing of the Peking "dogmatists." This is something that can be checked on right in Peking. The Soviet Embassy is still there and wide open. There are a great many Russian correspondents (from *Tass, Pravda* and *Isvestia,* Soviet Radio, etc.) as well as correspondents from the other Iron Curtain countries, and Yugoslavia. Both diplomats and reporters are anxious to meet the "Westerners" and they do have interesting things to say. They are all very much on edge when the conversation turns to China. To hear them proposing a thaw in East-West relations while they level the harshest criticism at their Chinese allies can make one think that there is no longer any "iron curtain" or that it has moved eastward and now hangs along the Sino-Russian borders.

These men told me the Russian version of the withdrawal of Russian technicians and aid in July, 1960. Far from being a surprise and a stab in the back from Khrushchev personally, as the Chinese claim, the break had been expected for a long time and had become inevitable—given the actions of the Chinese. What happened was this: over the years the Chinese became less and less docile disciples of their Russian teachers and finally became absolutely unmanageable.

"The Great Leap Forward went to their heads," a Russian told me. "Having decided on a breakneck speedup of production, they thought that they knew better than we did what the necessary precautions and technical norms were. They drove the machinery too hard, built plants in a slipshod fashion, even sacrificed human lives stupidly.

"For instance. We asked forty hours per pilot to train them for a certain model we were delivering. The Chinese said that was too much time. Chinese pilots could learn as much in twenty hours. It was no use protesting. We explained that the results would be catastrophic. Nothing helped. They wasted an incredible number of lives and amount of material. All right, they said, we'll try twenty-five hours. Further protests, further obstinancy— and the same disastrous results. And do you know what they came and said? 'We will *compromise* on thirty hours.' There was no way of convincing them that forty hours had been arrived at scientifically and that a Chinese is like anybody else!"

Analogous forcing had occurred in every domain, the Russians said, and in every sort of factory and shop. They cited a hydroelectric installation where thousands of tons of rock caved in, another where the cofferdams broke simply because Russian experts were not listened to—there were many casualties in both cases. As soon as the Great Leap was under way many Russian technicians found that they were no longer being listened to, many that they were being avoided. When they got to work they found posters on their doors or walls inscribed "Conservatives! Rightists! Revisionists!" They were handed pamphlets directed against their own regime. They were even expected to join with the Chinese against their own government's position on Marxism and the international situation! And the exhaustion of machinery and personnel continued, the Russians say, due to the Chinese philosophy that given revolutionary ardor such as theirs and leadership such as that of the Chinese Communist Party no miracle would remain impossible. . . .

However history will finally apportion responsibilities in this business, it is true that at the moment China feels a deep and lasting resentment. From 1960 on, a passionate loathing has been unleashed against Khrushchev. What they refer to as his "perfidy" will never be forgiven. He did more than simply leave them in the lurch, he picked the worst possible moment to do so, the moment when their sufferings were at their greatest, the industrial crisis obvious, the food shortages increasing, and China hungry. But it is interesting to recall that the ideological quarrel broke out before aid was discontinued. For Lenin's 90th birthday *Red Flag*, on April 21, published long columns of doctrine. For the first time the public had spread before it the profound disagreement between the Chinese and Russian parties—at the very moment when Khrushchev and Eisenhower were doing their best to understand each other.

Once the ideological war began it was carried on without mercy. The Chinese seized every opportunity to publish their indictment against the "revisionists" whether in public through the press or behind closed doors at international congresses. They contradicted the Soviet theses on war, peace, the atom, and disarmament; instead they proposed their own hard line, preaching "just wars" of liberation among oppressed peoples, take-overs in the advanced nations through revolutionary activity rather than by parliamentary means. They attacked the idea of Peaceful Coexistence as it is interpreted in Moscow and satellite capitals. They accused the Soviet camp of surrendering to the "paper tiger" of American imperialism. They maintained that the Russian leaders had disqualified themselves for the leadership of the international movement, and that the true Marxist-Leninists—meaning the Chinese and their friends—must grab and relight the torch to arouse the flames of revolution among the oppressed peoples, especially those of Asia, Africa and South America, the chosen lands of the anti-imperialist battle.

The true dimensions of this quarrel vastly exceed the narrow framework of Sino-Soviet rivalry, or the personal animosity Khrushchev feels for Mao and vice versa; in fact they exceed the definition of a mere quarrel. This conflict covers more territory than most observers realize—it is an accusation of the entire occidental leadership of Communism. It is not of the recent date that is most often given as the beginning of the rupture; instead it goes back at least as far as early 1956, when the 20th Congress of the Communist Party of the USSR was held. As far as Mao is concerned, things began going from bad to worse from the moment the Internationale lacked the iron fist of Stalin. Khrushchev alone is not to blame; there are Thorez, Togliatti and Tito, to name a few of the bad shepherds, and tiny Albania remains the only country in the West that has not slid downhill into Revisionism—and from there Communism can degenerate into a mere reformist socialism.

At the same time this ideological dispute hardly covers up the close political rivalry that it duplicates. Little by little the texts published by Peking have given us an insight into this too. The many acts of this drama that so rapidly destroyed the cohesion of the Communist camp are worth running through briefly. First act, 1956–1959: the conflicts (which were all secret at this time) included a profound disagreement on de-Stalinization (1956), the demotion of Molotov and Malenkov (1957), and China's opposition to any detente or Summit Conference (1958). Next, China found reasons for anger in Russian criticism of the communes and the Leap, Moscow's failure to back her up during the attack on the islands in the Formosa Strait or during her trespassing on Indian territory, and Khrushchev's meeting with Eisenhower at Camp David (1959). The second act begins in 1960 with the recall of the Russian experts in July and the violent disputes at the conference of eighty-one Communist parties in Moscow. At the 22nd Congress of the Soviet party, Chou En-lai left before the end, but not before visiting the body of Stalin (October, 1961). The third act begins with each party blaming the imminent schism on the other. China's military operations against India, and, even more than that, the Cuban crisis, brought the affair to a climax (autumn of 1962). Little by little the Chinese win over the other Far Eastern Communist parties—North Korea, North Vietnam, Indonesia (the three largest CP's in Asia, after China), Laos, Burma, Thailand, Malaysia, Singapore and Japan. Soviet influence in Vietnam is almost completely replaced by Chinese In the early part of 1963 the anti-Soviet dossier begins to appear in the pages of *People's Daily* and *Red Flag*, and answering shots commence from the Russian big guns in *Pravda* and *Kommunist*. Fourth act: in July, 1963, the Sino-Soviet conference meets in Moscow to attempt some sort of reconciliation—it fails, just as it was expected to. At once China makes new revelations by adding to the dossier of the political dispute two more items that had added to the bitterness.

The first concerns the five-year-old dispute over China's atomic weaponry. It had angered both parties. A sensational admission was that in autumn of 1957, when relations were temporarily happy, Khrushchev, in a secret military pact signed October 15th of that year, had promised to deliver to China atomic bombs and the technical know-how that would allow the production of such bombs in China. But in 1958 Khrushchev went back on his word and made suggestions that the Chinese angrily rejected, since, they explain, they tended to place China under the military domination of the USSR. No more details have been released, but it is easy to guess that Khrushchev proposed to put China under Russia's "atomic umbrella" and therefore asked China to give up her ambitions of being an atomic power. Finally, on June 20, 1959, the Russians informed the Chinese that they had abrogated the pact. But it was only at the end of 1963 that China's fury reached its height. Russia signed a treaty with the United States which put a partial stop to nuclear testing. Chinese propaganda saw in this an attempt on the part of these two powers to ally themselves in preventing a Chinese bomb or at least slowing down its production.

The second affair which came to light in 1963 concerns the border disputes with the USSR in Sinkiang, the largest and most distant of China's provinces. Serious border incidents had occurred there in the spring of 1962, and tens of thousands of inhabitants had fled to the Russian side of the border—at Russian instigation, the Chinese claimed. This conflict, which has its own history, points up the additional quarrel that China has with Russia, a territorial one, and one that covers much territory. . . . In fact the *People's Daily* in March, 1963, announced that People's China could not possibly recognize those unequal treaties forced upon her by the Tsars and that at some time that suited her convenience she would assert her claims to part of Siberia and the Soviet Far East beyond the Amur and Ussuri—which includes Russia's door to the Pacific and the industrial regions of Kabharovsk and Komsomolsk.

One man went even further and accused the Russians of occupying territory that does not belong to them, and that man is Mao Tse-tung himself. I was in Peking when he received a delegation of Japanese socialists, and the extraordinary interview that they published shortly after their return has not been denied by the Chinese authorities. In substance Mao says that there are quite a few other countries with just causes of complaint against the USSR besides China. Illegally occupied or annexed territories and regions include Mongolia and parts of Rumania, East Germany, Poland and Finland, and he ends with the Kurile Islands, north of Japan, which Japan lays claim to. and which indeed, Chairman Mao goes on, ought to be returned to her. "There are too many areas occupied by Russia," he continues, according to the text published in *Sekai Shuho* (Tokyo, August 11, 1964). He goes on, "The Soviet Union has an area of 13,750,000 square miles, while her population is only 200 million. It is time for some sort of redistribution. . . . Japan has an area of only 231,250 square miles and a population of 100 million!"

These statements coincided with China's decision to boldly attack the Soviet Union, at least verbally, on some points that had thus far been prudently avoided: Russia's internal conditions and policies. This final assault took aim against the central positions of Revisionism, and following the very best Maoist strategy was the culmination of a guerilla politic that had concentrated first on peripheral positions and allies of Khrushchevism. Did Peking have an inkling of how close the fall of its enemy was? Three months later it came as a great victory, for the Chinese. The whole world was told how Russia's internal policies had caused a scandalous "bourgeoisification" of the Russian Revolution. Even before the necessary texts appeared in print my Chinese hosts gave me horrified descriptions. In their travels through the Soviet Union, they told me, they had run across veritable capitalists, speculators, proprietors, bourgeois! They had watched Soviet beatniks dance the twist! They had heard intellectuals boast of the advances being made in Russia by degenerate art of the Western sort. Thus it was no surprise when, in the course of my travels, I saw the publication of a major document in which this offensive against the internal policies of the USSR became official: "On Khrushchev's Phoney Communism and its Historical Lessons for the World" which *People's Daily* and *Red Flag* published simultaneously on July 14th.

Armed as always with quotations from Marx and Lenin, the Chinese theorists thrashed the "Khrushchev clique" and the entire ruling echelons of the Communist Party of the USSR. These men, according to Peking, "have abolished the dictatorship of the proletariat in Russia while camouflaging this very destruction as a pretended 'Government of all the People.' They have opened the door to a restoration of capitalism while preaching 'Communist Construction.'" Thanks to this betrayal of real Marxism, continues the Chinese accusation, the former exploiters can again lift their heads as a class in the USSR, and new bourgeois elements flourish. Free enterprise and capitalist speculation have an open field. Socialism is in retreat before the attacks of a new privileged class composed of degenerate elements of the Party and its cadres who have been taking over since the time when Khrushchev first "usurped" the leadership of the Party and the nation. The indictment cites a whole series of concrete examples, sometimes even lifted from Soviet publications, to demonstrate the "bourgeoisification" of Soviet Communism and the betrayal of revolutionary doctrines and ideals. Khrushchev "has opened the gates to a revisionist deluge. . . . He is a peddler of bourgeois ideology, of 'liberty, equality, fraternity,' in short, of bourgeois humanism, among the Soviet people. He is inoculating that people with bourgeois idealism and metaphysics, with the reactionary ideas of individualism, humanism and bourgeois pacifism. He degrades socialist morality. The degenerate bourgeois culture of the West is now fashionable in the Soviet Union while socialist culture is under attack or banished."

For the more than four years this conflict has been out in the open, Peking has always insisted as one of its official doctrines that the Chinese people are tied to the Russian people by bonds of friendship that remain unbreakable, and that China's anger has only the Khrushchev clique and revisionist elements for its objects. But ever since those invisible centers that indicate to the Chinese people what they are supposed to think have ceased asking for praise of the Soviet Union, one wonders if there hasn't been a resurrection of the people's former anti-Russian feelings. Isn't it visible in the disturbing reawakening of the question of Sino-Soviet boundaries? That problem antedates Khrushchev and has very little to do with Revisionism. Whatever happens, the seriousness and openness of the quarrel has initiated a process of "de-Russification" that has intensified itself to the point of modifying the totality of Chinese life by reappraising everything that was accomplished in the fifties. This political readjustment duplicates the economic one and, like it, tends to liberate China from dependence on Russia.

Ten years ago the "Russification" of China was a phenomenon that repeatedly struck me on my travels through the country. It was all the more startling for being the result not of any invasion planned by the Russians but of the fact that a whole sea of ideas, methods, and practices had swept across China—in answer to a request on the part of that country's regime. And there really had been much more of an invitation than an invasion. It was Chinese and not Russian propaganda that repeated to six hundred million Chinese, "Study and put into practice the experiences of the Soviet Union." The Chinese Revolution had rolled in from the countryside in 1949 with its own original characteristics, nothing like those of the Russian Revolution. But it immediately entered on a long phase in which it became the rule to imitate Russia in everything. It was understood that all the stages that Russia had passed through would also have to be passed through by her faithful ally, China—at a distance of thirty years. Peking went to Moscow in search of ready-made ideas that presumably resulted from the experience dearly bought by Russian revolutionaries. By adopting them right off, the Chinese leaders and the Chinese people would spare themselves wasted energy and vain sacrifices. They would be applying formulas whose success seemed guaranteed. They would save time.

But in 1958 China began to look for her own road to Communism, in practice if not yet in theory, with the communes and The Great Leap Forward, and in 1960 she began to propound her doctrinal independence, after the economic break. The all-embracing imitation of the fifties has come to an end, and that old saw about "applying the superior experience of the USSR" has been retired. People used to repeat, "The Russia of today is the China of tomorrow!" That slogan is no longer on anyone's lips. I have even heard one important personality denounce it as odious and inadmissible. And how could anyone in China accept it now that "the Russia of today" is that horror, a Russia both Khrushchevian and revisionist?

Paradoxically, just about the only Russian to be seen in China today, other than the diplomats and journalists I've mentioned— is Stalin! His pictures still hang on many walls. Generally he hangs beside other non-Chinese prophets of Marxism. Marx, Engels, Lenin, Stalin—those are the four great ancestors. A more malicious visitor might incidentally notice an amusing transition from the woolly head and face of Marx to Stalin's simple mustache: their faces undergo a progressive liberation from invading hair which ends in a complete "de-beardification" when we pass from Stalin to Mao Tse-tung, whose round, beardless portrait is usually framed on the opposite wall. . . .

Today a foreign visitor who takes a walk in the city or in the country will no longer hear as he passes little Chinese applaud and say the words they used to be taught as soon as they reached kindergarten: "Soviet older brother!" The former "Palaces of Sino-Soviet Friendship" that were found in every town and always in the purest imaginable heavy Soviet style of architecture have been rebaptized and are generally used as exposition halls dedicated to the glory of Chinese technology and industry instead of to Russian propaganda as in the old days. *Pravda* and other Russian papers have disappeared from public places and are hardly to be seen nowadays anywhere but in specialized libraries. (However the scientific periodicals of the Russians are still authorized—for reasons easily understood.) In railroad stations, hotels or other places which foreigners frequent, no one has bothered to remove the Russian signs that formerly duplicated a great many Chinese signs, but little by little English signs replace them. The teaching of English is regaining importance, and the authorities have shown some interest in developing the teaching of French.

The pro-Russian element that is known to have been very powerful, although it has generally been difficult to name names, is now silent. According to Suslov's report in February, 1964, between 1951 and 1962, Russia trained 10,000 Chinese engineers, technicians and qualified workers; 11,000 Chinese students received Russian diplomas; and 1000 scholars made use of advanced facilities. Higher figures have been published in the West: 14,000 students and 38,000 workers trained in Russia between 1949 and 1958. These figures come from the *China Quarterly*, published in London, an authoritative review. Of course one cannot ascribe pro-Russian sentiments to every Chinese who ever lived for a time in the USSR, but the number of Chinese influenced or even formed by the Russians must be significant; and besides, showing pro-Russian attitudes was formerly the same as being a good Chinese. Since the break however, anyone returning from Russia finds that his opinions are carefully watched.

It has even been possible to catch a few signs of a purge of pro-Russian elements. In 1958, such a purge struck Marshal Peng Teh-huai, commander-in-chief of the army, as well as other less important personalities. The more recent nationwide campaign against Revisionism has had among other objects that of remolding after the fashion of Chinese Communism a large number of cadres who received their early training in Soviet Russia, or who had close contacts with Russia before the rupture. An example of this has been the attacks that the philosopher Yang Hsien-chen has been under since October, 1963. He was trained in the Soviet Union. Newspapers and other publications devoted columns and pages to denounce a thesis called "Two unite to form one" which this philosopher wrongly supported when the proper thesis is really "One divides to form two." Such a quarrel appears Byzantine merely to us. For the rulers of China today these arguments have importance because for them the union of contraries entails the revisionist theses of the reconciliation of class enemies or the compromise of countries whose systems oppose each other, while the revolutionary "truth" is that the conflict of opposites leads through class struggle to a victory of the proletariat over the bourgeoisie, and of socialism over imperialism. Many points of resemblance to ideas of Soviet philosophers occur in the philosophy of Professor Yang, who spent many years in the Soviet Union. The attack launched against him has been broadened to take in other thinkers. Among those recently singled out we find Feng Ting, another philosopher of the Russian school, whose books, formerly widely circulated, are now severely criticized.

During those years of "Russification" it was the rule in China to emphasize Chinese backwardness and inadequacies in relation to their Soviet older brothers. They were asked, "Help us since we don't know how to do anything." Repeatedly they were told, "You are our guides and masters." The Chinese people were informed that anyone who had anything to do with a Russian must behave humbly—this was during the Sino-Soviet honeymoon. Now that their liberated pride is seeking revenge, we are learning just how much such behavior cost the Chinese in self-esteem. At least twice, in May, 1962 and November, 1963, Moscow vainly proposed that Peking once again accept Russian aid, at least for the development of the petroleum and the mining industries. They got short shrift.

In its letter of February 24, 1964, the Central Committee of the Chinese Communist Party added another document to the

Chinese side of the extensive dossier of this quarrel when it replied rudely to the Soviet Central Committee: "Frankly, the Chinese people no longer have faith in you and won't be taken in again!" The letter went on to add with an irony that borders on insult that China was worried about the state of the Soviet economy and would, if requested, send Russia help in the form of Chinese technicians! So the humility vis-à-vis the Russians is a thing of the past. . . . The new refrain that I heard repeatedly all over China and that propaganda relays to the outside is that the Chinese are capable of doing anything, and of doing it themselves.

Thus the necessity for "de-Russification" was the first step in the direction of what might be called "a return to China." Historians may very well look back on the first years of the sixties as marking the end of a long adventure in which China attempted to flee from herself and find her happiness in those lessons taught by the outside world. For thirty years now, ever since Communism came to China, or even for half a century, ever since Sun Yat-sen's revolution, all the best people in China —humbled by Western insults to their country, and both frightened and disgusted by the decadence of their own government, people, and almost Chinese civilization itself—have turned toward the West in hope of borrowing its secret formulas for success in the modern world. Without ever losing sight of their goal—the liberation and moderization of their country—they accepted and even partly organized two successive invasions: first that of the liberal, democratic and capitalist West, and then the Marxist, Russian version of the Occident. This period seems to have reached its conclusion. China once more is China.

This return of China to itself is first of all a resurgence of Chinese nationalism, again vigorous and freed of all its former inferiority complexes and temporary counsels of humility. Copy foreign models? Not only has China no need to any longer, but the time has now come when China can offer itself as a model for the world. In the old days one had to carefully sift documents from Peking for any hint of an important place for China in the leadership of the world revolution. For example there is this

quote from a statement made during the Korean war by one of
the regime's foremost propagandists, Lu Ting-yi: "The prototype
of all revolutions in imperialist countries remains the October
Revolution. The prototype of revolutions in colonial or semi-
colonial lands is the Chinese revolution" (*People's China*, July 1,
1951). But such examples were rare and Peking was careful not
to pretend to any role that might cause offense in Moscow. Today
China's aspirations in regard to leading the world revolution are
spread across the pages of *People's Daily* and *Red Flag* in official
statements asking every Communist, whether in a developed or
underdeveloped country, to look to Peking for inspiration. Walls
all over China sport posters depicting the valiant Chinese proletarian leading his black, yellow and white brothers into battle.
A principle that they never tire of repeating asserts the betrayal
of Marxism-Leninism by Communists in the West, beginning with
the Khrushchev crew. True Marxism-Leninism has found a new
home in China. True revolutionaries, wherever they may happen
to be, will be able to quaff the unsullied spring of revolution in
studying the works of Mao Tse-tung, and China will send scouts
into Europe itself to recruit supporters—in the private preserves
of the Russians.

In diplomacy the "return to China" entails the end of a super-
vision or even a direction of Chinese foreign relations by Moscow.
Until quite recently China was willing to allow a good number
of her relations with the outside world to pass through Moscow.
It was all right with the Chinese if they were absent from the
international scene, or at least their internal problems gave them
good reason to be. Any diplomatic vassalage to the Soviet Union
would be unthinkable today. If the world is to look to China,
then China must be present all over the world. Thus she must
open embassies everywhere. She wants to see her exclusion from
the UN ended. "The economic Great Leap is dead, long live
the diplomatic Great Leap Forward!" said an occidental diplomat
in Peking, and he added, "When China isn't jumping in one
direction, it's jumping in the other!"

This new chauvinism is another affirmation of the principle
of economic independence. "Let's count on no other efforts than
our own," says a slogan I saw all over their factories—it was

painted across walls in mammoth characters, delicately sketched onto fluttering strips of red paper hanging above machinery, or scrawled in chalk upon the blackboards that each shop uses as a newspaper. This is a brave slogan. It asks the Chinese worker to fill that enormous emptiness left by the pull-out of Russian aid and Russian experts. It is also a very useful slogan. China repeats it to all the underdeveloped nations, urging them to "do it all themselves"—not to count on external help. But is it anything more than a mere slogan? Wouldn't it really be dangerous for China to go it so completely alone? Isn't it still a bit premature for China to expect herself to be able to do everything alone, and by so doing wouldn't she be adding an impediment to her economic development—and all because having once had trouble with foreign aid she deprives herself of all outside help and even of copying some of the methods of the more advanced nations? However these questions are to be answered, one thing is certain: at every opportunity China reaffirms her independence of the world. Everywhere I went, from factory workshops to schoolrooms in which I was shown aids for teaching physics to high school students, no guide ever failed to say at the beginning of the unavoidable briefing: "All our equipment is 100 percent Chinese!"

Mr. Yung Lung-kwei, an economist whom I have already quoted, sketched out for me his country's economic progress, and since he had to refrain from all statistics he went at great length into the "level of technical independence." For instance he emphasized that now China is self-sufficient in 90 percent of her steel needs, thus reversing in a matter of years her almost total dependence on the Soviet Union. In addition, China now produces 80 percent of her own machinery, and 60 percent of that equipment is made according to Chinese blueprints. (Which implies, although it was not Mr. Yung's intention to do so, that 40 percent of those machines marked "Made in China" are only copies of foreign models, for the most part Russian—China is is still far from independence in this quarter.) China is capable now, Mr. Yung continued, of producing 1500 m³-blast furnaces, 500-ton iron furnaces, 350-ton cranes, 1150-millimeter rolling mills, and 72,500-kilowatt hydroelectric groups. He might have added, "and of making her own atomic bomb." However, when I put the question he sidestepped with, "I am only an economist. . . ."

Through its multitude of changing forms, the return to China shows as a return to many of the deepest and oldest attitudes of the Chinese people. For example at the present time the Chinese are in the process of taking Marxism to themselves in order to give it their own imprint, or more precisely the red seal of Mao Tse-tung. This is part of that ancient Chinese art, played down recently although many experts were predicting its reappearance, of conquering their conquerors by finally turning them into Chinese. In years past Peking touched very lightly on that aspect of Mao Tse-tung's thought which showed originality. The official formula contented itself with something like: "Chairman Mao has combined the truths of Marxism-Leninism with the concrete situation of China." Today, on the contrary, his originality is recognized and asserted. Old texts are paraded in which the chief himself says that Marxism must be made Chinese. "The sinicizing of Marxism," he wrote in 1938, "which will make it universally carry marks of China's situation, is a problem that the entire Party must accept and solve immediately. The importation of ready-made formulas must stop."

Today an even greater care than usual is taken in the defense of Mao's statements by a battery of citations from the works of Marx, Engels, Lenin, and even Stalin. It is important that he be proven faithful to his great predecessors. But at every opportunity it is emphasized that he continues their work as well. This is as much as to say that thanks to him, and thanks to the China he leads, international Marxism has been enriched. The Marxism that he has received, he has prolonged and developed. He has added to it a new body of doctrine and writings. In Chinese texts on the Sino-Russian quarrel a curious new phrase has surfaced: "Marxism-Leninism and the thought of Mao Tse-tung." This is a pregnant phrase. One thing it means is that from now on Communism has a trinity of prophets, Marx, Lenin and Mao. It might be audaciously taken to imply that Maoism isn't exactly the same thing as Marxism-Leninism; it is to be distinguished even though it is also true that one won't do without the other.

There are many subjects on which Mao Tse-tung has spoken and to which he has brought a Marxist interpretation of his own construction. One oft-cited example is the doctrine of "contradictions" which is central to Mao's thinking. Nowadays a great deal of noise is made about this new idea that no one had ever developed before Mao. According to this doctrine there is always the possibility of a backsliding from socialism to capitalism by the primrose path of Revisionism. In the past, Communist thinkers have always maintained that there was a one-way street which led through socialism from capitalism to Communism. And as for actions and methods based on doctrine, since the beginning of the de-Russification, there too they are less guarded in asserting the originality of "the Chinese path to Communism." In the thirties, while he was forming the Party and assuring himself of power, Mao already saw something quite opposite from what his Russian theoreticians and agents saw, namely that the urban proletariat in a country as largely rural as China could not be— no matter what Communist orthodoxy might say—the class that would create the revolution. In China it would have to be the peasantry.

Much more recently it was the same concrete sense of Chinese reality that underlay his bold decision in 1961 to reverse the order of economic priorities. From the very beginning, the Moscow brand of Marxism-Leninism placed industry first, agriculture second. For a time, China too applied this rule. After the adventure of the Leap and of Russia's perfidy Mao Tse-tung reversed the priorities by proclaiming "Agriculture first!" In so doing China was again faithful to herself and to her own conception of Communism. The country of 500 million peasants rediscovered that its own brand of Communism had to be what it had begun as, an agrarian Communism. Following the Soviet line of all-out rapid industrialization with its goal of absolutely modern technology was not to be China's destiny. In agrarian Communism China found new and original lines of thought—such as the communes—that promise, it is believed, the final realization of Communism.

In refusing the Russian version of Communism, the Chinese seem to me to be following the same instinct that made the old

Empress Tzu-Hsi, three quarters of a century ago, reject the Occident. Chinese civilization seemed to her, and not without reason, to be of a higher order, worthy of imitation rather than transformation, much less humiliation! China after all was the Middle Kingdom, and that means the center of the world. . . . Even after the Westerners had forced her gates no Chinese— unlike the Japanese—wholeheartedly accepted the task of learning Western methods and ideas. For the most part the liberal-capitalist West "went down the wrong way," mostly, we must admit, because of the brutality and clumsiness of the Westerners themselves, but also in part because of the incurable "Sino-centricity" of the nation's outlook. When China again attempted to absorb the West, this time on her own initiative and under a new form, that of a Russian and communized West, she ended once more by spewing it out.

A century and a half ago, in 1816, Emperor Kia K'ing wrote a letter to King George III of England in which he haughtily refused all the presents the English ambassador had offered him: "O King, the imperial court does not place a high value on objects brought from a great distance, nor can all these curious and ingenious things from your realm be accounted of rare value here. . . . In the future there will be no need for you to call upon your servants to undertake so long a journey. . . . Simply learn to know your own heart and apply it to good works . . . and you will be said to make progress in the direction of a civilizing transformation." When Mao Tse-tung sends Khrushchev packing is the tone really much different?

Confronted with this complex amalgam of China and Communism, a visitor who did not know China in the old days may very well wonder which is which. It seems to me that the two phases are now easier to separate. Today there is more China in the mixture and it stands out more clearly.

"Eternal China" (as General de Gaulle has called it) seems to be showing through the constructions of Communism much more obviously now. The mandarins may have perished, but not the sense of a mandarin caste: the Party knows this and continues the battle against "bureaucracy," and the arrogance of some of its agents. Chou En-lai in a recent report to the National Assembly mentions "a tendency on the part of certain cadres to behave themselves like bureaucratic overlords," and he goes on to condemn those who "issue orders from on high" without ever "descending to the masses." Education is now so widespread that the monopoly of culture which the mandarins formerly enjoyed is no more. But has the spirit that made it possible been abolished? There is still a real monopoly there, and it differs little from the old one, although this time the monopoly is the Party's and the object of it, though still thought, is political thought. While the gates of the old Forbidden City are now thrown open to the people, and workers walk up and down in chambers formerly closed, secrets remain everywhere and secret is a watchword of the regime. I know of several "forbidden cities" in the Peking of today. Among other mysteries protected by long walls topped with electrified barbed wire, by sentinels whom no one gets past, is the mystery of the life led by China's present masters—their unpublicized comings and goings, their unknown private lives.

Assuredly no one would go so far as to claim that the life they are keeping secret contains luxury or dissipation. As far as we know they all lead lives of exemplary austerity. Mao Tse-tung, leader of the most enormous population ever gathered into one empire, lives a life of unrelieved hard work. All the same, modern China, like the ancient Empire, has kept its sense of the necessity of rites, and the new regime has found the proper ceremonies— I have given a few images from these festivities. "The most important thing in a state," Mencius wrote, "is the people, but the altars and rites come next." These words, soon to be twenty-four centuries old, still apply in the China of today. Formerly the rites were practiced in the luxury of the closed imperial city, on that north-south axis that led straight to the dragon throne, and their sounds and colors never reached the masses standing beneath the high red walls. Now, since it is the people who perform the rites, they take place outside the walls. And their axis too has changed: now they follow the east-west orientation of the great avenue running through Red Square. Chinese architecture, still enchanted by the rectangular space such ceremonies demand, has reproduced on a magnificent scale the great square, that noble form of the old China, in which flows the pageantry and red flags of the new order.

And today as yesterday it is the sovereign who forms the heart of these rites whose climax is his meeting with his subjects. When on the 1st of October Mao Tse-tung presides high above Red Square in the reviewing stand atop the Gate of Celestial Peace it is against a backdrop of imperial splendor. And just as the former emperors did, he follows the most ancient geomantic traditions by turning his back against the malevolent North to receive from the beneficent South the shouted good wishes that rise from below. . . .

But let's not push these analogies too far. There is no reason to believe that the new China will simply turn into the old. Such chauvinism will always find well-defined limits beyond which Communism will never allow it to run. It is one thing for China to rediscover her "Sinocentricism," a sense of her differences and independence, and an awarenes of her grandeur and influence. But Marxism has indelibly marked this country. There can be no return to all that China formerly meant. Communism will only go along with this "naturalization" of everything foreign as long as it is in the interests of the Party. The Party has never been slow to disclaim and condemn any tendency springing from social orders that it had destroyed or ages that it had disowned: feudal or capitalistic practices, superstitions and religion, epicureanism, love of profit, etc. Even at the risk of oversimplifying by reducing reality to a formula, I am tempted to say: "A return to China will never become a return to the Chinaman." By that I mean that the Chinese as we knew them in the past will never be allowed to exist again, with all their old individualism, mercantilism, liberty. Against all that a very high dam continues to hold.

But it is not always easy, even for absolute rulers with the resolution and experience of the men in Peking, to draw the line decisively nor to fix irrevocably the best means of holding it. I feel indeed that deep in this nation there is some sort of hesitation, perhaps a struggle between tendencies, between two possible paths. A "return to China" ought to contain at least in part a return to the old sense of realism and compromise that was formerly a mark of this country. And such a movement is there to be seen. I can think of more than one example of it. Look at how the commune system was modified, or at the compromise between Party and Capital in Shanghai. But Marxist rigidity is there too. Even if we admit that de-Russification leads back to China, it is certainly a China of Maoism we're led to. . . . And these compromises are probably no more than temporary, a tactic for extricating China from the bad years by means of concessions that prejudice her revolutionary goals and that will be rescinded as soon as the economy is on its feet.

The same thing goes for foreign policy: China's actions are not without their ambiguity. Sometimes supple and realistic, they are at other times based on nothing more than the intransigence of the Marxist faith.

CHAPTER ELEVEN

SEVEN HUNDRED MILLION MAO TSE-TUNGS

IF THERE IS ANY DOMAIN IN WHICH THE NEW REGIME HAS ALREADY scored a tremendous success, if there is one in which the leadership of People's China has given incontestable proof of its desire for a better China, it is the domain of public education. In Manchuria, Peking, and Central China, I visited kindergartens, primary and secondary schools, universities, and night schools, and a tremendous progress impressed me everywhere—I remember the days before the liberation when an average of something like only two out of every ten Chinese was able to read and write. The time is not far distant when there won't be one Chinese child out of ten who won't be able to. If there is to be any true restoration of the Chinese nation, it is in the schools that it will take place. Manufacture of machinery, construction of factories, creation of heavy industry and a reform of agriculture? How else attain these objects than by "producing" equally *new* men and women with a will to construct this new world? Very well, they're on their way. . . . After fifteen years of Communism a powerful reinforcement has begun to appear, made up of those young people whom the regime has formed after its own image in its own schools. A new type has appeared on the Chinese scene, turned out in millions of copies, the schoolchild, boy or girl, in a red neckerchief, as disciplined as a soldier, yet noisily joyous, because he's bursting with health and good will.

Abroad there has been much talk of the efforts made by the new regime from the very beginning to teach the Chinese characters to the innumerable adults it found illiterate when it came to power. That effort was made and it continues. Millions of peasants and workers have learned to read. But this does not touch on the most important point. If China, as every appearance indicates, is in a few years to contain only a very small number of illiterates, it is because of the rise of new generations among which the percentage of those who have attended schools keeps growing. Today the proportion of literacy still varies, depending on the age group under consideration or the urban versus rural character of the population tested. In the cities among people under seventeen the revolution is already victorious—almost every little Chinese is going to school and knows how to read, write and add. In Shanghai, a city of ten million, 2,400,000 young people are in school or at the university—that's almost a quarter of the population. In Peking, taking the population under 40, only two inhabitants out of ten fall into the category of illiterates. I am told that in the entire urban population, without regard to age, the rate of illiteracy has already fallen to less than 25 percent.

It is certain however that the situation in rural areas lags behind that in the cities, and besides this the statistics are weighted in favor of illiteracy by the vast numbers who were formed by the previous regime—that is to say completely deprived of education. The American writer Edgar Snow reports that in 1960 the rural population was still 66 percent illiterate. And in Peking I was told by a spokesman at the Ministry of Education that the state is not yet in a position to decree universal and compulsory education. In underdeveloped regions or far out in the country, and also among certain non-Chinese minorities, parents won't always send their children to school. But for China as a whole, 80 percent of the children are in school. That 20 percent which is missing can also be explained by the inability of teachers and buildings to keep pace with a galloping population. . . . Yet before the end of the century it is quite possible that China will have caught up with Japan, where in spite of the difficulty of their writing system (which is even more complex than China's) the percentage of literacy is the highest in the world. We can easily imagine the implications of such a revolution victoriously brought to completion in half a century by one of the most intelligent—and the largest—of this planet's peoples.

This revolution by education has other remarkable characteristics. Learning is now accessible to the children of peasants and workers—formerly it was accessible, with few exceptions, only to the children of the rich or of professional people. I am told that at the University of Peking, the best in the country, 52 percent of the students are of peasant or working-class origin. The rest are categorized as "other classes" and this does not necessarily mean the former bourgeoisie. Often they come from what we might term the "official class"—children of functionaries and professional cadres of regime and Party. Education is free throughout its course of six years of primary schooling (which begins at age seven), six years of secondary (from 13 on), and four to six years of advanced training. The teaching of adults, in spite of the reservations that I have expressed, has great importance in the eyes of the regime. It is handled by special schools with accelerated programs and even more by courses given workers after hours. For many workers the factory has become a school. At a factory in Peking, for example, I saw a beginners' class where the beginners were all in their 30's and 40's. There they sat around their teacher after the day's work was done, listening to her instruction in correct syntax and enrichment of vocabulary. Her students had each written an essay on the theme: "Old worker Wang loves the common good. How shall he show his love?" This "off-hour" education goes as high as the college level. In 1964 more than 400,000 adults all over China were taking courses at the factory or in the village. I was told that in Shanghai 19,000 men and women working in factories were engaged in courses leading to a diploma in engineering or the like. Between 1958 and 1962 a million workers and peasants obtained diplomas for the completion of their primary education, 600,000 a "secondary technical" diploma, and 15,000 a college degree. More than nine million adults have had some sort of training.

One of the ideas dearest to the regime, and from the pen of Mao Tse-tung himself, one which he has been drumming into his fellow Chinese since the beginning of his career, is that the distinction between manual and intellectual labor must be destroyed. The opposition of one to the other was particularly marked in China in the old days. The literate Chinese of the past knew no manual labor; he felt an extreme distaste for it and anyone engaged in it. Even if he was that exception, a literate member of a working-class family, with his entry into the world of ideograms and culture he let his nails grow and never dirtied his hands again. The regime wishes to remove this prejudice left over from former classes of "exploiters." In their new China the manual laborer is encouraged to become "a working intellectual" and even more strongly the regime recommends that every intellectual become, at least part-time, a worker or peasant. "We expect to increase production of course," a highly placed official in the Ministry of Education told me, "but more than that we hope thereby to give socialist training to intellectuals. Intellectuals must know and share the life of the masses. In this way they will learn to love the masses." Children in the primary schools I visited in Peking were learning at the age of ten to work with their hands —carpentry, gardening, maintenance, etc. In a secondary school they were already engaged in more difficult tasks: they had made their own desks and done the landscaping themselves, and a month and a half out of every year they devote to work in the country, especially at harvest time. At the college level, besides vacations, every student must spend a month to a month and a half in a factory or commune. (In my visits to factories and communes I could spot quite a few of them.) Although the system has merits there is much to be said about its inconveniences, at least when, as so often, it is pushed to excess. Frequently college students find their education interfered with and must needlessly sacrifice courses. During the frenzy of The Great Leap Forward, from the summer of 1958 on, the regular schedule of studies not only in primary and secondary schools but often on the college level was repeatedly disrupted by sudden mobilizations, postings to public works, trips to factories and communes. Some students spent months at a time as agricultural "shock troops." In spite of having their professors there with them, no serious study was possible. Since the beginning of the "readjustment," the regime has seen to it that such abuses were discontinued. The period of manual labor has been arranged now so as to disrupt the normal course of studies as little as possible.

How many young people are in school or at the university? "We have no figures for publication," I was informed at the Ministry of Education in Peking. The secrecy that applies to economic statistics extends to other realms, as we have seen. The last figures published were for 1959. In that year there were 80 million children in primary schools, with two million teachers; seven million in secondary schools, with 500,000 teachers; and 800,000 young people in universities and technical schools, with 100,000 professors and instructors. Nevertheless I did obtain a few interesting statistics. In 1964 200,000 students graduated with diplomas from technical schools, colleges and universities. That year there were three million teachers of all kinds. There were something like 90 million children in primary schools.

Between secondary school and any sort of advanced training there is a competitive examination that is the same all over the country. The authorities tell those students who pass where they will receive further schooling and what they must specialize in. The student's preferences will be taken into consideration, but the state does not guarantee satisfaction since the needs of the country come first in the planned creation of cadres. It is into science and technology that students are most often directed. Besides more than sixty universities, China has set up many specialized advanced institutes. Foremost are 250 engineering schools or scientific institutes. There are more than 150 normal schools and a few less than 150 medical schools. There are something like one hundred agricultural schools. But there are less than thirty faculties for law, the humanities and political science. I was told that at the University of Peking 70 percent of the students were in the sciences. And after graduation it is still the state which assigns profession, position and location—taking into account *or not* the wishes of the person concerned. . . . Actually, I'm told that 40 percent of the graduating class go into industry, 20 percent into teaching, 10 percent into medicine, 10 percent into general science and letters, another 10 percent to agriculture, and only 2 or 3 percent go into law and finance. In the final grading of the student and thus in his assignment after graduation, his political evalution has a great deal of importance. The best positions are given to those who show the most revolutionary zeal and get the best marks in Marxism and political science.

Here we have touched upon a most important aspect of education in Communist China. The Party and state have completed only half their job in making basic education and culture available. Such training would be useless and even harmful in the eyes of the regime were it not accompanied and directed by the most disciplined course of political and ideological indoctrination. Education submits to political theory from the lowest grades on. Once out of the cradle the child begins to receive the molding that state and Party expect will turn him into their future citizen. But just as political education begins before school age, it continues long after. Not even the student's entry into his profession puts an end to it. Political indoctrination will in fact make a claim on his time as long as he lives! In this sense too the factory and the commune are schools, schools for the teaching of Communism, in an education no adult Chinese ever completes.

In Peking I paid a visit to a kindergarten. It was overflowing with well-behaved and well-dressed little moppets of four to six years old, with round faces. Their principal said, and I quote: "We teach them to love their friends and hate class enemies." And who are those enemies, I asked. "Landowners, reactionaries, and American imperialists!" These tiny children, these sweet Chinese dolls, surrounding me with their babble, are taught political love and hate! A colleague of mine, another foreign correspondent, saw something more at about the same time. He was visiting a kindergarten when he noticed the infants dancing in a circle, but this was a round dance where each child shouldered a little wooden gun. "Is this the struggle against American imperialism?" he asked and tried to laugh. "No, this dance is called *We come back from the rifle range."* A bigoted political indoctrination begins the moment a little Chinese begins his education. "As soon as our babies can talk they know how to stammer 'Chairman Mao!' " the *Workers' News* wrote in April, 1964. "In kindergarten they play at marching past under red flags, singing revolutionary songs. . . . They already know what scoundrels the American imperialists and other reactionaries are. . . . They shout 'Long live Mao, long live the Communist Party!' "

A teacher in a model school in Peking tells me that the children from seven to twelve in primary school receive the rudiments of political education. "We give them patriotic and internationalist training," he tells me. "We give them some idea of the meaning of socialism, Communism, class struggle. We explain capitalist exploitation and imperialism. We demonstrate why we must give our support to the downtrodden peoples of the world." On the wall a poster presents a fitting image: a yellow hand grasps a black one. This teacher continues: "It is we, the schoolteachers, who are the new regime's engineers for the reconstruction of the human soul. We wish to produce a new generation of revolutionaries. . . ." Then he went on to describe how the school teaches "the Five Loves:" love of fatherland, love of the people, love of science, love of manual labor and—love of parents, perhaps? No, "love of public property." . . . We arrive in a classroom after the children have left. On the wall a bulletin board has disappeared under a sea of political posters made by the children themselves. For example one panel shows the life of Chinese children as presented by photos cut from Chinese newspapers; on the other panel also by means of pictures from the same newspapers, the life of little capitalists. On one side little Chinese boys and girls cut flowers, sing songs and climb around in "Uncle Mao's" lap, etc. On the other side thin little Americans sit in rags before their wretched shanties, little Koreans stand behind barbed wire guarded by sentries, little Japanese lie in hospital beds between life and death—a caption explains they were poisoned by American powdered milk.

In a secondary school, in Peking also, an instructor explains the curriculum to me. At thirteen the children begin to receive political training from a special teacher who does nothing else.

Until they are fifteen the youngsters study the evolution of society, the history of the Communist Party, the works of Chairman Mao, etc. Those at the next stage (16 to 18) learn the rudiments of Marxism. All of them are drilled on "the four concepts of class"; they are: the role of the proletariat, manual labor, love of the people, and atheist materialism. In order to explain class struggle the teacher invites workers or peasants to come and explain to the children what life was like before the liberation. The students, I am told, have often been marked by certain of their parents' bourgeois attitudes, marks that must be effaced. Naturally some children come from formerly upper-class families and seem to have inherited their bad habits from the previous state of society. Yet children with other than proletarian backgrounds are not subjected to special surveillance, my informant hastens to add, nor are they "tagged" as such.

Beginning in the primary grades and continuing through the first half of secondary school, a political organization exerts its active influence on the children: the Pioneer movement, the first step in the direction of Party membership. This movement resembles nothing so much as boy-scouting plus politics and serves as a breeding ground for a second organization, The Young Communist League. And the League, whose members are between 15 and 25, is the breeding ground for the Party itself. In principle every child in school becomes a Pioneer—except for the bad eggs blackballed by their classmates, I'm told. The red neckerchiefs they wear are "corners of the red flag," reddened by the blood of revolutionary martyrs. Both boys and girls become members. They elect patrol leaders. They meet once a week and pay visits to heros of the production front, or to pilot industries, or they do manual labor, or listen to children's programs on the radio, etc. Their leaders come from the League, which has control over the movement. There are 50 million Pioneers in the whole of China, with a million and a half members of the League to lead them. In their ranks, as on school benches, the little Chinese never stops learning of heroes and hero-worship. The movement instills in him a taste for work, the spirit of sacrifice and an almost military discipline. As are few other students in the world, they are continually given lessons in morality, in the differences between good and evil. But of course this morality is deeply tinged with politics and the good often turns out to be whatever serves Party, government and socialist construction, while anything that smacks of bourgeois or revisionist attitudes is hateful evil.

And finally at the university emphasis is placed on Marxist doctrine. Here somehow indoctrination comes from every side. For one thing every student's schedule requires several hours per week of Marxism, including historical materialism, economics and political theory. Then there are extracurricular meetings and work periods that teach them "to join forces with the masses." There are also meetings specifically devoted to political education by groups under the direction of Party cadres, or members of the League. In these meetings students are informed of what's going on in the world from a political point of view and informed too of what they are expected to think about it. Official positions are communicated and explained, deviations pointed out and condemned. Criticism and autocriticism, so frequently on the agenda, assure the Party a close surveillance of student opinion, and allow students to keep tabs on each other. In addition, the League itself is a channel of ideological and political indoctrination. This organization is made up of both the best and the average elements, about 70 percent of all students. It is to the young what the Party is to adults. The attitude that it continually drums into each student has a military character. It gives a political twist to all activities, organizes propaganda campaigns— and its drives are unending. The League is a powerful influence, source of watchwords and slogans, ever watchful over behavior, harsh when necessary. And again "correct" political thinking is absolutely necessary for doing well at a university, just as later it is expected of all Chinese in their professional and everyday life.

One hardly need add that socialist education not only leaves the young Chinese no time for religious training, but finds time to combat religion. The regime has run into difficulties when it has attacked adults on their religion—an example of such resistance is given by the Christians of Shanghai, whose strength has never been broken completely, and whom persuasion has not converted to the regime. From their first experiences in the anti-religious struggle the leaders seems to have gathered that the education of children and young people supplies them with the proper terrain. Just as illiteracy will disappear in a relatively short time thanks to all children being sent to school, it should be possible to finish off religion at the same time by seeing to it that all education is socialist, thus by definition atheist, and that no source of religious education remains open to the children. Such a policy requires nothing more than patience for one or two generations. Besides it allows the regime to brag that there is no religious persecution in China and to point to article 88 of the constitution, which guarantees freedom of belief. Foreign visitors can be shown churches in which people are hearing mass, mosques and the temples in which Buddhists and Taoists are at prayer. But what has not been announced is more essential: an organized drying up of recruiting sources for these various religions will inevitably lead to their extinction due to the lack of both ministry and laity. What has already happened to the Catholics is significant. It can be boiled down to the following three points.

First of all no more infants are baptized. Catholic parents can no longer celebrate a baptism shortly after a birth. An eighteen-year-old, fully aware of the meaning of the ceremony, will be baptized if he asks to be. A result of this is a very striking reduction in the number of baptisms. In a political climate like that of present-day China, for an eighteen-year-old to demand baptism amounts to nothing short of heroism. For this age group the pressures of the environment and the government have reached their maximum. There is no persecution, but there is that "persuasion" which never lets up and never loses its temper. A course in atheism is forced upon him. Against the "superstitions" of his faith they offer the total assurance of modern science and materialism. Attempts are made to discredit the persons of religious leaders. *Red Flag* recently wrote that "under the cloak of 'Religion,' all sorts of pernicious practices flourish," such as "the extortion of money under false pretenses, rape, death or incurable wounds, disturbances of the social order and disturbances of production."

The second point of the program is to close down all places

of religious education. Not a single Catholic school stayed open anywhere in China after 1949. Catechism, although not forbidden, must be accompanied by a prescribed dose of socialist and patriotic education. In school any child who goes to catechism is subjected to counter-propaganda in favor of atheism. He is advised to give up this path that leads to mere superstition. He will assuredly receive bad marks in political science if he continues. He will not receive the Pioneer's red neckerchief. Later he will be among that 30 percent who do not belong to the League. Of course Catholic parents can give their children religious instruction at home—and such instruction has more staying power too. But it cannot be without the Party's knowledge because the Party has its ears everywhere. It exerts pressure on both children and parents to make of their home a place in which nothing but socialist truth is taught.

The third point regards the complete lack of new priests. All over China, Catholic seminaries, large and small, have closed their doors. No priests are being prepared in China. Of the 2500 Chinese priests who celebrated mass before the liberation more than half have been eliminated. They refused to rally to the new regime and are now either being "reformed through work" or in prison. Or they have died. The shepherds decrease as do their flocks.

For the flock does decrease as its age increases. You need do nothing more to check that statement than find one of the few churches still open and walk in. There are no churches in the countryside and very few in the towns. In the cathedral at Peking, for instance, the average age of the participants certainly differs greatly from that of an average Chinese crowd. Children are almost completely lacking, except for a few babes in arms, and young people are very rare. While everywhere else in China children and young people are in the majority, here it is mostly the elderly, men and women in their forties and fifties and older. All of them are members of the Association of Catholic Patriots which the Party created and controls through its own cadres and representatives—even the priest is a member. He is a public official, in other words. They are all members because it is obligatory, because the pressure put on them by the authorities is so great, because they were willing to do anything to save what they could. They should not be condemned for this by Catholics abroad, and certainly schism has nothing to do with it. Their faith is not dead. It is very much alive, to judge from the fervor of the faithful whom I saw. It is probable that the Church would regain part of the ground lost if only the authorities would lower the antireligious pressure.

But events are not developing toward such an outcome. Since the beginning of 1964 the antireligious campaign, which had smouldered during the difficult years, has flared up again along with increased emphasis on socialist education. The government no longer makes any secret of its long-range plans. *Red Flag*, in an article from which I have already quoted (February 26, 1964), has detailed the means of fighting "the battle that will promote the extirpation of religion." We can predict a new hardening of the line from a phrase like "religions must be gradually eliminated." Islam and Buddhism, with both of which the regime has had serious difficulties in the West and in Tibet, are singled out particularly and accused of favoring "the most barbarous and cruel systems of oppression and feudal exploitation." Religious groups "even organize insurrections and counterrevolutionary activity," says *Red Flag*. The journal warns the faithful of whatever religion, and notifies its own cadres, that the only religious activities authorized are those carried on in the bosom of its own patriotic religious associations. There are five of these answering to the five religions practiced in China: Buddhism, Islam, Taoism, Protestantism and Catholicism. All religious activity outside these associations runs the risk of stigmatizing its practitioners as class enemies and counterrevolutionary elements.

Thus each flock of faithful is watched, isolated, and condemned to gradual death, in the midst of a multitude who preach without letup socialist education and atheist materialism. And within the next two or three generations China may very well be the first of the People's Republics to have completely jettisoned religion.

Just as among school-age children mere learning means nothing as far as the regime is concerned unless it is backed up by solid political training, so labor, whether professional, or in factory, office or field, cannot exist without the accompaniment of what is known in China as "study" or "political work"—which means an organized, systematic indoctrination. Politics and propaganda fill every factory. They never leave the worker alone, either surrounding his machine, or following him home. Take the shops of the steelworks in Wuhan, Central China. Gigantic portraits of the chiefs watch the worker from every wall. On the same whitewashed walls giant characters in red or gold remind him of national slogans: STUDY THE WORKS OF CHAIRMAN MAO! COUNT ONLY ON OUR OWN EFFORTS! FOLLOW THE EXAMPLE OF LEI FENG, MODEL SOLDIER! The shop newspaper, chalked up on a blackboard, bears only such announcements as the party cell that manages it thinks expedient, and among factory news of a general nature occur the usual slogans and local notices like "Meeting tonight of workers from such and such a shop for a discussion after work," etc. A loudspeaker blares patriotic and political songs from time to time, and during breaks it reads an article from *People's Daily* or offers its commentary. Even after the eight-hour day has ended the workers very often aren't free: after supper they must return for night school, where courses in technology and general culture contain much pure politics.

The Wuhan steeelworks sets aside one evening a week for the study of the works of Mao Tse-tung; another, but not regularly, for news and discussion; two others for culture and technology. Each course lasts two hours. I was told that the instructors mix a strong dose of politics with the culture.

What is true of the factory is also true of the office or the commune. On a commune the head of each team uses the break to discuss that day's editorial or give a simple political lesson. I saw this for myself. In the evening after work some meeting or other for discussion or information will call together teams, brigades, young people or even the whole village. Radio has become an important means of indoctrination in rural areas. In one widespread system—I was able to see it in operation near Shanghai—a commune organizes its own programs around network material that it receives from the city. The commune places little radios in each cottage—actually they are nothing more than loudspeakers. The listeners have no choice; their fare in the case I happen to know about consisted of Shanghai programs seasoned with a girl announcer reading political lessons from the commune's high command.

In the cities as well as in the villages the Party does its best to fill the workers' leisure. Its greatest success has been with unmarried workers, housed, as we have said, in dormitories beside the factory. And the dormitory system has the Party's approval: it allows the most nearly perfect control of free time, and an almost uninterrupted flow of political propaganda. *People's Daily* (February 7, 1964) announced a campaign for the proper method of filling "the other eight hours" during which a worker isn't on the job or asleep. The article boasts of the Party's success in organizing the workers in their factory dormitories "for the pursuit of many sensible ends: the study of Chairman Mao's writings, the recital of stories of the Revolution, the comparison of the misery of the past with the good life of today." Another article in the same issue implies that a few workers "waste their time on the street or in parks looking at flowers or moonlight." The article goes on: "Since our eight working hours subject our minds and hands to the inspection of others"—read "the Party"—"our eight hours of leisure cannot fail to be of interest to the proper authorities." In the country too a program began in 1964 with the object of organizing the leisure time of young people on the communes, Rural Youth Clubs. The Young Communist League has been instructed to aim for more than the progressive element by giving membership to as many young people as possible. Fairs, theater groups, book clubs, choral societies, etc., of course all aim at what the review *Chinese Youth* (organ of the League) terms "aiding politics and production."

That politics and production stand on an equal footing is a fundamental principle, and the foremost objective of "political work" is the stimulation of production. And this answers to a fundamental aspect of economic life: in Communist China as in every socialist country—and even more than in any other socialist country—profit and personal interest are forbidden and have ceased to motivate production. Thus new stimulants are needed to replace them. This explains why China has organized her immense program of "political work" which exceeds anything of its kind anywhere else in the Communist world: it hooks up with the "economic work" that it must encourage and accelerate. The reasons for a worker to labor disinterestedly for the collectivity must be drummed into his head without letup. The collectivity would vanish, they say over and over, and he would go with it, if he did not demand unending zeal of himself, breakneck labor. In a new country as poor as China the creation of a modern state provided with advanced technologies depends on every worker forgetting himself out of a maximal devotion to the collective good. To become a good producer one must have become a right thinker—that is, learned the mission of socialism and the sacrifices it demands. In its January, 1964 number (the first number of the year is important; it sketches out the program for the next eleven months) *Red Flag* explained the reasoning behind the "political work" program. If there were any letup in political work, a letup in economic work would necessarily follow. On the other hand, "when ideological work has been done properly and elevated the political conscience of the workers, their wisdom and talents can be put to maximum use." The article goes on to explain that when material stimuli are used— salary, bonuses, etc.—what actually happens is a reduction in the value of each worker's output along with the spread of bourgeois individualism.

Since the most important role of unions in China is relaying directions from the state to the workers, and the stimulation of production, "political work" is very much their work. This is the substance of what a militant organizer, Mme. Tsang Wei-chen, told me in Shanghai. She is an enthusiastic, robust woman, her energetic face framed in short bangs; she is built along the energetic lines of a tank or truck. Mme. Tsang covers political propaganda as assistant director of the Department of Propaganda of the Shanghai Federation of Unions. "For the worker the union is a school of Communism," Mme. Tsang told me. And what is taught in that school? In answering this question Mme. Tsang gave first place to information, which the worker receives in meetings and lectures, from the shop blackboard, from group readings of newspapers, at work, in the dormitory, etc. By all these various routes come the facts about the international situation (machinations of the imperalists) and an exact knowledge of the Party line. Workers must constantly have explained to them the reasons for decisions made by the authorities. The cases Mme. Tsang cited are significant: the decision to place industry at the service of agriculture, and the necessity for an acceleration of the rhythm of production. "A worker does better if he knows *why* he's working and for *whom*."

She might have also added ". . . if he knows what he's working *against* and against *whom*." And she did say that in the factories class struggle forms a central feature of the curriculum—the same is true of commune, office, etc. "Those social classes overthrown by the revolution," continued Mme. Tsang, "have not yet acquiesced in their fates. The imperialists still plot China's destruction. Chiang Kai-shek's gang still attempts to land armed agents on the mainland. Our vigilance must be unceasing." To create the necessary spirit she tells how the union has retired workers return to the factory and describe to the younger men both their former miserable life and their revolutionary struggles. In this way the young are given something against which to view the good life available to them today. For instance an old stevedore recalled "the 200-pound test." In order to obtain a job as an ordinary stevedore he had to carry a 200-pound load from the banks of the river to the delivery platform of the factory, about a third of a mile. Once there he had to pass a further test: not collapsing under the blows and kicks rained down by foreign overseers. Mme. Tsang's comment: "We tell the workers 'Never forget! Stand guard around the fruits of former victories!'"

Study the thought of Mao Tse-tung. . . . At the moment this is the Party's first commandment and the theme of a current campaign for socialist education which took on new and unheard-of proportions in the winter of 1963–1964. From Harbin in the North to Canton in the South, from Shanghai in the East to Urumchi in the West; in universities, offices, barracks, neighborhood committees, women's clubs, chapters of the League, in unions, literary guilds and societies for the arts and in organizations whose existence I may have overlooked, indeed in the Party itself, cell by cell, at every level, hundreds of millions of Chinese have gotten together to "study the thought of Mao Tse-tung," source of all *correct* political thinking. All together, wherever they are and whoever they are, they devote to this study hundreds of millions of hours over and above the eight-hour day. For a minority this really is a labor of love—penetrating the mind of China's leader, enriching their own minds with his abundant, complicated writings studied in complete editions. For the many this difficult task has been simplified: instead of complete works, selections—or even single sentences—give the group something to repeat and comment on under the eye of a Party cadre who extols the wisdom of Mao and points the moral. . . . For the broad masses Mao's works are boiled down to nothing but slogans and comic books, so that even the simplest minds can absorb the elements and duties of Chinese communism decked out with the authority of the new China's teacher and hero. The "study of the thinking of Mao Tse-tung" has become Maoism's catechism —and everyone goes to catechism.

One day when I visilted a factory in Peking I was able to mix with a group of workers and for a moment even take part in their work. Had they asked me to approach their machinery and get a better idea of their jobs? Not at all! It was nothing more nor less than political work, and the period was devoted, of course, to the study of Mao Tse-tung's thought.

In a small room they sit all around me on benches, like school children, about 20 boys and girls, quite young all of them. They listen carefully to the instructor at the blackboard. The lesson for today is an article, or actually a story, that Chairman Mao wrote in his youth. The tale relates the manner in which a good peasant named Yukong moves a mountain from his front yard. . . . This mountain makes life difficult; it interferes with his farming. He goes at it, shovelful by shovelful, and removes rocks and earth in little baskets. The whole village turns out and hoots Yukong, but he replies to their jokes: "I have sons and my sons will have sons and all together if we work long enough we will move this mountain."

The instructor explains that this is a *fable* and admirably chosen by Chairman Mao—the worker students fill their notebooks avidly. And what is a fable? The fable is a literary form of a popular nature. Fables prove the artistry and profundity of China's masses—the instructor's lengthy explanations find their way into twenty notebooks. The profundity shows in a fable's *moral*. What is a moral? A moral is a profound lesson that comes from the people. A lesson such as Chairman Mao, as he moved through the Chinese countryside, had many opportunities to learn —and to teach so well to others. My companions are still taking notes, imperturbable, and if you ask me, impenetrable. . . . They never smile, but they don't yawn either. They note down the part fiction plays in fables, and how in the guise of fiction animals are made to speak. The instructor explains how this reflects the class struggle of the past. Lions and wolves stand for the feudal classes and exploiters. To escape punishment people spoke of them in these disguises. . . . How many parts has Chairman Mao divided his article into? And how shall we apply the moral to our own situations? "Because that's essential," the instructor tells us. "Mao's thought is universal in its range but always of practical value. It has something to say to each of us, since each of us has everyday problems that require solutions. All of us have mountains in our front yards. China has a mountain in her front yard. But the power of the people is such that no limit can be set it, and we have sons and our sons will have sons. . . ."

I leave the class on tiptoe. It lasts an hour and a half—and I lasted a third of that. It is 10 A.M. but for those workers sitting there it is already night. My guide wishes to emphasize their zeal by pointing out to me that these children work all night and then reassemble to learn their lessons before returning home to sleep all day.

This lesson on Crazy Yukong gives us a good idea, I believe, of the level at which Mao Tse-tung's thought is studied by China's workers. I have been told how workers by the thousands in the Anshan steelworks have formed groups to "study the thinking of Mao Tse-tung" on their own time. In Wuhan, for instance, the subject when I visited the workers in the great steel combine was —Crazy Yukong. He turned up again in Shanghai. This demonstrates the organization and uniformity of propaganda achieved by the Party throughout the country. All over China groups have formed as they did in Anshan for the "study" of Mao Tse-tung. The peasants do the same, either in the villages after work or in the fields during breaks. In a commune I visited near Peking they had formed more than 100 groups. In factories these groups form "of themselves," but in Shanghai Comrade Tsang Wei-chen, the union representative, added that the union "aids in this free formation." The union trains instructors such as those I saw performing in Peking. The unions organize lessons and discussions of Chairman Mao's thought, and distribute his works. They keep a close watch on the activities of these study groups. Mme. Tsang assured me that all this "interests our workers very much. They know that it makes them better socialists and more efficient producers. Every day we wash our faces. We must wash our minds as well, our workers say. If knives aren't sharpened, they don't cut. If we neglect political work, production falls off. . . . Do you know the story of Crazy Yukong? Yes? Well, we still work by hand in our factories with little baskets, but we will move the mountain of poverty. Nothing frightens us anymore. . . ."

The Chinese press also brings its tremendous influence to bear in this campaign. It adds voices to the movement throughout the country with edifying articles and editorials written to be read aloud by workers assembled to read the papers or for "political work." The dailies strain their invention in supplying thousands of true stories that are intended as examples. They show how thousands of workers have seen the light and become devoted servants of the common good, and even more essential, have increased production—all from reading Mao Tse-tung. Very often these stories sound quite silly.

A poor peasant in a commune learns to count and work an abacus to tote up his fellow team members' work-points because he's heard that Mao considers that man worthy of praise who bears the heaviest burdens. In a hospital a seriously sick woman whose husband knows nothing of her condition is able to get him on the phone because the operators know by heart Mao's phrases about their duty to serve the masses—they move heaven and earth to reach him. In the Shenyang market a vegetable vendor has learned enough to advise her clientele on the nutritional value of cabbages, roots, squash, fruit, and so on, because she read in Chairman Mao, "What we don't know, we must learn." She therefore learned about vitamins and calories. In Shanghai students who complained about having to interrupt their studies to go to work in a bicycle factory for their period of manual labor went off full of zeal after the Party had Mao's ideas on youth and ideological reform read to them. In Peking a professional athlete became a champion after having discovered Mao's works and studied them, and a ping-pong champion owed her most splendid victories to this very study.

But let's not laugh too quickly at such simplicity. . . . This tremendous campaign for "political work" with its piercing "Study the thought of Mao Tse-tung!" certainly produces significant results in worker productivity. It mass-produces right-thinking workers—which means workers who follow instructions and therefore work at breakneck speed. The model held up to the masses for their admiration and imitation is no longer a champion of economic production. Today's hero is political, and it is only his conformity that reaches heroic proportions. No longer do they look for that rare phenomenon, the herculean Stakhanovite—he is only imitated with difficulty. Now the hero is an everyday hero whom millions can copy, a simple worker whose zeal is heroic because it results from absolutely correct political thinking.

Lei Feng, the prototype of this variety of everyday heroism, was sprung on the people amid unbelievable publicity when the regime began the period of economic readjustment. All China echoed with the episodes of his almost legendary life in which every action was a textbook situation, every word said was straight out of Mao, and every musing he committed to paper a model of absolutely conformist thought. Lei Feng had not yet turned twenty in 1960 when, as he said, he "enlisted in the army so as to march in the footsteps of revolutionary martyrs and be a soldier for Chairman Mao." He showed such zeal that his comrades treated him like a half-wit. But he merely wrote in that intimate diary that the Party reads to the entire country: "I wish to become a half-wit. The Revolution needs half-wits like that. I have only one desire: to give myself body and soul to the Party, to Socialism, to Communism." On July 1, 1961, he wrote:

"Today is the fortieth anniversary of the Party. I cannot find words to express my gratitude. One might almost say, had there been no Party, I would not be here." On October 1, 1961, National Day, he wrote: "Beloved Chairman Mao, all day long I have been dying to see you and I've looked up at your picture countless times, and as in my dreams I see the goodness that's in your face." In April, 1962: "A human being is a screw in a machine. The screw may be small but its importance is capital. I wish to remain a screw forever, in good shape and well cared for, one that will never rust."

A short time after the death of Lei Feng (which took place in an accident I'm told) the *People's Daily* could editorialize: "All over the country among the young a grass-roots movement has sprung up: learn the lessons of Lei Feng. In villages and towns young men and young women talk about Lei Feng, learn from Lei Feng, compare themselves to Lei Feng, and resolve to imitate the grandeur and simplicity of his revolutionary spirit. . . . Newspapers, radio stations, TV, posters and all other media publicize Lei Feng. In a thousand meeting rooms the first secretary of the Party or the president of the League, in the provinces or in the cities, urges on groups whose program is—learn the lessons of Lei Feng."

Did Lei Feng ever really exist? Whether he did or not millions of Lei Fengs are born every day. For instance in a machine-tool factory in Wuhan the shop paper, as usual a blackboard written on with colored chalks, sings at great length the praises of Comrade Pan Sing, one of the shop metal workers. "Comrade Pan Sing learns the works of Chairman Mao. He works at them every day. He takes notes. When you pass his bed in the dormitory you'll see the works of Chairman Mao in a pile. Thanks to this penetrating study he never tires. He is the leader of his team. During his rest periods he often returns to the shop to see if he can discover any production problems. He watches over tools carefully. If his comrades haven't gotten everything shipshape he pitches in. He's always thirty minutes early for work. Every minute of his eight hours is devoted to production and quality. Not a single piece of his has been turned down in a year. . . ."

Pan Sing is Lei Feng. And what is Lei Feng, the humble hero

of the lower orders? He is nothing more than a reflection of the great hero at the top, Mao Tse-tung!

Never before has the adoration that surrounds the person of Mao Tse-tung been as intense as it is today, thanks to the "study of his thought"; and never before was it so universal, so well-organized. This has led to a superficial comparison with the cult of Stalin. The differences between the two personalities are large, and it is easy to show that there are better reasons for Chinese feelings about Mao than for the Russian cult of Stalin. Above all, the adoration of Mao appears to me to have an essential originality. At the summit of power Stalin was all-powerful because he was the supreme, the unique motive force. Mao Tse-tung receives unequaled temporal power because he stands at the apex of the pyramid from which all thought flows.

One man at the top does all the thinking for the masses. From his mind flow forth rivers and streams that water "the hundred flowers," but none of those flowers dare show any color but the red of socialism. This mind illuminates millions of brains—but none can be brighter than it. The ideal would be a China populated by seven hundred million Mao Tse-tungs. But that can never be: the model is too great and can never be equaled. The project then is a China populated by seven hundred million Mao Tse-tungs—in the abridged version.

In the meantime the choruses of organized praise mount upward toward the great genius who purveys ideology to the nation. Some idea of what these choruses must sound like during the meetings for political work in a factory or on a commune can be gotten by reading a few of the encomia that follow. "Mao's thought is like the sun," writes the *Journal of the Army* (March, 1964). "It is the highest wisdom of the Chinese people. . . . The least deviation from his line of thought and we would be lost and defeated." In this same paper a soldier muses, "I am a green shoot, the masses are my soil, my officers and the Party are gardeners, but the thinking of Mao Tse-tung is my dew and my sun." *Chinese Youth* (July 1, 1963) writes: "As a fish cannot leave the water, nor the child his mother, revolutionary cadres can never leave the works of Mao." *Red Flag* (August 1, 1963): "In the past, present and future the thinking of Mao Tse-tung exists as the single correct compass for the work of our army." "It is the lighthouse that illuminates our work and China's compass," said an announcer I heard on the air. And the *People's Daily* (March 26, 1964), national party newspaper, proclaims, "Without the sun the moon would give no light. . . .Without the study of Mao Tse-tung's thought, even if we kept our eyes open, we would be blind men."

CHAPTER TWELVE

THE ARTS AND CULTURE IN THE SERVICE OF SOCIALISM

AT THE BEGINNING OF JUNE, WHILE I WAS IN THE CHINESE CAPITAL, an unusual congress was meeting in the Hall of the People, a congress of "workers in the theater" called by the minister of culture to discuss ways and means of reforming the classical Chinese theater. Actors, musicians, authors, directors, etc., two thousand strong, had come from the four corners of China. All of them work in a genre called "Peking Opera," the noblest form of classical theater, and in its many provincial and local varieties popular throughout the country. "Discuss" is a euphemism— unless we simply take it in its Communist acceptation. In reality all that the participants in this "congress" were called upon to do was sit listening to long speeches explaining decisions already made in high places by cultural dictators acting in concert with Communist cadres from their professions; as model citizens of a socialist state they then, either on the spot or later in the committee sessions, developed in their turn all the reasons for approving, applauding, and finding this reform both admirable, and welcome—and promised to return to their theaters and zealously apply the new directives. The discussions were held behind closed doors. After the congress though, there were a few echoes in Peking. Evidently the congress unfolded in a charged atmosphere in which the organized enthusiasm of the majority rubbed elbows with the powerless dismay of the minority. And indeed the decisions arrived at "unanimously" (as is somehow always the case) amounted to much more than a mere reform. Their object was to "revolutionize" (that's the official term) not simply the opera but all the artists connected with it.

Nor did the revolutionizing wait for the approval of the congress before going into action. While the congress was meeting, the city of Peking began a festival devoted to "The New Peking Opera." Five of the city's theaters, accompanied by loud journalistic fanfares, premiered thirty-seven new plays that answered to socialist specifications. And if there were one or two participants who hadn't gotten the sense of the congress before it opened, they could not have entertained any doubts after the first session: the lightning of ideological revolution which had so far spared their stages had blasted them at last. Chen Yen-ping, minister of culture, Kuo Mo-jo, assistant minister and respected dean of literary and artistic progressives, and a few other personalities and propagandists made the whole situation crystal clear. "The Peking Opera is a product of feudal society," the minister told them. "It is simply inconceivable that a stage dominated by emperors, warlords, mandarins, and concubines can accomplish the task expected of the theater, which is to militantly promote a proletarian ideology and to extirpate a bourgeois ideology." (I am quoting from *Red Flag* and *People's Daily*.)

For the last few years the government had been content merely to "improve" ancient plays, to "purge" passages that were susceptible of encouraging reactionary or feudal ideas. The repertory contains plays that are progressive in certain respects but insufficiently so, and it also contains a remnant of truly feudal plays "that must now be eliminated." It is not only a question of drastically "adjusting" the traditional repertory by further purging and adapting, but of creating a whole new socialist theater to serve the aims of the revolution. A few of the ancient plays will be preserved because they are really masterpieces and very celebrated, but today China needs, the minister told the press, "new plays of a historical character but written from the viewpoint of historical materialism and with true educational significance," plays on contemporary themes, the class struggle for example, or production, or the progress of socialist education since the liberation. For heroes it will no longer be possible to choose lovely ladies, literati, or feudal China's warriors; instead there is choice between soldiers of the Long March, soldiers of the Korean War, workers in the steelworks or on the Great Bridge over the Yangtse, peasant activists on the people's communes, and so on. . . .

And to assure that these new plays be well acted and well written, one last revolution is decreed by the congress, one which will "revolutionize" all workers in the theater—by sending them off to learn the metiers of their new heroes! As soon as the congress ends, actors and actresses, directors, costume designers, stars and bit players, in short everyone who is connected with the Peking Opera, will have to set out for village, factory or barracks, in order to "mingle with the people," as the papers put it when they reported this item, and thus to acquire living knowledge "of the places where the history of modern China is being made." "Whether members of the older or the younger generation," said the minister of culture, "they ought to become revolutionaries—and stay revolutionaries! They ought to steep themselves in the class struggle and the struggle for production so that this reeducation can teach them the execution of roles in the socialist theater and contribute thereby to the great cause of socialism." In the end, several actors, mostly of the older generation, decided to leave the theater after the congress, but for the most part they abandoned themselves to the enormous revolutionary wave that had at last reached their art and their world.

Only a few weeks before the congress a Peking Opera company from Shanghai had toured Europe under the auspices of the Chinese Communists. Its reception had been wildly enthusiastic, particularly in Paris. But what Paris applauds, Peking now condemns. Soon the theater of the old days will be nothing but an article for the export trade. Until very recently it retained a dizzying amount of vitality in spite of the "improvements" demanded by ideological censors. Its color, buffoonery and beauty cut through the grayness of socialist life and gave it tremendous popular appeal. Tomorrow it will go down before an invasion of right-thinking, socialist plays. But we must put aside our useless regrets unless we want the minister of culture to brand us as "enemies of China"—who have already decided, he tells us, to attack the new plays, registering their low quality, joking about them in the Hong Kong press and elsewhere. "We on the other hand consider them excellent!" he says by way of reply. Their primary intention is to communicate revolutionary spirit to the spectators, and next to "revolutionize" both the author and the actors.

And this is nothing more than an intermediate stage in a revolution: the new plays have not completely broken with the past. After the subject matter of the Peking Opera has been "revolutionized," the papers go on to say, it will be the turn of operatic form itself; a whole new manner of delivery, a new musical style must be invented. But this final stage has not yet begun, and for the moment modern subjects experience a strange mixture of socialist realism and traditional stylization. The results are silly and uneven. There have been some successes: *The Spark in the Reeds* has become the box-office attraction of the new repertory. Diplomats and foreign journalists invited to the gala premiere that opened the festival were served up a series of children's book illustrations from the war against Japan. At least they were able to applaud all of the color and buffoonery of the old days that remained under the modern costuming. The peasant girl who hides Chinese soldiers wounded by the Japanese miaows her words and songs in the style of a princess in the old theater. Mao's soldiers in their khaki uniforms act out their battles with the same acrobatics used by ancient warriors in the old plays, while the Japanese officer retains all the makeup and gestures of the traditional bandit—down to the deafening accompaniment of gongs and cymbals.

Another play, exaltedly talky, deals with the theme of people's communes. We are in a village. There is a husband, a wife, and —the Party. This brings "the eternal triangle" up to date. These three argue passionately over a large and unexpected object in the center of the stage: a crock of fertilizer, of natural fertilizer, I'm afraid. Will they spread it upon the soil of the commune— the socialist solution? Or will they reach an antisocialist solution and save it for their individual plot? You can imagine who wins. . . . And as the *People's Daily* writes without cracking a smile: "The greatest skill in the use of traditional conventions is demanded in order to put this over, and without that skill, this theme, no matter how excellent, will not be able to effectively move the public." Moreover success will not be immediate, as *Red Flag* explained on June 30, 1964, at the termination of the congress. It is unavoidable that for a time the plays will be "rather clumsy" or tainted with "minor faults." They must be "improved and perfected from performance to performance," by following "advice from every quarter" and making continual revisions. (Note in passing that a work of art is widely regarded in the new China as something basically alterable. The criticism of the masses can and should revise a work to the point where it carries the properly vigorous, and correct, socialist message.)

As far as *Red Flag* is concerned no one but a revisionist or a reactionary could say that the performance of "new revolutionary operas on contemporary themes" means the "decline of the Peking Opera as an art form." The facts point in precisely the opposite direction, the Party review maintains: "It is not simply the connoisseurs of the Peking Opera who adore these new revolutionary plays. A whole segment of the population which formerly hardly ever went to the opera has become enthusiasts." I therefore don't wish to include myself among the ranks of those who maintain that the public dislikes the new repertory. Besides, this doesn't seem to be the case. In Hankow, for instance, in the Palace of People's Recreations (the *Grand Monde* of the old days, like the one in Shanghai) five or six plays, as socialist as can be imagined, were playing on the same night in several different halls to full houses. Even "revolutionized," the Chinese theater retains the keen sense of style and timing which was always its hallmark, and the Chinese are still the born actors they always were. In addition, the Chinese public lacks diversions and receives gratefully those which it is offered. Finally, since the total willpower of the authorities has been mobilized to "intensively promote" the new plays, as the papers put it, we can be certain that the theatrical revolution will end in triumph and spew out as reactionary and backward anyone hateful enough to dare shed a few tears over the condemned funeral processions of emperors, mandarins and the lovely ladies of the past.

To anyone who knows how to see and hear it is evident that in striking at the Peking Opera the government and Party have set out to create what I might call a "spectacular" opening for an ideological campaign aimed quite broadly at the whole artistic and intellectual fraternity. In fact, as soon as the congress was over, the same issue of *Red Flag* from which I have already quoted let its readers in on what it called "some new measures of a revolutionary nature which are in the offing for popular songs, films, books, music, dance, fine arts, and other literary and artistic provinces." The reform of the Peking Opera it calls "a great achievement" that forms an important part of a much broader cultural and social revolution.

It is also significant that these thoughts of *Red Flag* should be preceded by a vigorous analysis of class struggle that takes on an almost violent tone in places. In such a transitional society as present-day China, although on its way toward socialism, there is always the danger of a "capitalist restoration." This can happen most insidiously, the enemy doing its utmost "by means of deadly poisons in sugarcoated pills" to cause an imperceptible degeneration of socialism into capitalism by way of Revisionism. So the fundamental question will be, "What class occupies the ideological positions in the arts and literature?" And the answer to it determines "whether or not socialist political institutions and their economic basis can be consolidated." The question is to discover "in which camp" art and literature are, socialist or capitalist? And further, Marxist-Leninist or revisionist? "Let there not be the least doubt in anyone's mind," writes *Red Flag*, "about this fact: we absolutely cannot tolerate any literature or any art that breaks with socialism, or that opposes socialism." The watchword that has been given the theater and that will be extended to the rest of culture is then as follows: "Weed out the old, cultivate the new!" The old means feudalism and capitalism; the new means socialism and Communism. We must give culture a new content and new forms in keeping with this socialist era, the Party review explains, and adds: "Times are changing. There ought to be corresponding changes in the content of art and literature."

After such general warnings, *Red Flag* takes aim with greater precision and launches an offensive against the artists and writers themselves. In truly combative language the review continues: "On our country's literary and artistic fronts there are some sincere comrades who have solved these questions, but there are others who have not at all, or only incompletely. Working-class people have performed miracles on every front. But certain workers on literary and artistic fronts have refused to recognize this, or feel no enthusiasm for it. They simply do not wish to praise or describe that struggle, or they do very badly. They are completely absorbed in capitalist and feudal attitudes. They still hide in their ivory towers. They still stubbornly refuse to go out among the mass of workers, peasants and soldiers or into the fire of combat. At the bottom of their hearts they still belong to the bourgeoisie. Continuously, obstinately, they persist in the pretentions game of expressing their egoism and remodeling the world according to their private notions of that world. Certain of them have already begun to degenerate and to stink. Others, if the truth were known, have been on the side of the exploiting classes ever since their birth. . . . Such a state of affairs cannot be tolerated; it cries out for change. . . . The most important problem, the crucial problem in revolutionizing literature and the arts, is how to revolutionize the artists and writers themselves."

This personal revolution that it is each artist's duty to fight to a victorious conclusion was given method and goal by Mao Tse-tung himself way back in his heroic past in the caves of Yenan. The goal? Put the arts and literature at the service of socialism. The method? Go out among the people and share their work and hardships. It is in the fires of struggle, the struggle for production and the class struggle that they must "harden themselves and remold themselves." Mao has said (*Talks at the Yenan Forum on Literature and Art,* 3rd revised edition, Peking, 1962), "The life of the people is always a mine of raw materials for literature and arts . . . an inexhaustible source, the only source."

Thus the call for a departure in the direction of "the people" has already sounded and not just for the actors of the Peking Opera. Writers, painters, dancers, musicians, film makers, philosophers, scholars, etc., will soon be "going out among the people." Taking a trip to the factory, the commune or the barracks will be a part of their lives. Indeed some of them, as that passage already quoted from *Red Flag* says, "feel no enthusiasm" for these new socialist obligations and do their best to avoid them. This system of detailing intellectuals to manual labor is two-edged. It can serve the regime in "improving" those artists who have already rallied to it or been won over, but it can also be used as a means of punishing those who have earned its displeasure or anger. The good elements, those who have gotten good ideological marks, are certain to hold round-trip tickets. Those elements who are aware of their insufficient orthodoxy, who have received bad marks, can justifiably fear that their stay among the peasants or workers will be long. . . . For these the obligation of "going out among the people" can become a real period of "rectification through labor," which is simply the Chinese version of "hard labor for subversive opinions." It can even send them to the very end of the world—Sinkiang, China's Far West, feared by all as a land of deportation and exile from which no one is certain to return. Later on in the article quoted above, *Red Flag* emphasizes that just as there are some comrades who have already begun to mix with the people and have learned "to make use of artistic and literary weapons to depict the struggle for socialism," there are "several other. categories who have not yet begun to do so." Some of them are attempting to gain time, the article says, while others have adopted the "stance of resistance." *Resistance* is a word that does not often make an appearance in official documents.

Here we have reached the heart of the problem of the indoctrination and formation of Maoism's "new Chinese." When the regime sets a hundred million little Chinese on school benches and, with the very first ideograms they learn, tries to inculcate the "five loves" of socialism, the task may be enormous but it meets no resistance. When the regime takes it upon itself to bring culture to the illiterates it has inherited from the previous government, and at the same time to teach them socialism, the task is demanding but the people dealt with are already docile and even grateful. The "tough customers," so to speak, are members of the old intellectual and artist classes. Thus the task that really gives the regime trouble is the indoctrination of this upper stratum of "intellectual workers" who neither by their origins, their careers, nor their studies have been provided with minds cut out for the ready-made thinking of Communism. Since the very beginning of the regime the business of permanently molding them, or remolding them, has been an enterprise fraught with many serious obstacles for the regime. Even though it is true that the intellectuals cannot rally together to organize an opposition to the Communist Party—in a country run like People's China there is absolutely no means of doing so—nonetheless they exist as a sort of party, though scattered and sporadic, yet all the more difficult to combat for that very reason. Because they are the party of independent thought (if that isn't the same as thought), perhaps they are the only party outside the Party.

Fundamentally the Chinese Communist Party is animated by a prejudice against the intellectual as he has so far been conceived anywhere. I felt this very sharply for instance during my visit to the University of Peking when a young professor, a Party member, recited to me a list of complaints against intellectuals. "Since the beginning of history," he said, "the intellectual has lorded it over the worker, despised the worker. For thousands of years it has been the rule that the intellectual must not work with his hands, nor have any respect for working people." Without using the word once, my guide denounced what amounted to an "exploitation," in the Marxist sense, of the manual laborer by the intellectual, whose very learning has placed him in the camp of the exploiters of the people. A profound anti-intellectualism is latent in that attitude. . . .

In the same way, the regime blames its disappointments with

the intellectuals on its excessive kindnesses, on an insufficient demand of discipline. The regime believed that mere persuasion would be enough to win their gradual conversion. It counted on reforming their habits of thought without reforming their manner of life. It believed that heads could be changed without hands being changed. But what do you have after you've convinced an intellectual of the virtues of socialism? Another intellectual, the Chinese complain, a man whose mind, although colored with Marxism-Leninism, keeps right on "lording it over" the manual laborer, a man who thinks of himself as superior to the masses, thanks to his culture. That an intellectual should be an intellectual and nothing more is something that the authorities are not going to allow much longer in China. Their project is the hybridization or amalgamation of the worker and the thinker. What they are trying to realize is one of the guiding ideas of Mao Tse-tung. What the intellectual is being called upon to do is to graft upon his intellect a second self, a manual worker's self. This new self must be one that he has never had but now must develop. He must become a double man. Alongside the mind that thinks as a writer or feels as an artist a new mind must appear, that of a worker for economic production, a mind sunk among the laboring masses and their problems.

But the reverse of this process also exists and gains increasing importance as the regime realizes that it produces another variety of intellectual whose ideological point of view can be depended on. This process begins with a manual laborer and adds the intellectual's gifts. "Periods" of intellectual work either at night school or within the factory, and of course only with the aid of the Party, transform a peasant or worker into a genuine intellectual proletarian—a worker-poet or a peasant-artist, for instance. To this end every organ of the Party has been asked to harvest a new crop of artists and intellectuals among the people—working-class artists and intellectuals. A sharp lookout is kept for potential talents among manual laborers who are aided in their development and directed toward socialism and the creation of works that actually "spring from the bosom of the people."

I had the good fortune of meeting one of the proletarian artists of this "New Wave" during my stay in Hankow. Comrade Hong Yang of the Wuhan branch of the National Union of Writers had been a sailor and a worker before becoming a professional writer. An intelligent and agreeable man in his forties, he explained to me how peasants, metal workers, former rickshaw boys, etc., are all becoming the novelists, poets, painters and musicians of the New China. One of his friends who was once a dockhand is now a celebrated poet. A peasant girl whom her own father sold at the age of twelve under the old regime had just had a show of her untutored paintings in Hankow. In the Houhsien district of Shensi in the Northwest every sizable village has at least one painter, and last year more than 450 peasants produced more than 5000 paintings of socialist life.

My informant explains that in Hankow as elsewhere the state and the union of writers does its best to develop new writers from the working class and then directs their works and their thought. "But their supply cannot keep up with the demand," he tells me. The most important thing as far as they're concerned is that they share the people's life. "Even our way of life we share with the masses. We work among them. We find our subjects among them. Naturally they love us." The next thing in importance "is unceasing study of the policies and line of the Communist Party so that we will be properly armed on the ideological front," he continues. "Thus a writer will be able to do more than merely observe life correctly; he will be in a position to analyze it." In art and literature, Comrade Hong Yang continues, warming to his task once he realizes how happily I'm taking notes, "when new tendencies make an appearance or new problems come up it is absolutely necessary that we attack them in depth with group action." (In other words they work it all out with a representative of the Party.) "In such a discussion each of us has total liberty of expression for his views. We always arrive at the correct solutions. It often happens that our readers, by means of letters to the press, or literary critics point out weaknesses in a work and demand rectifications wherever socialist reality has been departed from. The author can then make such corrections. Literature must serve the three struggles of our society: the class struggle, the struggle with Nature, and the struggle for experimental science. Descriptions of our personal pleasures, any sort of egoism, etc., these have nothing to do with our socialist existence."

Hong Yang spoke to me at great length of one of his fellows who has his admiration, the worker-poet Hwang Shen-shiao who had been a dockhand on the Yangtse at Itchang when the Liberation overtook him; he had been in his thirties and almost illiterate. Realizing that life had suddenly taken a turn for the better under the new regime, he began to compose short poems, just four or five lines, which he would scribble in chalk on the decks of ships. Workers and dockhands took them up and made work songs of them to replace old songs that no longer applied. One day a reporter passed through. He discovered the new poet and his new poems, and published the poems in Peking, thereby making the poet famous. Hwang kept on working on the wharves, but the Union and the local Palace of Culture helped him to educate himself and today he is one of the editors of the *Long River Literary Review,* published in Hankow. Hong Yang recited one of his poems:

> *I am a stevedore toiling on the Long River,*
> *River stretching on one thousand miles.*
> *With my right hand I'm tugging at Shanghai,*
> *My left hand pushes back Chungking.*

Hong Yang has written both poems and novels. He quotes a few titles, among them *Song of the Ocean* and *Song of the Whole World.* He has written stories about his days as a sailor and as a factory worker. What size printings do today's authors get in China? My informant mentions a bestseller that sold three million copies, *The Red Crack,* a story of the Resistance in one of Chiang Kai-shek's camps for political prisoners. Another, *Song of Youth,* about the Student Movement of 1935, has sold two million copies. Figures like that should interest Western publishers on the lookout for foreign bestsellers to translate! But although works like these may fascinate a Chinese audience, they would prove absolutely unreadable to a Western one. At least that is what I was told in Paris at a publishing house that has followed Chinese publications for months and months without finding anything. And for my part, what little I could read in translation struck me as often incredibly naive and conformist. Take this poem by a peasant poetess:

> *The Party is the sun:*
> *Chairman Mao is our father.*
> *When I dream of Chairman Mao*
> *The sun drives out the shadows.*
> *When I dream of Chairman Mao*
> *I feel strength from feet to head.*
> *When Chairman Mao appears*
> *Red banners fill the sky.*

A sixteen-year-old daughter of poor peasants has written a poem, quoted all over China, that goes like this:

> *The Party has showered us with benefits*
> *Too numerous to mention!*
> *Like thousands of new flowers*
> *red and all perfumed.*

On her first trip to Peking she writes:

> *O Peking our beloved capital,*
> *How can I sing your merits?*
> *Thousands of quills and a sea of ink*
> *Would not suffice for all that's in my heart.*

However, her inspiration returns to her as she sings of model workers:

> *Which watermelon is the sweetest in the garden?*
> *Many of them are good enough but which is best of all?*
> *From all there are in the world which one comes first?*
> *We will choose it in Peking.*

Let us not make fun of these poems. Besides, I am certain that there are better ones than these which I happened upon in the Chinese press. And aside from all questions of esthetics or criticism there is something quite touching in the way artistic talents have awakened among the masses, the way in which a

tremendous audience has been found for them. There is proof
here of the sincerity and magnitude of the regime's efforts in
the realm of culture. At the same time that the regime has encouraged the appearance of new talents from the masses, it has
created in both villages and cities vast numbers of cultural
circles, little theater groups, choral societies and orchestras,
mobile film-projection units, exhibitions of paintings, etc. It is
true that this cultural undertaking is completely political in nature
and that the culture it brings the people is a culture without
freedom. All the same the first shock of this intellectual revolution,
it seems to me, might have far-reaching consequences for the
development of China. An extraordinary metamorphosis is taking
place quite rapidly. The Chinese masses were certainly "cultivated" by the ancient Confucian standards, but they remained
for the most part illiterate, without money or leisure. In a few
years the masses will know how to read and write, be in possession of the means and the time to educate themselves further.
With the talents which the Chinese incontestably possess, will
they remain for long at the level of the poems I've quoted? Not
very likely. . . . People with their intelligence will one day discover their old taste for seeing beyond those barriers constructed
around them. Has anyone yet seen the case of a culture which
grew without secreting freedom?

But I believe we can say that the regime has already taken
cognizance of this possibility and profoundly mistrusts it. While
bringing education and culture, or at any rate a sort of culture,
to the masses whom they have awakened, they are also making
extraordinary efforts to isolate "socialist culture" from the old
Chinese culture—which they feel to have been merely feudal
and now outworn completely—and from the cultures of the
West—which, in their eyes, purvey noxious poisons.

However, we must admit that in its handling of the ancient
culture of China the regime has made tremendous efforts to
preserve the nation's heritage. From Peking's Imperial City to
the ancient Manchu palaces in Mukden, from Shanghai to
Hankow, much more often than ten years ago I saw old monuments restored, and sometimes even over-restored (too much

paint, too bright, etc.), former palaces opened to the people as exposition halls, and scattered works of art assembled into great collections. The regime obviously believes that it is a good idea for the people to see proofs of China's perennial greatness. But past is past and the masses must be protected from an empty "passeism" only a little less than from contamination by the feudal or capitalist ideas that such works of art might suggest, ideas that pervert the socialist spirit.

In May, 1963, a nationwide campaign undertook the "criticism" of China's past. It was directed by a National Conference of Artists and Writers, which had already set up its goals at its 3rd Congress back in 1960. According to the formulation adopted by the Congress, old China had left to the new China a heritage that contains on the one hand a precious elixir and on the other hand pernicious dregs. The trick will be to keep the elixir while rejecting the dregs. Or to make use of a statement by Chairman Mao, one which the conference often made use of: "We must knock down the dead things so that the live things can make their way." Thus China's heritage can be accepted only conditionally. It must be submitted to socialist criticism.

As soon as this conference ended, the literary and artistic world began its great task of "reevaluation" according to the critical guidelines of Marxism and socialist construction. This cultural purge—that is what it is—has been pushed to different lengths in different fields. Certain works, no matter how famous they may be, deserve their place on the new index because of their complete contamination by feudal and capitalist "dregs." Others can be censored so as to offer only the pure elixir. Works that would be almost totally destroyed by such tampering will be saved as is, but only presented to the public preceded by warnings and necessary precautions—for instance, with critical introductions and notes that will furnish antidotes to whatever poisons the works contain. It may even be possible to "rewrite" certain passages of an ancient classic. This has already been done to many of the plays in the Peking Opera repertory while the more total "revolutionizing" that I⸱have already described is being waited for. Such rewriting is only an element in this much broader purge. And last of all there are certain forgotten or insufficiently appreciated works from the past which are in for a rediscovery that will place them very high in the estimation of a socialist public.

Since 1963, artistic and literary journals have been full of this "criticism of the cultural heritage." In its December, 1963 special number devoted to literature, the journal *New Construction* wrote: "This criticism is a sort of disinfectant. We must suppress what can be suppressed and revise what can be revised. When neither suppression nor revision are possible we must explain wherein the dregs lie, and give the reader an idea of the evil that they can still cause today." This same number contains a whole series of articles in which authors and critics give their ideas on the subject of "reevaluation." One author says that the most important thing is to praise those works that come from the people or deal with the people, works that reflect the class struggle in the past and attack the oppressors. One must be on guard against works that from an artistic point of view have a seductive quality but conceal a pernicious political message. Literary criticism must "arm itself with the weapon of class struggle and take its inspiration from the interests of the proletariat."

What must be rejected, another article points out, are all works which lead toward melancholy, which speak of phantoms or present us with the Taoist Immortals. Bravo, says a third, for those stories that teach courage, for the story of King Kou-chien, for instance, who slept on sticks to toughen himself so that he could conquer his kingdom! Bravo for the Emperor Yu who did all sorts of physical and mental exercise so that he could overcome the flooding river! But we must totally reject all works that complain about old age and poverty, just as we must reject all those that counsel us to seize the moment because time passes swift as a dream. Works that do nothing more than describe the countryside may very well be beautiful but ideologically they are harmful and only some must be retained.

Another critic warns us that there is a "significant proportion of bad" in the works of famous poets like Li Po, Tu Fu, Po Chu-yi, etc. The celebrated authors of the past still influence us today, and because there are now more readers than ever before their

influence is perhaps greater than in the past. A famous novel like
The Dream of the Red Chamber can only be allowed distribution
in a critical edition that would warn the reader against two
dangers, very marked in this work—too much sex and too much
ennui. But let us look into an article on poetry in this issue of
New Construction. Readers must be warned off poetry that
throws a haze over the soul, that leads to fatalism or softness.
The same subject can be treated so that it exerts an optimistic
influence, benefiting struggle, or exerts a loathsome morbidity
in favor of pessimism. Let us consider two poems on wine. The
first is by Tao Yuang-ming:

> *Gathering chrysanthemums by the eastern gate*
> *I gaze and gaze toward the mountains in the South.*

This is not good. It favors mere strolling and "detachment." Here
is another, by Su Shih:

> *After three glasses*
> *I sweep away the Warring Kingdoms!*
> *After one whole bottle*
> *All-overpowerful Chin's in flight!*

Now that poem is excellent. It expresses the poet's "refusal to
merely tolerate his enemies." Now let us examine two poems
about flowers. The first is by Han Wu:

> *Last night the rain came down.*
> *A wave of cold cut through the dawn.*
> *Are you still down there, my begonia flower?*

We must definitely reject such poems because of their negative
attitude and laziness. But we can have nothing but applause for
poems, like this one by Lu Yu, which teach an active love:

> *I am absolutely mad about that peony.*
> *Each day I fear what wind or rain might do.*
> *Tonight I will pray to the Emperor of Heaven*
> *To ask that he force the sun to protect this flower.*

There is another domain in which the heritage of the past
is open to criticism: morality. Both the Confucian morality and

the bourgeois morality deserve condemnation. Every effort must be made to stamp out any trace that remains and any partisans that they still may have in today's China. Loyalty, filial piety, uprightness, etc., as they were understood in the past were nothing but "class" virtues utilized by the oppressing classes to hold the people's souls captive. A great debate took place in 1963–64 in the pages of a newspaper called *Light,* which is published in Peking for academic and intellectual circles. In reality this "debate" was a propaganda campaign. A prominent historian, Wu Han, was under attack for having maintained that certain portions of the morality preached in the past might still be of use in today's society. Wu Han was a president of the Peking Historical Society and had been a vice-president of the municipal council. He was attacked specifically for maintaining that the proletariat could usefully practice the virtues of loyalty, honesty and industry as they were known in the feudal past, and the bourgeois notions of foresight and personal interest too. No, *Light* explained to its readers, these so-called virtues were nothing more than prejudices created by a class of oppressors and exploiters to further their own interests. Wu Han has been guilty of spreading ideas that lead to the pernicious belief that a morality that transcends class distinctions and is favorable to the ideas of coexistence and the interpenetration of classes can exist (*Light,* November 1, 1963).

Another and less celebrated academic, Professor Liu Chieh of the University of Canton, was guilty of teaching something even more scandalous! He said that Confucian philosophy contains some values worthy of application even in a socialist society. *Light's* attack on this man was even more lively than in the case of Wu Han. It is clear that this is intended as a warning to all and sundry. Liu Chieh had gone so far as to maintain that the Confucian doctrines had been just as much the doctrines of the people as of the ruling classes, that class analysis has no place in historiography, and that humanity still has need of the Confucian doctrine of attaining harmony with the mind of Heaven. That the paper (*Light,* June 18, and August 17–18, 1963) mentions counterrevolution and treason allows us to infer that stern measures were taken against the Cantonese professor.

Recently *Light* has undetrtaken another purge, this time of a more trivial nature, but one that indicates the lengths to which criticism of China's cultural heritage has been pushed. This campaign agitates in favor of socializing celebrated sites by removing any "shocking" traces of the feudal or bourgeois past. For instance, it will no longer be possible for places to bear names like Mountain of the Jade Emperor, Bridge of the Fairy, Filial Piety Street, Good Acts in Past Lives Alley, Thousand Benedictions Hotel, etc. This campaign in *Light* was launched simultaneously with an analogous action on the part of the *Shekiang Journal.* The city of Hangchow, famous for its ancient sites with their ancient Chinese atmosphere, came in for special criticism. For instance, near one of the ancient bridges stands the tomb of a courtesan famous in times past, Su-Siao-siao, who lived under the Chi dynasty. Even today young people come to this tomb to touch a particular stone because legend says that whoever does so will enjoy prolonged happiness. Such actions release a poison and the Chinese paper demands that they cease. These famous places are now visited by the laboring masses, thanks to the leisure that the new regime has brought them, and such bourgeois and feudal thinking must be destroyed. In Hangchow too, near the West Lake, there stands a monument to the Northern Expedition—shocking! The general in command was Chiang Kai-shek. And it is no less repugnant for the paper that quite near this site lie buried a score of poets, mandarins and courtesans. "These can only remind the visitor of the noisome system of government practiced by the reactionary classes. These tombs should be leveled."

In many famous places the calligraphy too often offers inscriptions expressive of decadent sentiments, or there are wall-hangings that paint a landscape of the past instead of depicting the new socialist landscape of today. What can we think of the paintings in a famous teahouse which show the four seasons with inscriptions like these: "Summer: the wind wrinkles the lake's mirror and scatters the captivating perfume of the lotus. . . ." "Winter: with my flute for sole companion I watch the snow fall upon a bridge in ruins." *Light* comments on these: "Isn't there an attempt here to inspire the visitor with the decadent and demoralizing sentiments of feudal literati who merely wasted their time, and to dampen the revolutionary spirit of workers, peasants and soldiers?" This paper also has it in for the names borne by flowers. At the recent chrysanthemum show in Hangchow socialist ears were shocked by the names still attached to certain varieties: Ancient Temple at Sunset, The Great Hero, Lover Powdering his Beauty, Long Fingers Applying Rouge, Drunken Ballerina . . . And on a trip to the city parks among the four hundred varieties of roses inspected quite a few bore names which had to go: Elisabeth, Beauty Prize, Lovely Lady of the Kingdom of Kuo, etc. Names like these are "a poison left behind them by degenerate feudal literati and decadent bourgeois men of letters." It is important that in our day the names of flowers and plants "give off the delicious perfume of a socialist epoch, and that the very names of flowers invite the visitor to consider by association the happy perspectives of a new society."

The article ends with the ardent wish that "the proper authorities put these affairs in order immediately and choose judicious means for the preservation of historical monuments and cultural objects that have any educative significance, and the elimination of all those that spread the decadent and demoralizing ideas of feudal periods or of the bourgeoisie."

Now that we have seen how China reacts today to her inherited culture, let us see what her attitude is to foreign culture. When I asked Comrade Hong Yang, the proletarian writer, about this, he explained how an "Institute for Research in Literature" had been set up by the Hankow writers' union for the systematic study and evaluation of famous foreign classics, as well as the criticism of China's heritage. Similar institutes have been set up by artists and writers all over China. Once again what the writers and artists are expected to do is carefully filter the entirety of foreign culture. Comrade Hong Yang draws my attention to the principles formulated as early as 1960 by the Third Congress of the Federation of Arts and Letters. Chou Yang, associate director of the propaganda department of the Central Committee and a specialist in the problems of the intelligentsia, detailed these principles in a long report delivered to the Congress.

Chou Yang begins by sketching out "the frightening spectacle of demoralization of the spirit and degeneration of morality" offered by capitalist countries. Their literature, according to him, contains an immense arsenal of bloody writings directly dedicated to the service of wars of imperialism, "openly preaching wars of aggression, colonial domination and racial discrimination." If we wish to see "the image of the putrefaction and decadence of the capitalist world," all we need do is visit the Film Festival in Cannes where the offerings are "an amalgam of sensuality, obscenity and criminality." For this reason the battle between capitalist and socialist countries ought to become particularly violent on "the literary and artistic fronts." Chou Yang attacks with particular vigor the so-called bourgeois humanism, of the theory of love of humanity as a whole, bourgeois pacifism, and "other absurd notions of the same stamp," preached only by capitalist and revisionist authors.

"We believe that in a class society there can be no abstract principle of humanism which transcends the epoch and the social classes concerned," he writes. "In a class society humanism as an ideology will always have a class content no matter in what epoch. . . . As for us, we are partisans of a proletarian humanism whose object is the final liberation of all mankind from every mode of exploitation." He reminds us that Engels severely criticized the love of humanity as preached by Feuerbach, who aimed to reconcile the warring classes. It all adds up, said Engels, to nothing more than intoning: "Let us all love one another." Chou Yang adds, "No Marxist, no true revolutionary, will aid in the spread of this abstract humanism or this pretended love of humanity. In this vast world of class antagonisms how can there be any 'love of humanity' that transcends class distinctions? True Marxists do not boast of some sort of 'unilateral' love, but they will aid the growth of love for the masses while they aid the growth of hate for all exploiters and oppressors. . . . That is the meaning of proletarian humanism."

Mao Tse-tung has issued an even more vigorous pronouncement on this subject: "There is absolutely no such thing as love, or hatred, without reason or cause. As for the so-called love of humanity, there has been no such all-inclusive love since humanity was divided into classes. . . . We cannot love enemies, we cannot love social evils; our aim is to destroy them." (Quoted by Hu Yao-pang in his Report to the Congress of the Youth League, *Peking Review,* July 11, 1964.)

Chou Yang also takes bourgeois pacifism to task. The Chinese people love peace and Chinese literature condemns wars of aggression, he explains, but "our writers can only have praise for just revolutions." Bourgeois writers are unable to distinguish between the two and thus paint an equally gloomy picture of both, to the point that "the reader can only envisage war from a viewpoint as sentimental as it is decidedly pessimistic." And yet the truth of the matter, Chou Yang reports, is that "although a people might very well suffer terrific losses in a war of liberation and that a great deal of blood might be shed, anyone with a developed political conscience will know that the individual ought to sacrifice himself for the liberty of his fatherland, for the historical progress of society and for the happiness of all the people."

Chou Yang announces in this report to the congress that in literary and artistic circles and in the departments of literature and the arts of various institutes and universities all over China a program has begun "which will critically study and reevaluate the principal European masterworks of the 18th and 19th centuries." As in the case of China's own heritage, the literary and artistic heritage of Europe can only be accepted after the most severe critical examination. The arts of the 18th and 19th centuries in particular "represent the reaction," to an important extent. Thus for the most part our reason for studying it remains a negative one—"the discovery of what not to do." The results of this tremendous task of reevaluation began to appear in large selections covering page after page of newspapers and magazines, in 1963, the year in which anti-Russian and anti-revisionist propaganda intensified. What this reevaluation has amounted to in the end is a *devaluation* and a call to rally against Western culture. This campaign behaves no less mercilessly with the classics of the past than against those of our day: in fact, on the contrary, it takes no pains to spare reputations that have been considered safe universally. Judge for yourself on the basis of these examples culled from recent publications.

Shakespeare: "If this old man could return to earth he would be ashamed of what he has written. . . . Today is the epoch of class struggle. . . . If old Shakespeare could only learn that, he would think, 'Although my works do contain a few patches of reality, compared with the accomplishments of the Chinese people it is far away as the earth is from heaven. . . .' To suppose that Shakespeare is some sort of god who cannot be surpassed is to lose direction and proceed contrary to the spirit of this epoch and our people who are in the act, at this very moment, of refurbishing the objective and subjective worlds." (*Liberation,* a Shanghai paper, January 5, 1964.)

Balzac: These false foreign devils are hard to kill. . . . Anyone who kneels before the shrine of Balzac or Shakespeare or other artists and writers is guilty of favoring moribund capitalism." (Same paper, January 21, 1964.)

Beethoven: "In his last years the old warrior, the brave fighter who had always fought to win, was transformed into a mouther of prayers for peace. No, the hopes of a Beethoven cannot possibly become today's hopes! The music of a Beethoven cannot possibly be today's music." (*People's Music,* Number 4, 1964.)

Debussy and occidental music: "One of the fundamental obstacles, for our musicians and students, in coming to a solution of the problems of our own music, is their idea that anything that comes from the West is superior and that anything native is inferior. The analysis and discussion of problems relative to Debussy will make a good point of departure. Research and critical analysis devoted to the musicians of the 18th and 19th centuries can help us to destroy and liquidate the cult of all things foreign and that blind adoration extant to the present day in the minds of certain people. The music of Debussy is by no means a correct national and popular music. Young people who are under his influence are actually under the influence of bourgeois ideas and ideals. They follow the artistic line of the decadent occident. They lose their desire and intention of serving the working class, peasants and soldiers. (*Liberation,* August 19, 1963.)

Every aspect of occidental culture may not be condemned with such sweeping severity and there are some judgments that often seem more reasonable than those quoted. Chou Yang's report does not ask us to condemn *en bloc* but to proceed by the scientific analysis of individual works. To Goethe, Tolstoy, and the good fruits of critical realism and of positive romanticism he gives his approval. But even these, he goes on to say, proceed from a bourgeois point of view and describe individualist heroes who offer models that go against the current of collectivism and that cannot fail to develop a deplorable individualism among the young. Works, authors, and famous heroes fall equally under the purifying fire of socialist criticism, from Stendhal to Romain Rolland, both Julien Sorel and Jean Christophe; from Beethoven to Debussy by way of Bizet and Verdi (*Carmen* is condemned, *Rigoletto* loathsome—for the famous *la donna è mobile* more than anything else, which one paper describes as "full of ideological poison, of decadence, of degeneracy, of a licentious spirit, of shamelessness, of insults to womanhood.") In fact music comes in for special criticism, as though China's rulers wished to close a possible escape route, one last exit open to those Chinese who would like to avoid indoctrination and enjoy a few hours far from the difficulties of reality. A real dislike of foreigners appears from time to time in these articles, and strengthens the ideological distrust by rejecting or deriding occidental culture—how deep are the scars left on the Chinese spirit by a century of Western brutality and occidental exactions! A spokesman for the Ministry of Education in Peking went on at great length to remind me that in China under the previous regime there had been schools and universities staffed by foreign professors and for the most part founded and financed by Western countries, but he only brought the subject up in order to condemn them harshly as "bases for cultural aggression against China by the imperialists."

No, as far as the leadership of China is concerned, no "eternal China" exists to furnish the Chinese with deathless values. Conversely, there can be no universal occidental values capable of reconciling China, on some higher plane, with the imperialist capitalistic world that surrounds her. The willful intolerance natural to socialism counsels China to cut herself off from much of her own past, to reject audaciously and with determination a great portion of ancient China. The same intolerance counsels the rejection of the majority of the cultural goods of the West. Any "return to China"—and this has become clearer than ever—

means a return to a China that never before existed and has no intention now of acknowledging anything other than innovations of its own devising. Chou Yang makes this clear in a striking way: "We should have new ideas of our own, new techniques of our own, new artistic methods of our own, and new avenues for creation." And he ends on a note of ambitious hope: "New geniuses will make themselves known among us. Their creations will surpass anything realized by the artists of the past."

In the meantime, China has never before seemed so cut off from the outside world by walls of her own making, nor so completely introverted. This defense against anything getting in from outside is particularly effective against the foreign press and information services. A trip to China amounts to saying good-bye to the world we know. Only an occasional, oddly chosen, story gets through the bamboo curtain; passed through the filters of censorship and propaganda, it issues colored by politics. The sort of calumny, misunderstanding and criticism that China suffers in a portion of the occidental press cannot equal what the West suffers in the Chinese press. Especially in news about the United States information bows to the political necessity of caricature and hatred. A foreigner residing in Peking is as totally cut off from his homeland as if he were living on another planet. He will look for occidental papers in vain. A Frenchman will not find his *Figaro*. An Englishman will have to go without his *Times*.

A few years ago a Frenchman in Peking could still keep up with life in the world outside by reading the Communist *l'Humanité*, or for literature their weekly *Les Lettres Françaises*. But *l'Humanité* has disappeared along with *Pravda, Isvestia, Unità* and the *Daily Worker*. They no longer turn· up in hotel lobbies and public places. There is only one bookstore in the whole of Peking which stocks them and that's where you'll have to go for them. The newspapers that one still sees in Peking form a curious collection indeed: Albania's *Zerit Populit,* the Hanoi *Nhan Dan, Akahata* from Tokyo, a few Cuban and Indonesian reviews, and little sheets published by the pro-Chinese splinters of various Western Communist parties.

The window that formerly opened on the world by way of the Soviet block has been banged shut. For the Chinese, except for

items about Afro-Asian and underdeveloped countries—from
which they can expect very little cultural return—there is almost nothing to read but local news. They get no outside air to
breathe. Do their rulers plan to open any windows in the near
future? Let us hope so! But, at the moment, the new contacts
that China has made on the level of foreign affairs appears to
require that the Chinese people undergo an interior discipline,
one which is becoming all the more rigorous, to protect them
against the dangerous miasma of Western culture.

CHAPTER THIRTEEN

THE NEW GENERATION AND CHINA AFTER MAO

MORE THAN 3500 REPRESENTATIVES OF CHINA'S YOUTH CONVERGED on the capital from the four corners of the country for a great congress, *another* congress. They held their meetings in the very heart of the city, in the mammoth Great Hall of the People. Their deliberations stretched over three long weeks. Morning and evening, lines of buses provided them with transportation. The first day, Mao Tse-tung himself put in an appearance to speak to them. The highest dignitaries of the regime also enlightened them. And unlikely as this may seem, not one of us, not a single Western reporter or special correspondent got wind of this—that's how well secrets are kept in Peking! We had to wait a whole week after the end of the meetings for an explosion of publicity (whole pages on the decisions approved by this congress appeared in *People's Daily*, *Red Flag* and other organs of the press; there were programs on Radio Peking; releases from the New China Agency, etc.) that told the whole world—and our small world of foreigners in China's capital—that this congress had taken place. And yet it was a congress of the greatest importance, the congress of the Communist Youth League of China. And the younger generation had been told that its time had come, that their elders were on the point of delegating grave responsibilities and tasks in the system.

The "changing of the guard," and the rise of the younger generation are questions that have preoccupied the regime for some time and that become more serious as the regime ages. First question: Who has been slated for the top posts in the government? They should already be visible, ready at a moment's notice to take over the controls near the top of the pyramid of power. Second question: What sort of young people make up the base of that pyramid? It will make a tremendous difference if instead of being militant they are bored, if instead of favoring a hard line they are revisionists.

That the problem of "changing the guard" could apply to the very summit of power in China no one in Peking would so much as suggest. It simply is not mentioned. There is no change of personnel, or almost none. A few minor changes were announced in December, 1964, but these were only shifts that suggest no real change in the overall picture. And there is still nothing like an unambiguous answer to the first of our questions. Yet during my stay in the capital I felt certain that there were real signs of change. New phrases that kept making an appearance point to the advent of new times. We hear of *cheh pan-jen,* "people who take their tour of duty" (which means simply "the new shift which is taking over"). Propaganda is now full of a phrase that everyone repeats: "heirs of the revolution." The heirs of the revolution are all those who without having actually fought the revolution themselves have reached the age when its responsibilities become theirs. It is true that these words refer to a change of the guard which will take place on the lower levels, but it is easy to see that it also implicitly applies to that change no one ever mentions—the change that must eventually affect the summit of power.

Although no one ever speaks of it, that does not make it seem any the less an obvious necessity. The dictatorship of the proletariat resides in the Political Bureau of the Central Committee of the Chinese Communist Party. In the beginning this Bureau numbered twenty-six members, but at the moment it has fallen to nineteen by death, sickness, and—in spite of the unusual stability of the political team that runs China—because a few members have been kicked upstairs. . . . This Bureau itself is controlled by a smaller informal group that forms the nucleus of an all-powerful collective power and is made up of Mao and his closest comrades. This is the Permanent Committee of the Political Bureau. Now of the seven men who originally belonged to this group there are only five active members left: Mao Tse-tung, who as chairman of the Chinese Communist Party is in reality the sole leader; Liu Shao-chi, president of the People's Republic; Chou En-lai, premier; Chu Teh, who presides over the permanent committee of the parliament; and Teng Hsia-ping, first secretary of the Party. Two others are inactive: Lin Piao, marshal and commander of the army, absent on sick leave very often (said to have contracted TB), and Chen Yun, former economic chief who seems to have fallen into disfavor, or something close to it, in 1958—some say for having opposed The Great Leap Forward.

In 1964 the average age of the members of this Permanent Committee was 65. In a country that has given such importance to youth the increasing age of the highest echelon appears more and more of an anomaly. It is this absence of replacements at the top of the pyramid that makes the age difference between the governing body and the body of the Party so striking. There are hardly twenty members of the Central Committee who were born after 1907. Of the total of 187 members (permanent and suppletory) 81 had already reached their sixieth birthday by 1964, or were close to it. Two of the most important members, Tung Pi-wu, vice-president of the Republic, born in 1886, and Chu Teh, "father" of the army, born in 1877, are truly "grand old men." It would take a congress of the Party as a whole to fill the empty positions and undertake the necessary rejuvenation. For seven years now no congress has been called; the last, the eighth, ended in 1958. The hesitation to call the ninth congress becomes all the more striking when we realize that the task that awaits it has swollen with the passage of time. Not only must personnel be replaced and a higher proportion of young people injected, but the programs of the Party too must be brought up to date. On a certain number of subjects the Party has not even replaced documents and texts that still speak of close collaboration with the Soviet Union, or even of Soviet leadership of world Communism, or imply that The Great Leap Forward has remained unchanged since 1958.

Will we have to wait for this *aggiornamento* until Chairman Mao is no longer with us? Such a supposition is probably too pessimistic, and besides the Party would not want to risk letting the situation deteriorate that long, since Mao, born in 1893, may have quite a few more active years left. Observers in Peking are more often of the opinion that all that the Party is waiting for is the announcement of the third Five Year Plan (scheduled for 1966) and perhaps for a day when the quarrel with Russia will have reached dimensions that no longer admit of any kind of whitewashing and promise to remain lasting. But even so, Chairman Mao, from recent photos, does not appear to be in good health. He looks fatigued, aged and even thin. European visitors who have been allowed to see him recently describe him as in full possession of his faculties, but from time to time in need of an aide to help him get up or keep him from stumbling. Rumors flourish. Does the old man have rheumatism? Is it his heart? Has he had trouble with his eyes? The consensus certainly is that "something is the matter." After seventy-one years of adventures and tiring duties may not the old conqueror's days be numbered?

Thus the hypotheses, the speculations—foreign observers in Peking have to fill their spare time somehow. . . . But why the hypotheses, why keep our eyes peeled for the slightest indications, the wrinkles, the signs of fatigue, anything that could let us in on the secrets of the condition of China's chief of state when, as I believe, if we know how to judge what is under our noses we have incontrovertible proof of the fact that the "end of a reign is in sight?" The proof is simply the nationwide campaign that deifies Mao and seeks to make his model life a legend during his own lifetime in order to spread and glorify his ideas. What better explanation can be given for this universal organized veneration, this hymn of seven hundred million human beings to the founder of their state, this whole nation of students reciting his lessons, than that everyone is aware of his imminent departure and feels a profound desire to set him up while still alive in his niche in China's Hall of Fame. Just as in the Nō theater of Japan the star remains before the public even after the end of the play, only disappearing slowly along a catwalk that leads into the wings, Mao Tse-tung has already begun his exit. In the view of the whole people and aware of their applause, he enters with open eyes into History.

But for this reason it is absolutely mistaken to suppose, as people often do in the West, that Mao's end will usher in a time of uncertainty, wavering, and possible upheavals. History of course is mainly the history of surprises, and we should avoid making prophecies; yet all the same it seems to me that the opposite is the case. The energies of the regime have been concentrated for some time now on precisely this possibility of maintaining Maoism after Mao goes, and every effort is being made to assure that there will be no uncertainty, no reversals. We can already be sure that post-Mao China as the regime plans it will not differ in any striking way from present-day China because post-Mao China is also planned by Mao! This is the meaning of the nationwide campaign for the study of his thought. The master has finished his great life work. While he is still present the disciples recite their lessons so that they will know them all the better when he has departed. And who will be their leaders after he has gone? What difference can that make as long as we are certain that whoever they are they will be faithful continuators? The decisions that they will take cannot of course be predicted, but we can predict their sense, and that they will be taken in the name of Mao. Changes, if there should be any, will only be made while claiming them as continuations of his policies. No "de-Maoization" will occur in China, not if her present leadership has its way. Once again, Russia has supplied them with a model of what not to do. They have decided not to follow in the footsteps of de-Stalinization, but instead to maintain the general line and the cohesion of the governing clique even after Mao is no more—his pictures will not be taken down, nor his statues unbolted from their pedestals. Replacements will reach the summit, but not in a spirit of repudiation.

It is only with all this in mind that we can understand the changing of the guard that has already begun quite frankly in favor of the young among the lower echelons. This is nothing more nor less than a preparation for the days to follow Mao's departure. Precisely in order to preserve the continuity of the system by establishing these many links between an epoch that is ending and the new era that must soon begin, Mao Tse-tung while yet alive and still giving the orders has already opened the doors to a new generation that has been a long time waiting for these offices. "To train proletarian revolutionary men to take over the job is a task of grave strategic importance proposed to the whole Party by comrade Mao Tse-tung. The consolidation and development of the revolution, the fate of the Party and of the state, depend on whether this is done well," wrote *Red Flag* on July 31, 1964, at the end of the congress of the League. "The consolidation and development of the revolution, the fate of the Party and of the state depend on our being certain that this job will be done properly."

Who are the younger generation? Of course they are young Chinese from eighteen to thirty years of age, but what sort of young Chinese are they? This generation differs totally from the one that is now in power; but what makes that difference? This generation did not fight the Chinese Revolution; it was an already "revolutionized" China that their elders gave them. Its benefits were not fought for over the decades but dealt out to them in the cradle and at school. And all the same the regime decided to make the theme of this congress of the League the increased importance of the younger generation just now reaching adulthood—"the heirs of the revolution."

Significantly it was Teng Hsiao-ping, head of the Party (he is secretary-general of the Central Committee) who came to announce the big news to the congress. First of all a great number of posts in the League itself were thrown open to younger people. The new governing body of the congress contains 217 new members out of 252—only 35 of the former members have been retained. The same sort of renewal took place on the provincial and local level after the closing of the congress, and the League itself has undertaken a recruiting program to increase its forces, especially by enlarging the number of its young women members.

The Party itself received a veritable transfusion by giving membership to the best elements who had reached the maximum age for membership in the League. And last of all a renewal of party officials began in the second half of 1964 with elections to the provincial and local assemblies and to the National Assembly as well. The new National Assembly has twice as many members as the last one and has greatly decreased the average age of its members. And the administrative positions will progressively be filled by younger people. *Red Flag* revealed that before this new program began, the average age of minor officials, just like that of Party members, was forty years of age. This explains why "a transfusion of new blood" was necessary, *Red Flag* continued.

But there was one surprise. At the same time that the leadership announced this good news about the younger generation's new responsibilities, all their speeches, reports and propaganda began showering this younger generation with warnings and reservations—which can only lead to one unexpected conclusion: the younger generation does not have the complete confidence of the regime and therefore the regime feels it necessary to stiffen the discipline demanded of them. It was especially to say this that the head of the League, no young man himself, Hu Yaopang (the leader of the younger generation was born in 1915 and is fifty), came before them. "It is wrong and dangerous," he said, "to think that youth, born in the new society and brought up under the red flag, is 'born red' and can automatically be heir of the revolutionary cause. . . ." The younger generation still bears the marks of various ideologies left over from previous states of society. He also explained that since they have only known the present stability of society, they cannot comprehend the tempest that preceded it and thus run a risk of "lapsing into a false sense of peace and tranquility and looking for a life of ease and security. Because they have not been through the severe test of revolutionary struggle, they lack a thorough understanding of the complex and exacting demands of revolution. Thus it is that, under the corrupt influence of bourgeois ideology, a certain number of new bourgeois elements and revisionists will inevitably crop up among the young people." (*For the Revolutionization of our Youth,* Report by Hu Yao Pang, First Secretary of the Central Committee of the Chinese Communist Youth League at its ninth Congress, *Peking Review,* July 10, 1964.)

So Revisionism is the real enemy. . . . And this is an enemy particularly dangerous in its pursuit of the young. It is the same in every socialist country, explains the First Secretary; the country's youth is at stake in a struggle between "the Marxist-Leninist line" that seeks to transform them into true proletarian revolutionaries, and another group that follows "the revisionist line." If allowed their freedom, the latter group would corrupt the revolutionary spirit of the younger generation with the poisonous theses of class reconciliation dreamed up only to ease a return to bourgeois capitalism.

We used to believe in the West that Revisionism for the Chinese meant an external enemy only, an evil outside their gates, "the Russian disease." But if there was one thing I learned on my trip through China it was this: the campaigns against Revisionism are just as much directed against internal foes. The regime isn't merely attempting to nullify any influence that Russian Revisionism may still have in China, nor is it attempting merely to prevent the formation of a Russian "fifth column"— de-Russification, as we have already seen, should be able to prevent that. No, they are concerned with preventing something much more disturbing to them than either of those possibilities: the spontaneous growth on Chinese soil of a new Revisionism, a Chinese Revisionism. The perils of Revisionism have taken on a new dimension. . . . No longer is Revisionism the concern only of the Foreign Office; now the Department of the Interior too is concerned. Anti-Revisionism has become a war on two fronts. It calls for a continuing offensive against Khrushchev but also for an offensive on the very soil of China against other Chinese. The leadership in Peking has been sincerely shocked

(as I said in the chapter on de-Russification) by the evolution
of the situation in the Soviet Union since the death of Stalin;
in their opinion what is happening cannot fail, unless reversed,
to return a capitalist regime to power in the Soviet Union. They
do not intend to allow anything of that kind to happen in China;
but to prevent such a degeneration it is the younger generation
that must be most carefully educated.

This explains why a take-over by the rising generation must
be combined, as the congress was told, with a parallel take-over
of the minds of that very generation by political control. In other
words a terrific "turn of the screw" for the younger generation
began in the summer of 1964, and it was to announce this that
Hu Yao-pang went before the congress. The League will be in-
strumental in this. First of all, the League must toughen discipline in its own ranks, and to that end the executive committee
has been enlarged and its constitution reinforced. Then the
range of the League's activities must be increased. Until now
the League really has only been concerned with activists, that
is to say only with those elements with the most ambition and
zeal. From now on the League is expected to organize the
greatest possible number of young people and take special pains
with those who might otherwise avoid them. Everybody must
become involved in a new and intensified campaign for socialist
education (in other words, ideological indoctrination) which
will lean strongly on the energetic practice of class struggle.
Young workers and young peasants from the poorer classes, according to the report, will be the nucleus around which the
others will be expected to rally. Youth must learn to distinguish
friend from foe, and particularly must become adept at iden-
tifying the hidden enemies of socialism. The children of former
bourgeois parents, of rich peasants, and of other exploiters of
the people will become the objects of special attention intended
to "turn them against the classes in which they were born." In
the future the League will spend more time systematically and
energetically organizing the leisure of the young people and also
scheduling more "political work." Thus they will read more revolutionary books and pamphlets, stage revolutionary plays, sing
the right songs, enjoy healthy fun . . .

These young workers and peasants, at work in factory or on the commune, must take the lead in a movement for the glorification of production and ideological development. "Educated youth" (the increasing numbers of young people who have graduated from secondary school at 18) must be repeatedly reminded, and with greater energy, that only a small minority can count on entering the university or even going into industry or commerce or government. The vast majority must be prepared not only to end their educations at 18, but to accept the directives of the regime and head for the countryside to work on a commune. Distaste for manual labor is a revisionist attitude, Hu Yao-pang emphasizes in his report. It is the source of all evils —along with a taste for leisure. Love of work and the desire to live in the middle of the laboring masses must combine with contempt for personal interest and a total devotion to the public good. And last but not least the youth of the country must realize that the final victory can only be had at a price. The price is temporary sacrifice on the part of a minority to assure the happiness of future millions. . . .

This is the meaning of the *revolutionization,* to use Hu Yao-pang's very title, which is absolutely necessary if the young are to take over and rise to posts of the first importance. The posts will only go to the most superior and the renovation of cadres can only be achieved by the most careful selection. According to the published documents it is Mao Tse-tung himself who has set up the specifications demanded of young people who wish to become cadres in the regime. There are five specifications:

(1) That he be a genuine Marxist-Leninist filled with the thought of Mao Tse-tung.

(2) That he serve the interests of the Chinese people and of the world, not his own personal interest or merely nationalistic ends.

(3) That he be capable of leading the masses and joining with them, and also of becoming reconciled with those who were previously in disagreement or active opposition but who have recognized their errors and recanted.

(4) That he know how to practice democratic centralism without any of the marks of dictatorship.

(5) That he be modest and admit his errors.

When *Red Flag* and the *People's Daily* reproduced these orders from Chairman Mao they emphasized that it is necessary before appointing a young man to a post that he have been thoroughly tried, well known to the people concerned, and chosen from candidates who have all received their formation by a long process of "struggle for the masses." And the text that appeared July 14, 1964, in these two publications added: "This series of principles emitted by comrade Mao Tse-tung represents a creative development of Marxism-Leninism. Herein he adds to his theoretical arsenal important weapons that should be decisive in preventing any restoration of capitalism."

When so many precautions are taken and so much discipline thought necessary against any development of Revisionism among Chinese youth, are we to consider these measures simply preventive, and the deviation they aim at merely hypothetical, a possibility; or are we to suppose that the regime has begun to have difficulties with the young? Since the very beginning of this work I have pointed out repeatedly that one thing my trip to China convinced me of unshakably is that in today's China any organized opposition to the regime would be unthinkable, and that any opposition as such has been eliminated. But it would be extremely risky for a journalist who has only passed through China to pretend to know what was going on inside the minds of the Chinese people, and I can only offer a few personal observations, the limited nature of which I am aware of.

(1) I was not able to converse with many young people, but those whom I did meet never showed anything but the most unconditional faith in Communism. It struck me as being without reservations and totally sincere. I recall in particular my conversations with the two young cadres who served as my guides in Manchuria. Even when I had gotten them on to the subject of The Great Leap Forward and the people's communes they were unwilling to offer any criticism of the period beginning in 1958: the policies of the Party for industry and agriculture had been absolutely correct from the beginning.

(2) All the young people I was able to observe living their

everyday lives seemed to me equally right-thinking, and satisfied with their lots; in other words, an unconditional surrender to the Party's demands for obedience and applause.

(3) The few qualified foreign observers with whom I was able to speak all described the youth of the country as for the most part completely won over by the regime, and yet less conformist than it seemed to me judging from appearances. Behind that unconditional obedience lurks a variety of opinions and even a feeling of class distinctions!

(4) These same observers emphasize something that everyone must be aware of—the Communists admit its existence in their declarations and proclamations—and that is that good relations between the regime and the young do not exclude the possibility of difficult problems and real subjects of discontent.

One of these problems, one that is spoken of most often, is the lack of enthusiasm for agricultural labor felt by so many young people once they have had a taste of city life or the rudiments of an education. Since the readjustment of the economy gave priority to agriculture, tens of thousands of young men and women have left school for the countryside. Official propaganda has repeatedly had to take cognizance of the fact that it is only "over their dead bodies" that a great number of young people will allow themselves to be "buried in the country." Work in the city, labor in factories, a bureaucratic post, a place in officialdom, the intellectual's prestige, that's what they want. . . . Unless they come from a peasant cottage they will consider this return to the land just as their family does, as a catastrophe.

The loathing for agricultural work is even greater among young intellectuals, that is, among those young people whom the regime, even after university training, persuades to "voluntarily" return to the soil. The magazine of the League, *Chinese Youth*, has not ceased since 1963 to combat these prejudices, this regrettable resistance. Since the congress held in July, 1964 furnished the League with new orders, all recalcitrants have been dealt with more harshly. They now run the risk of being accused of a distaste for manual labor—punishable manifestation of Revisionism. It can lead to much worse than being sent to a commune. It can lead to Sinkiang, or some far off camp, and under a sentence of "rectification by work."

Another delicate problem concerns "social labels" applied to young people who come from families of the former bourgeoisie or other exploiting classes. The labels remain. The young complain often enough, in the papers for instance, of the difficulties and the distrust these labels cause them even after they have been transformed into loyal socialists. The regime however has not wanted to erase these old signs of social origin, and indeed it appears that thanks to the present hardening of the line the problem may only become more acute.

Some young people, particularly at the university level, complain about the way their educations are constantly being interfered with by politics. Even since the beginning of the "readjustment," which corrected the worst excesses of the Great Leap in this quarter, their studies are too often interrupted by extracurricular activities, manual labor, militia duty, propaganda campaigns, and parades and political rallies to which they must run and applaud some visiting dignitary or denounce the most recent crime of the imperialists. In the factories and communes too there are a certain number of young workers and peasants who wish the Party would just let them work in peace. They feel that someone is always on their backs with political lessons. They would like it better if they were not continually being asked to imitate some hero or become heroes themselves.

And last of all, a series of articles recently published in the press points to something that has thoroughly scandalized authorities and all right-thinking readers, the appearance among Chinese youth of such decadent phenomena as beatniks and "hooligans." Even the Beatle haircut has attempted an invasion of the Mainland in places as far apart as Shanghai, Tientsin and Sian! And in Shanghai too, that most dangerous of cities, girls suddenly sported toreador pants and the boys were out in tight trousers of the worst capitalist cut or wearing pointed shoes! Last summer the papers were denouncing a vogue for photos of movie stars and phonograph records of music that sounded like it came from Hong Kong. But "fortunately" there has been a socialist reaction to such excesses. The Shanghai tailoring union, warned by its more wide-awake members, decided to refuse the requests of clients who asked for anything extravagant. Tientsin hairdressers and barbers decided to force a uniformly short haircut on their clienteles, something more in keeping with socialist youth. The waiters in a Shanghai restaurant called to order some customers who had the nerve to ask for two bottles of rice wine per person.

I am tempted to guess (although I am aware that I can hardly have been said to have examined the subject from the inside) that the conflict between youth and the regime never exceeds such small differences as those I have just reported. I believe that only a minority, a very small minority, is involved. I cannot credit the existence of any large-scale disagreement between these two parties. In fact I believe the opposite: after fifteen years of Communism there are between two and three hundred million young people ready as never before under any totalitarian regime to act the parts of docile, right-thinking applauders of their chiefs. The vast majority of young people are as ready as faithful sheep to follow their Party.

But that may very well be the trouble as far as the regime is concerned: what has been happening indicates a fear on the part of the leaders that the majority of Chinese citizens, and particularly those who were already grown up when the Party came to power, had never learned anything but the obedience of sheep and never accepted the active faith with which Communism attempts to inoculate them. There is also the deeper fear that the younger generation might be similarly lacking in enthusiasm. Taking orders, applauding the chiefs, repeating lessons and slogans, for thousands of Chinese this might not be more than a strategem, a useful manner of having a little peace that in no way indicates any interior commitment to the Party. Mightn't it really be a way of escaping from the system rather than a way of giving oneself to it? There is evidence, unavoidable evidence, no matter how disappointing and even dangerous for the regime, that millions of Chinese only accept Communism inasmuch as it supplies tangible material benefits (and another thing, chauvinistic satisfaction thanks to the prestige the new regime has won for the country). However, these same millions may not have been able to generate any enthusiasm, but remain indifferent or sceptical of the ideology that they are constantly plied with. Even though this state of affairs admits of no cure when those concerned are adult or aged, this sickness must not be allowed to contaminate the young.

It would also seem that the Communist leadership has become nervous about the survival of Chinese types from the old days, those of the capitalist past who may outlast Communism, and that they have begun to wonder how much longer it will take for the "new man" or the "new Chinese" whom they have been forging over the years to have completely replaced the old models. And in reality nothing could be further from Communism than the old-fashioned Chinese, at least in the character traits obvious to the foreign observer. Lovers of profit, motivated by a real mercantile spirit, incredibly gifted in financial matters as soon as they have any capital to work with, open-minded even in slavery and poverty, as sceptical of the powers of this world as of the powers of the next, gourmets and artistic. In addition, there is that one talent that they still seem to have and that would be even more dangerous if they were forced to conceal it: they are among the world's greatest actors! And how many of these traits have been removed? And the ones that have been —mightn't they reappear? Luckily for the Communists they have the coolness to withhold a too optimistic answer. They are proceeding carefully. . . . In fact they are doing more than just that: they are very outspoken about the possibility of a backward step toward the old China and the old Chinese of the capitalist era, and this is therefore a possibility that is real and dangerous.

The possibility of this restoration of capitalism, I hear in Peking, is a new truth that Chairman Mao Tse-tung has recently discovered and published. It is in fact the most recent of his contributions to the development of Marxism-Leninism. Until that moment of truth Marxist orthodoxy viewed history as humanity's ineluctable march toward Communism, even though there might be defeats like the Paris Commune of 1871 or accidents like the Hungarian Revolt of 1956. The new thesis that Chairman Mao defends denies that this trend is irreversible. If a socialist economy is badly managed we may expect society to degenerate in the direction of captalism, by way of Revisionism. This is a greater peril for Communism than armed counterrevolution because it proceeds by "peaceful evolution" that gradually replaces the revolution and diverts the dictatorship of the proletariat into Revisionism, to produce a degeneration of the leading cadres of the Party and state. This has already happened in Yugoslavia. It is happening right now all over again in the Soviet Union.

There is every indication that Chairman Mao communicated this new thesis to the Party during the course of the Tenth Plenary Session of the Central Committee in September, 1962; thus it came after the crisis of The Great Leap Forward had been successfully resolved in spite of the perfidy of the Russians. His thesis on capitalist restoration was kept secret for some time. In his report to the League at the recent congress in Peking its chief revealed that at that epoch Chairman Mao developed "a historical directive." *People's Daily* and *Red Flag* gave more details in reporting this speech: this historical directive consisted of "an aggregate of theories and policies." Chairman Mao had reached his formulations "after having added up all his practical experience of the dictatorship of the proletariat in China, and the fruits of his study of the positive and negative experiences of other countries, in particular the Soviet Union, in the light of the fundamental principles of Marxism-Leninism."

The report on the revision of the League's constitution confirms from another angle the existence of a "series of declarations and instructions from the chairman." Among these, there is reason to believe that we will find a "plan for youth" which will cover the entire evolution from socialism to Communism. Chairman Mao analyzes the nature and the role of youth. He defines the manner in which youth must be won for socialism. He gives instructions for assuring its proper formation and particularly ways of maintaining its revolutionary character and its sense of class from generation to generation.

It is easy to imagine that in view of the predicted economic upsurge after the great crisis of the black years, Mao Tse-tung on the eve of his seventieth birthday, having published no

major political encyclical for some time, decided to publish a
series of documents about his experiences since coming to power,
particularly drawing on his experience of the crisis of the black
years and of Russian perfidy. Haven't we here almost a "political
testament of Mao Tse-tung"? And isn't this just one more sign
of the fact that arrangements have been made for the day
when Hu Yao-pang's "beloved master" will have made his last
farewell? However that may be, this historic directive remained
a secret for a year and half before even its existence was revealed. But perhaps it is to be found in substance in two extraordinary doctrinal texts published during the summer of 1964:
Hu Yao-pang's report and an almost endless editorial carried
by *Red Flag* and *People's Daily*, on July 14, 1964, "On Khrushchev's Phoney Communism and its Historical Lessons for the
World." (Comment in *Peking Review*, July 17, 1964, on the open
letter of the Central of the C. P. S. U. by the Editorial Departments of *Renmin Ribao* and *Hongoi*.)

Both these documents seem to be based on the same unpub-
lished text by Mao Tse-tung. They actually start off with a
rather lengthy passage by the master himself in which he warns
that despite the tremendous rally of the Chinese people to
socialism the enemies of the revolution continue their attacks;
this stubborn minority, because of the possibility of a restoration
of capitalism, remains a danger for the regime. The exploiting
classes are not yet resigned to their defeat. They are seeking
revenge and remain "very powerful even yet." Masked by a
pretended commitment to socialism, in every realm they continue
their sapper's work against socialism: they are working to overthrow the dictatorship of the proletariat; to infiltrate the government, the administration and the Party; to make raids on the
socialist economy in order to foster the forces of capitalism; and
to poison the country's cultural life with bourgeois ideology. In
agriculture, as long as there remains any hint of private enterprise "spontaneous capitalist tendencies" will appear among the
peasants—and once again "rich peasants" have begun to appear.
This same tendency toward capitalism exists among the small
producers in the towns. The last few bourgeois practices still
allowed and the bad habits inherited from the former state of

society exert their dreadful influences. . . . All these various factors (and here I quote "Khrushchev's Phoney Communism") "constantly breed political degenerates in the ranks of the working class, the Party, and government organizations; new bourgeois elements and embezzlers and grafters in state enterprises owned by the whole people; and new bourgeois intellectuals in the cultural and educational institutions and intellectual circles. These new bourgeois elements and these political degenerates attack socialism in collusion with the old bourgeois elements and elements of other exploiting classes that have been overthrown but not eradicated. The political degenerates entrenched in the leading organs are particularly dangerous, for they support and shield the bourgeois elements in organs at lower levels. . . . The old and new bourgeois elements, the old and new rich peasants and the degenerate elements of all sorts constitute the social basis of Revisionism, and they use every possible means to find agents within the Communist Party."

This text is both interesting and important. It demonstrates that no matter how "unanimous" the public facade of Chinese Communism may appear, there may still be hidden power struggles behind it, and that in spite of the great rally to the regime there is still some sort of countermovement. It demonstrates moreover that the regime is aware of all this, to the point that it posits the existence, for the entire development of socialism, of a permanent and organic reactionary conspiracy to restore capitalism! Against such a peril the regime has set up a defense which is basic to the Communist system. Mao Tse-tung doesn't seem to have any illusions about the inevitability of an opposition, but he has done all he can to assure the opposition of a vulnerable form. First of all he has forbidden any right of assembly outside the Party—the opposition and other malcontents might profit from it and this refusal to allow their assembly and hence their unification seems fundamental. No *organized* opposition, whether open or hidden, nor under any imaginable mask, will be allowed to come into being. Even if the opposition exceeded the million mark, that would make very little difference provided that they remained isolated and denied the chance of concerted action. Members of the opposition are thought of as weeds that must be pulled up as they appear—this too will lead to their eventual disappearance. The whole of society is organized for this, as I have already pointed out. Each Chinese must keep an eye on the rest. It's a duty. They are under an obligation to inform on each other by reporting to the authorities any word or action or thought that seems incorrect. The Party has a right to know as intimately as possible the mind and heart of each citizen. Rooting out the weeds only becomes truly violent when the weeds are "enemies of the people": against them rises the total power of the dictatorship of the proletariat, which means violent and pitiless action. In the case of "the people" (which in the parlance of the Party means nothing but the obedient masses) any opposition can be nothing more than a temporary misunderstanding and finds its proper treatment in the Party's arsenal of "persuaders." These persuaders are various pressures brought to bear by the environment "to kill the sickness while saving the sick man."

The anti-revisionist struggle and the Maoist texts of the summer of 1964 perfected the methods that were already quite refined. One novelty however was the appearance of the notion of the new bourgeois, of the new rich peasants, and of the new capitalist producer—as well as the notion of the political degenerate. In the West we used to ask (and I was still asking this question on the communes) how it was possible for class struggle to exist in the villages, in the factories, at the university, after fifteen years of revolution had purged, scattered, converted, and eliminated the former class structure. The answer must be that in the eyes of the regime these elements have had a chance to re-form sufficiently to show certain visible characteristics. In the villages a peasant who has managed to improve his situation too greatly, either by his way of life or his resources, and escape from the uniformity of the austere existence of the mass, runs the risk of being classed as "new rich peasant" and finding himself involved in class struggle—at the receiving end! And this in fact is what has begun to take place everywhere. In the towns the label "new bourgeois" fastens on anyone who by thoughts or actions of an incorrect cut allows himself to become separated from "the people." And last of all the label "degenerate," or more often simply "revisionist," is reserved for anyone—either in industry or the Party or even in government administration—who has been guilty of any act unworthy of a Communist or the least thought unfaithful to the regime.

The most novel thought in this analysis of "the social basis of Revisionism" is surely the idea that the opposition, or what I might call the "anti-people," not only forms around malcontents but also in the ranks of the contented. Revisionism finds fewer adherents among those who feel dissatisfaction with the regime, those whom the regime has deprived of position, or those who remain, in spite of their new leaders, poor and unfortunate, than among those to whom it has brought advantage, basic improvements and affluence of a sort—in other words, among those whom the beginnings of comfort and wealth have caused to place comfort and wealth, as personal interest, above the common good. And it follows that "embezzlers and grafters" will almost always be profiting from their position *within* the regime. "Degeneration" is thus more to be feared in periods of success and progress than in periods of crisis or difficulty. The Chinese cite the Soviet Union's progressive degeneration into a bourgeois society as a particularly loathsome example of this process. . . . Any hope for a reversal of this trend in the Soviet Union appears even less likely when we recall that a capital crime has been committed by its leadership over the years: how long has it been since they began to neglect the education of the rising generations in the doctrines of class struggle and the spirit of self-sacrifice? When the entire younger generation no longer believes in any other brand of Communism than "goulash Communism" and after they have been seduced by "American-Way-of-Life Communism" what will remain to prevent the restoration of capitalism?

But China has this "negative example" which Russia supplies to thank for her present awareness. . . . That sort of treason will never occur in China, the authorities proclaim, because they have learned their lesson: it is absolutely necessary to indoctrinate the rising generations with hardline thinking and revolutionary ardor. Hu Yao-pang's report ends by stressing that "the new generation will be ripened in struggles. Let the growing storm of the revolution grow ever more violent! The future belongs to youth, which never loses its revolutionary spirit!"

The conservative, wealthy and well-fed West used to be able to believe on the basis of what it could see of the evolution of Communism in Russia that a period of relaxation was in store for it. The nightmare of World Revolution had begun to fade. The revolution was losing its fire thanks to the inevitable and welcome process that sends the successful revolutionary in search of comfort and stability. The grandsons of Bolsheviks are beatniks. . . . Communism ceased to be a dangerous enemy when it became a mere rival anxious to find a compromise.

But China has upset these calculations. There will be no cooling off nor loss of bite in *her* revolution. Mao Tse-tung has already seen to that. He has formulated, not simply for China but for the entire world revolutionary movement, recipes that ought to prevent degeneration at the same time that they assure fuel for the flames of revolution until the final advent of true Communism. To begin with, he has, before his own departure, seen to it that the youth of China become shock troops of the revolution. . . .

At least so they think in Peking. . . . Could they be deluded? This much at least is sure: the younger generation, contrary to the calculation of many Westerners, does not appear to be any more manageable than their elders. Europeans and Americans who believe the children of the Chinese revolutionaries are "softer" than their fathers, and that thanks to a few comforts, better education and an enlarged horizon the younger generation will pick up flexibility and tolerance—well, they have made miscalculations, in my opinion. The majority of young people may very well be nothing more than the most conformist of conformists, but the leaders and cadres who will be skimmed from the very top of this group will have been so filled with revolutionary spirit, so well prepared for every weakness, that they will not be flexible, they will be *hard-line,* as much and perhaps more so than their predecessors.

"Political work," supported by propaganda and press, tirelessly warns the youth of China against the sins and temptations of Revisionism, and reminds them of the Spartan slogan of the regime: "A simple life and strenuous labor!" Sooner or later, everything which in other countries attracts boys and girls in their twenties comes in for the Party's denunciation as a pernicious goal unworthy of their attention. Well-being? "To aspire to mere material or personal satisfactions would be degeneracy and betrayal!" proclaims, along with many other papers, *Nanfang Jipao* (April 14, 1964). According to this paper we must denounce "the wrong road which goes under the name of the Welfare State." We must be ready for harsh combat over a period of many years. This means that we must consider the service of the people and the struggle for Communism as the greatest happiness that life can offer. . . . We must never be discouraged, we must never allow ourselves to feel hesitation or think of compromise, even if we are suffering hunger and cold, torture, blows, wounds, sacrifice of life itself." Love? "We must destroy," writes *Chinese Woman* (Number 5, May, 1964) "the notion that after work is over we can be with our loved one, arm in arm, shoulder to shoulder, in a park, or in the street, at a film or in a restaurant, dancing or billing and cooing." Marriage? Along with *Chinese Youth* every periodical aimed at the young people of China maintains the line that in choosing a mate politics is the important thing. A young woman who is a real socialist worker will see to it that her future husband is a true revolutionary fighter, while the young worker will only marry a girl who is a worker and "red." A good life? We must condemn, writes the same issue of *Chinese Woman* quoted above (and it is not alone in so doing), all reactionary or anti-socialist ideas such as "The good worker deserves the good life," or "Since we are not at war we ought to be allowed to enjoy life," or "A good husband is a good worker who is also a bon vivant." Happiness? Hu Yao-pang in his report to the congress teaches, as does all propaganda intended for the consumption of youth, that the end of life cannot be attaining personal happiness nor even the happiness of the family. The only worthy goal of life is the happiness of the people as a whole. "True revolutionaries," he maintains, "never work for their own interests but always for that of others. In time of emergency, they come forward without hesitation and sacrifice themselves in the interests of the public."

Thus at the very moment when the doors of the arena of action and power have opened to the new generation, Mao Tse-tung and his comrades, last survivors of the older generation that sacrificed itself to the cause of revolution in China, warn them that they too will go down in history as a generation that was sacrificed to the cause. Now young Chinese men and women between twenty and thirty can be certain, thanks to the Youth Congress of the summer of 1964, that they will know neither a pause in the revolution nor a relaxation of the struggle. No more than did those who took the Long March or made the Liberation possible will this generation know tranquility or comfort.

And there is more. All political education and propaganda in China teaches youth that it has more to aim for than the total liberation of China through socialism; they are expected to contribute also to the liberation of all oppressed classes and peoples throughout the world. No true Chinese revolutionary could allow himself to enjoy comforts, the papers explain at great length, while whole populations in Asia, Africa and Latin America live in misery and slavery simply because they have not yet been freed from imperialism and the old or new colonialisms. "We should not only be concerned with the destiny of our people, but should share the weal and woe of the world's people. We have always regarded the revolutionary cause of our country as part and parcel of that of the whole world," Hu Yao-pang wrote in his report.

And there is still more! To crown this Communist gospel of austerity and sacrifice, a sensational proclamation was delivered during the course of the League congress in Peking, a proclamation that is destined to echo through the whole Party and through the length and breadth of China. Not only will the younger generation of today have to be sacrified, but the next one—and the next one! It will be five generations, and it might be ten and it could even be more than ten who will have to sacrifice themselves one after the other. Then and only then will socialism have been definitely established in China without there still being a danger of a restoration of capitalism, and then the happy age of true Communism will be able to begin. . . . The report of Hu Yao-pang reveals that it was Chairman Mao himself who delivered this oracle "to insure that our nation will remain revolutionary and incorruptible for five generations, ten generations, and forever."

Complete victory for socialism cannot be brought about in

one or two generations. To resolve this question thoroughly requires five or ten generations or even longer. . . . Khrushchev's slogan of basically building a Communist society within twenty years is not only false, but reactionary. . . . Socialist society covers a very long historical period. . . . A very long period of time is needed to decide who will win in the struggle between socialism and capitalism. Several decades will not do it. Success requires anywhere from one to several centuries." (*Peking Review,* July 10, 1964.)

"How long is a generation considered ·to last in China?" I asked when I had heard this extraordinary piece of news. "A shorter time than in the West," I was told. "You consider a generation to last thirty years, but when we use the word we intend anything from twenty to twenty-five years." From which I conclude that the new schedule that Mao Tse-tung announced pushes the end of the socialist period with its termination in the advent of Communism in China to anywhere from a century to two and a half centuries in the future. Thus at least in Mao's thinking the work of political construction lasts longer, much longer, than the economic structuring of socialism. So that although we can expect a truly modern, and totally complete Chinese economy in thirty years, it will be a wait of four to eight times longer before China exists on the ideal Communist level. For that whole period, if Mao's heirs remain faithful to his thought, "a simple life and strenuous work" will remain the rules of life for the Chinese multitude. The benefits of such effort, of perpetual labor, will not be distributed among the people. Everything will be reinvested, so to speak, in the Chinese revolution and in world revolution. And it is only after five to ten generations that the germs of the reaction will have been sterilized for sure, so that the loathsome race of capitalists will have disappeared from the earth. . . .

If they remain faithful!

In Peking, however, no one would dare show the least doubt about the perpetuation of that faith. For the foreign visitor one of the most lasting surprises reserved for him by a study of these documents, the report, the commentary, and various editorials, is the announcement that the thought of Mao Tse-tung will reign supreme throughout this entire period of "transition to socialism." Mao Tse-tung will remain the venerated guide of successive generations. Mao's works will continue to shine like a beacon for China. "The historic directive of Chairman Mao," says the report of Hu Yao-pang, "traces out the League's route for the entire period of socialism. It lights the way that opens for hundreds of millions of our country's youth."

Just as in the old days China had in Confucius a master whose doctrines could work unchanged through the changing centuries, today it has found such a master in Mao. . . .

The first of October, fifteenth anniversary of the Revolution, I was no longer in China. But someone who had been there described for me what he had seen before the Gate of Celestial Peace. Mao Tse-tung, surrounded by the chiefs of the Party and the government, presided over the expected review. After the advance guard of gigantic red silk flags, the first waves of squads and squads of young people began to march past. The "heirs of the revolution" are in for many honors this year. Just for this festival they had learned a new song and this was the morning that they sang it publicly for the first time. And what was the refrain of this song that boys and girls in their twenties sang with one great vibrant voice as they passed before the greatest revolutionary China has ever known? They thundered this extraordinary promise in his direction:

CHAIRMAN MAO, WE WILL NEVER CHANGE!

EPILOGUE

A FEW LAST FRAMES OF MY "FILM" SHOW CHINA AS SEEN FROM the plane to Canton, where I will take the train that leaves China by way of Hong Kong. . . .

For tens of thousands of *li* stretching to the four points of the compass the earth is one great sheet of silk without tear or fold . . .

Not a single forest, not even a grove of trees, nor even a visible road. But ten thousand canals of jade, irregular in their patterning and hardly less green than the vegetation they serve, separate with their clumsy tracery a thousand million fields, all of them gray or slightly tinted with a gray-green and appearing to have been streaked, always in the same direction, by the same brush pulled along the earth's endless fabric.

One canal out of two betrays to the viewer's careful attention a mossy growth of a deeper tint: a village. And suddenly I realize that there must be thousands of villages like this one, that there's not a district that isn't inhabited, and that these plains, no matter how empty in appearance, support millions of human beings. . . .

Farther on all is changed and the fine silk of the land disappears in a cardboard surface lightly wrinkled by brown blisters. Dry hills without appreciable height have been created by the erosion of land offering no obstacles to winds and water, spreading far and wide a nervous system of wet-weather creeks that all lead toward the sandy serpents of real rivers.

No agriculture to be seen—and then at last the eye makes out among the pale veins of this ochre and tan cardboard those same gray blotches, tiny ones, and they have to be villages, and villages, and more villages. No cities, and no railroads and very few roads, but millions and millions of human beings. If our plane were to make a forced landing, we would be on a pale and denuded earth among millions of industrious beings everywhere acting under the orders of a Party and a Plan, never able to escape from universal laws of organized labor and group existence. Everywhere this innumerable multitude repeats the same watchwords and slogans, and forms another web, this one weaving an invisible system of endless labor and obedience across this frontierless land.

China? Human beings . . .

At 30,000 feet problems, like landscapes, become oversimplified. And since I am up here in the clouds, thinking, let me say that I believe that confidence in human nature, in the nature of the Chinese, might be the solution to "the Chinese problem." The Chinese is too alive, too intelligent, too humane not to be able to reach an understanding with the rest of mankind, and too gifted for any final abdication of personal thought.

"We will never change!" That would surprise me. . . . The China of the past said as much. Hasn't the continuous revolution replaced Confucius?

And China will change in a changing world, a world changed by China—among other things.

For after all China's entry on the international scene is simply one among many of the extraordinary changes that have taken place in the modern world. And it isn't even the most overwhelming of all those that will shake up this extraordinary century of ours.

China in thirty years? or forty? or even fifty—since Chou En-lai says "a matter of a few decades. . ."? But we must keep in mind that it will be a world of six billion people, rocket ships, food from the seas, thinking robots, round-trip tickets to the moon, cheap atomic bombs, the ocean as a water supply. . . . In thirty years man will be about to create life in the laboratory, to produce chlorophyll and rain, to land on other planets, to live to be 150. . . .

Why shouldn't China and its billion Chinese be in on all this?

Between now and the year 2000 the children and grandchildren of today's adults will have to adapt faster and faster to the transformation of the world and the acceleration of history. In the year 2000, day after tomorrow so to speak, a world broken by the whirlwinds of change may have less trouble accepting China than we have today, and China much less trouble in accepting the world.

DATE DUE

2/22			
MAY - 7 1968			
May 20 1969 OCT 2 7 1969			
MAR 15 1971			
GAYLORD			PRINTED IN U.S.A.